DOING EDUCATIONAL RESEARCH

This book collects together semi-autobiographical accounts of the research of thirteen major educationists, all of whom have been involved in prominent and influential projects. In recounting the ways in which their work was conducted, the authors focus on the practical and personal aspects of the research process, which are so often overlooked in conventional accounts. Coping with the complicated and the unpredictable emerges as a keynote in these descriptions of the reality of educational research.

The authors discuss the various stages of the research process, including conception of the project, obtaining funding, gaining access to the research site, managing research relationships, gathering information, analysing data, writing up the research report, publishing books and articles, and the reception given to the research by others. Educationists, policy-makers, and those involved in education research will all benefit from a greater knowledge of the research methods used in these major studies. The book offers new understanding for those who read and use educational research, and should be a source of comfort for students and researchers attempting to conduct their own.

Geoffrey Walford is Course Director for the MSc in Educational Research Methodology at the Department of Educational Studies, University of Oxford. He is the author of numerous books and articles, including *Restructuring Universities: Politics and Power in the Management of Change* (1987), *Private Schools in Ten Countries* (1989) and *Privatization and Privilege in Education* (1990).

Also by Geoffrey Walford

TEACHERS INTO INDUSTRY
(with Richard Thompson)

BRITISH PUBLIC SCHOOLS
Policy and practice

SCHOOLING IN TURMOIL

LIFE IN PUBLIC SCHOOLS

DOING SOCIOLOGY OF EDUCATION

RESTRUCTURING UNIVERSITIES
Politics and power in the management of change

EDUCATION TRAINING AND THE NEW VOCATIONALISM
Experience and policy
(edited with Andrew Pollard and June Purvis)

PRIVATE SCHOOLS IN TEN COUNTRIES
Policy and practice

PRIVATIZATION AND PRIVILEGE IN EDUCATION

CITY TECHNOLOGY COLLEGE
(with Henry Miller)

PRIVATE SCHOOLING
Tradition, change and diversity

DOING EDUCATIONAL RESEARCH

EDITED BY

GEOFFREY WALFORD

London and New York

The Open University

First published 1991
by Routledge
2 Park Square, Milton Park, Abingdon, Oxon, OX14 4RN
Simultaneously published in the USA and Canada
by Routledge
270 Madison Ave, New York NY 10016

Reprinted 1995. 1996, 1998, 2000

Transferred to Digital Printing 2005

Routledge is an imprint of the Taylor & Francis Group

Typeset by Laserscript, Mitcham, Surrey

British Library Cataloguing in Publication Data
A catalogue record for this book is available from
the British Library

Library of Congress Cataloguing in Publication Data
A catalogue record for this book is available from
the Library of Congress

ISBN 0–415–05289–0 (hbk)
ISBN 0–415–05290–4 (pbk)

CONTENTS

v

NOTES ON CONTRIBUTORS

Stephen Ball is Professor of Education at the Centre for Educational Studies, King's College, London. He is the author of *Beachside Comprehensive* (Cambridge University Press, 1981), *The Micropolitics of the School* (Methuen, 1987), *Politics and Policy-making in Education* (Routledge, 1990) and many articles and papers which deal with ethnographic research focussing, in particular, on school processes and struggles over policy. He is currently engaged in research into the implementation of the 1988 Education Reform Act in secondary schools.

Colin Bell is Professor of Sociology at the University of Edinburgh. He is a graduate of the Universities of Keele and Wales. He has been Reader in the Department of Sociology at Essex as well as Professor of Sociology at the Universities of New South Wales and Aston. He is the author and editor of numerous papers and books including *Middle Class Families* (Routledge & Kegan Paul, 1968); *Community Studies* (Allen & Unwin, 1971); *Doing Sociological Research* (Allen & Unwin, 1977); *Property, Paternalism and Power* (Hutchinson, 1978); *Inside the Whale* (Pergamon, 1978); *Fathers, Childbirth and Work* (Equal Opportunities Commission, 1983) and *Social Researching* (Routledge & Kegan Paul, 1984). Besides the work reported in this chapter, he is currently (with others) researching the impact on the environment of military activities and the social science policy process. He is the editor of the Edinburgh University Press Education and Society Series which he founded.

Martin Hughes studied philosophy and psychology at the University of Oxford, and obtained his PhD from the University of Edinburgh. He was a Research Officer at the Thomas Coram Research Unit and Research Fellow at the University of Edinburgh, before moving to his present post of Lecturer in Education at the University of Exeter. He has researched and written widely on the development and education of young children, and his books include *Children and Number* (Blackwells, 1986). He is currently directing projects on young children learning with the computer language Logo, and on parents and the National Curriculum.

Máirtín Mac an Ghaill is Lecturer in Education at the Faculty of Education, University of Birmingham. He previously taught sociology and economics at a state school in the Midlands. His main research interests include the sociology of 'race' and the sociology of education. He has a particular interest in Irish Studies. He is author of *Young, Gifted and Black: Student–teacher relations in the schooling of black youths* (Open University Press, 1988), and has also published work on teacher practices, post-16 education and the vocationalization of the curriculum. He is currently preparing for publication a co-edited book on teachers' work, and researching the construction of masculine identity.

Lynda Measor worked as a research fellow at the Open University with Peter Woods on the project published as *Changing Schools* (Open University Press, 1984). She is also co-author (with Patricia Sikes and Peter Woods) of *Teachers Careers: Crises and Continuities* (Falmer, 1985) and author of numerous articles. She is now a Lecturer in Education at the West Sussex Institute of Higher Education. She has recently published work on ethical issues involved in doing educational research, and is currently working on two projects. The first is a textbook about gender and education. The second is research in local primary schools on teacher–researcher techniques in relation to the National Curriculum and other policy initiatives.

Neil Mercer, who wrote *Common Knowledge* with Derek Edwards (Methuen, 1987), is Director of the Centre for Language and Communications in the School of Education at the Open University. Since the completion of the project described in that book, he has begun a project using similar methods to those described in his chapter in this volume to investigate the development of shared understanding between participants in employment training assessment interviews (in collaboration with the Training Agency).

Peter Mortimore is currently Deputy Director of the Institute of Education, University of London. Previous appointments have included the post of Director of the School of Education at Lancaster University, and the post of Director of Research and Statistics for the ILEA. He has also been a secondary teacher, a school inspector, a research officer and an educational administrator. His interest in school effectiveness stems from his work during the 1970s with Professor Michael Rutter and colleagues at the Institute of Psychiatry, London. This was followed by further work carried out during the 1980s with colleagues in the ILEA Research and Statistics Branch. In addition to his interest in school effectiveness, Peter Mortimore's current research includes school leadership, assessment of the curriculum and the teaching of English to bilingual learners.

Jennifer Nias is Tutor in Curriculum Studies 3–13 at the Cambridge Institute of Education, UK. She has taught, at various times and in different parts of the world, children from 3 to 15 and adults from 18 to 56. Her research interests include the lives and careers of primary school teachers and adult relationships in primary schools, especially as these relate to whole school curriculum development and implementation. Her publications include *Primary Teachers Talking: A study of teaching as work* (Routledge, 1989), *The Enquiring Teacher: Sustaining and supplying teacher research* (Falmer, 1988) (edited with Susan Groundwater-Smith) and *Staff Relationships in the Primary School: A study of organizational culture* (Cassell, 1989) (with Geoff Southworth and Robin Yeomans). In addition to the research described here, she has also been a member of the Cambridge Accountability Project (SSRC, 1978–80) and of the Teacher–Pupil Interaction and Quality of Learning Project (Schools Council, 1980–2); was director of the Primary School Staff Relationships Project (ESRC, 1985–7) and co-director (with Geoff Southworth) of the Whole School Curriculum Development Project (ESRC, 1988–90).

David Raffe is Reader in Education and co-Director (with Andrew McPherson) of the Centre for Educational Sociology (CES) at Edinburgh University. He has been a member of CES since 1975, and has worked on the design, conduct and analysis of the Scottish Young People's Survey carried out by the CES. His research has covered various aspects of secondary and post-secondary education, the youth labour market, and training. It has included studies of recent British and Scottish policy initiatives including the Youth Training Scheme, the Scottish Action Plan and (as described in this chapter) the Technical and Vocational Education Initiative. His publications include *Reconstructions of Secondary Education* (with John Gray and Andrew McPherson) (Routledge & Kegan Paul, 1983), *Fourteen to Eighteen* (Aberdeen University Press, 1984) and *Education and the Youth Labour Market* (Falmer, 1988).

David Reynolds is a Lecturer in Education at University of Wales, College of Cardiff and has an international reputation for his work into school effectiveness. He has researched schools in Wales for over a decade and is editor of *Studying School Effectiveness* (Falmer, 1985), co-editor of *Education Policies: Controversies and Critiques* (Falmer, 1989), *School Effectiveness and Improvement* (University of Groningen, 1989) and *School Effectiveness and School Improvement* (Swets & Zeitlinger, 1990) and co-author of *The Comprehensive Experiment* (Falmer, 1987). He has written over eighty papers, chapters and articles and is a member of numerous journal editorial boards.

Barbara Tizard was, until October 1990, Director of the Thomas Coram Research Unit, and Professor in the London Institute of Education. Most of her research has been concerned with preschool and primary education, and the care of children outside their own families. She is currently directing research into the social identity of adolescents. Her books include *Early Childhood Education* (NFER, 1975), *Adoption: A second chance* (Open Books, 1977), *Involving Parents in Nursery and Infant Schools* (with Jo Mortimore and Bebb Burchell) (Grant McIntyre, 1981), *Young Children Learning* (with Martin Hughes) (Fontana, 1984) and *Young Children at School in the Inner City* (with Peter Blatchford, Jessica Burke, Clare Farquhar and Ian Plewis) (Lawrence Erlbaum, 1988).

Geoffrey Walford is Lecturer in Education Policy and Management at Aston Business School, Aston University, Birmingham, where he is also course organizer for the University's Society and Government undergraduate programme. He has collected various degrees from the Open University and the Universities of Kent, London and Oxford and has taught in schools in Oxfordshire, Kent and Buckinghamshire. He has researched and published widely, mainly on topics concerned with private education, research methods and higher education, and is author of *Life in Public Schools* (Methuen, 1985), *Restructuring Universities: Politics and Power in the Management of Change* (Croom Hem, 1987) and *Privatization and*

Privilege in Education (Routledge, 1990). His edited books include *Schooling in Turmoil* (Croom Helm, 1985), *Doing Sociology of Education* (Falmer, 1987) and *Private Schools in Ten Countries* (Routledge, 1989). His most recent research, with which the chapter here is concerned, was published as *City Technology College* (Open University Press, 1991) and was co-authored with Henry Miller.

Peter Woods is Professor at the Open University, and Director of the Centre for Sociology and Social Research. After graduating in history at University College, London, he taught for a number of years in primary and secondary schools in Norfolk, London and Yorkshire. He studied education and sociology at the Universities of Sheffield, Leeds and Bradford, before joining the Open University in 1972. He has contributed to several courses there, including *Contemporary Issues in Education* and *Exploring Educational Issues*. His books include *The Divided School* (Routledge & Kegan Paul 1979), *Sociology and the School* (Routledge & Kegan Paul 1983), *Inside Schools* (Routledge & Kegan Paul, 1986) and *Teacher Skills and Strategies* (Falmer, 1990), and he has written many articles for the academic and educational press.

1

REFLEXIVE ACCOUNTS OF DOING EDUCATIONAL RESEARCH

Geoffrey Walford

There are many introductory books on social and educational research methods. Some of the most well known of these textbooks, such as those by Moser and Kalton (1982), Cohen and Manion (1980) and Hoinville *et al* (1978) are widely used on undergraduate and postgraduate courses in universities and colleges and have been reprinted many times to serve successive cohorts of students. These books, and others like them, present research largely as an unproblematic process concerned with sampling, questionnaire design, interview procedures, response rates, observation schedules, and so on. They present an idealized conception of how social and educational research is designed and executed, where research is carefully planned in advance, predetermined methods and procedures followed, and 'results' are the inevitable conclusion. In essence, such books take what they perceive to be the methods used in the natural sciences as their model, and seek to present social and educational research as being equally 'scientific' in its methods.

In practice, however, it is now widely recognized that the careful, objective, step-by-step model of the research process is actually a fraud and that, within natural science as well as within social science, the standard way in which research methods are taught and real research is often written up for publication perpetuates what is in fact a myth of objectivity (Medawar, 1963). The reality is very different. There are now several autobiographical accounts by scientists themselves and academic studies by sociologists of science that show that natural science research is frequently not carefully planned in advance and conducted according to set procedures, but often centres around compromises, short-cuts, hunches, and serendipitous occurrences.

One of the earliest and most well known of these autobiographical accounts on natural science research is that by Nobel Prize winner James Watson (1968), who helped unravel the helical structure of DNA. His revelations of the lucky turns of events, the guesswork, the rivalries between researchers and personal involvement and compromise gave a totally different view of how natural science research is conducted from that given in methods textbooks. The personal and social nature of science research (and of writing about that process) is underlined by the somewhat conflicting account of the same research given much more recently by Watson's co-Nobel Prize winner, Francis Crick (1989). Various sociologists of science have also looked in detail at the process by which scientific knowledge is constructed. The ethnographic study of the everyday world of the scientific laboratory by Latour and Woolgar (1979), for example, shows clearly how scientific 'facts' are not 'discovered', but are the result of an extended process of social construction.

Yet, while it is increasingly recognized that the individual researcher in natural science does not behave as an objective automaton, social and educational research has traditionally tried to justify its own research procedures by making them as 'scientific' and 'objective' as possible, and by aping what have been perceived to be the methods of the natural sciences. Most social science and educational research methods textbooks have abstracted the researcher from the process of research in the same way as have natural science textbooks. The social dimension of research is omitted and the process is presented as a cold analytic practice where any novice researcher can follow set recipes and obtain predetermined results. It is little wonder that when the novice researcher finds unforeseen difficulties, conflicts and ambiguities in doing research he or she will tend to see these as personal deficiencies arising from insufficient preparation, knowledge or experience. It is the belief of the contributors to this present book that the idealized models of research presented in traditional textbooks are a necessary part of understanding about research, but that they do not prepare novice researchers for the political and social realities of actual research practice. They need to be supplemented by rather different accounts of the research process in action.

The limitations of traditional research methods textbooks have gradually been recognized over the last decade or more, and there

2

has grown a range of 'alternative' books for students and practitioners, which aim to present more realistic accounts of the particular research practices that led to specific research reports. In these books the researchers themselves have written semi-autobiographic reflexive accounts of the process of doing research, in the hope that others will benefit from this sharing of practical experience. Sociologists, and in particular those engaged in more qualitative research, have tended to be the most forthcoming in their accounts, and Whyte's (1955) appendix to his ethnographically based *Street Corner Society* is widely regarded as a classic of the genre. Within Britain, the most widely known and used collection of such accounts are those edited by Colin Bell and Howard Newby (1977), Colin Bell and Helen Roberts (1984) and Helen Roberts (1981). All of these collections, in their different ways, give accounts of the 'backstage' research activities and unveil some of the idiosyncrasies of person and circumstances which are seen as being at the heart of the research process. Although some of the contributors to these volumes deal with quantitative research, the majority of cases discussed are qualitative in their nature and thus, perhaps, lend themselves more easily to this type of self-analysis of methodology. Anthropologists have written similar accounts of their fieldwork for some time (see, for example, Wax, 1971). In contrast, it is noticeable that psychologists have been more reluctant than sociologists to move away from the security of their natural science research model, and there are no similar collections of reflexive accounts on key psychological works.

Few of the articles in these general collections on sociological research methods were concerned with sociology of education. Indeed, the only article on education intended for inclusion in Bell and Newby (1977) was not published due to possible libel action, and a modified version only appeared much later (Punch, 1986). Nevertheless, there have now been several collections which present the practical, political and personal side of educational research. In Britain, the first of these was the collection edited by Marten Shipman (1976), who managed to persuade six authors of highly respected research reports to write about the origins, organization and implementation of their projects, including the personal and professional problems that they had to overcome. He was unusually fortunate in being able to include authors of longitudinal quantitative research as well as detailed case studies and qualitative work. As with all such collections, the authors responded with differing degrees of candour, but some of the accounts were eye-openers to students trained only in the 'scientific' method.

During the mid-1980s there was an outpouring of four books edited by Robert Burgess which gathered together similar revelatory autobiographical accounts by educational researchers. The most important of these was *The Research Process in Educational Settings* (Burgess, 1984) which presented ten first-person accounts of research experience in ethnographic or case study work. The book has since become an Open University Set Book and is widely used in other universities and colleges. Burgess produced three more rather similar collections in 1985 (Burgess, 1985a–c), which discussed strategies and tactics for research, and examined methods of investigation in relation to theories, problems, processes and procedures. The relationship between research and policy and practice was also given prominence. These four collections by Burgess contain many valuable accounts, but they have the drawback of only being concerned with qualitative research, and omit consideration of quantitative research. A critical reader might gain the impression that the 'flexibility' of method and the effect of the personal on the way in which research is conducted is a feature only of qualitative methods, and that the 'harder' quantitative methods escape from these problems.

That this is not correct was shown by some of the chapters in the recent collection by Walford (1987) on *Doing Sociology of Education* which did include contributions from quantitative as well as qualitative researchers. However, the fact that the majority of the chapters in that book were still written by qualitative researchers is an indication of the difficulty of persuading more quantitative researchers of the utility of such accounts. The present book can be seen as a sequel to that earlier volume.

The rise of evaluation work within educational research has brought its own literature on methodology. This has mainly consisted of 'how to do evaluation' books and articles, but there have also been several reflexive accounts of the evaluation process. An early collection was that of David Smetherham (1981) which included sensitive accounts on a diverse range of evaluation studies. This was followed by Clem Adelman's (1984) *The Politics and Ethics of Evaluation* which brought ethical questions to the fore. More general ethical issues have also been addressed in a recent collection of essays edited by Burgess (1989).

4

The present book seeks to place itself in what it is hoped will become a tradition of books which explore the practical and social aspects of doing research in education. The contributors to this volume have been asked to write reflexive autobiographical accounts about aspects of the major research projects with which they have been involved. The majority of the chapters examine particular segments of the process of a research project that led to a major book – often one which has had a significant impact on our understanding of education. In doing so, it is hoped that readers will be better able to assess the validity, reliability and generalizability of that particular research, but it is also hoped that these discussions of specific research projects will help students and others involved in conducting and reading research to understand the research process more fully. The chapters have different emphases. Some give the 'true stories' of a well-known research project, others elaborate the day-to-day trials and tribulations of research, while yet others are concerned with the process of publication of findings and the reactions of others to these reports. However, all of the chapters aim to share some of the challenges and embarrassments, the pains and triumphs, the ambiguities and satisfactions of trying to discover what is unknown.

With all such accounts, there is always some self-censorship. Some of this will be done to avoid harm to others or because there might be a threat of libel action, but the majority is likely to be the result of the reluctance on the part of the researchers to reveal quite all that occurred. In all the collections published there is, for example, a complete lack of comment on any sexual relationships that may have been a part of the research process, yet it is difficult to believe that these have been entirely absent. Perhaps the best that anyone can expect is that the *second* worst thing that happened will be discussed. Thus, these accounts do not pretend to present *the* truth about research or even about the research methods used in the particular studies discussed, but they do give a further perspective on the ways in which research is conducted. It is hoped that these accounts of doing educational research will help the reader to reflect critically on research methodology, and may provide a source of comfort to students and fellow professional researchers setting out on their own research projects.

THE CHAPTERS

The chapters in this collection include discussion of a wide variety of educational research. The range is from large-scale quantitative surveys to qualitative case studies of just a few pupils. It includes discussion of work on school effectiveness, learning theory, pupil experiences, teachers' careers and life histories, micropolitics, racism, and policy implementation. One of the chapters describes a longitudinal interview study, another a psychological investigation, another some teacher–researcher work and yet another an intensive period of participant observation. There is also diversity in the aspect of the research process which the authors choose to discuss, so that some deal with the problems of research access, others with the collection of data, the data analysis, the process of writing up for publication, and the public reaction to the research following publication. Yet, within this diversity, there are great similarities in the pragmatic and down-to-earth ways in which researchers set about their tasks. The real world in which they work, is one of constraint and compromise. Individuals and groups try as best they can to grapple with the innumerable problems that confront them, working within practical, personal, financial and time constraints to produce reports which are as sound and propitious as possible.

The first account, by Barbara Tizard and Martin Hughes in Chapter 2, is concerned with language and communication with young children. Their book, *Young Children Learning* (1984) has now become a classic, and has been the subject of considerable debate, for it questions commonly held assumptions about the ways in which children learn at home and in school. The book discusses the findings of a study of the conversations of thirty four-year-old girls (half middle and half working class) at home with their mothers, and at nursery school with the staff. At home, *all* of the children took part in conversations with their mothers that increased their knowledge of the world and stretched them intellectually. They found that, in all, there was four times as much adult–child talk at home as at school, and that children on average asked twenty-six questions an hour at home compared to two an hour at school. Most interestingly, the difference was particularly pronounced for the working-class children who, at school, appeared subdued, unassertive and immature. Tizard and Hughes argued that the myth of working-class language deprivation arose from the assumption that children who appeared inarticulate at school were the same at

6

home. But, far from compensating for these perceived inadequacies at home, the staff lowered their expectations of these children, asking them less intellectually demanding questions. The authors suggested that the kind of dialogue used by teachers actually made the child more confused and inhibited and did not help her to think and learn as much as the informal conversations taking place at home. The taped conversations with nursery staff showed with horrifying clarity how difficult the deliberate process of aiding intellectual growth can be.

However, the authors stressed that they did not wish to see nursery schools disappear: they emphasized that children have a wide variety of needs, some of which cannot be met at home. But they did wish to raise questions about why it was that working-class children were so socially insecure at nursery school that they *appeared* to be linguistically deprived, and thus started on the downward spiral towards underachievement.

In Chapter 2, Tizard and Hughes discuss the origins of their research project and the methods they used, describing the various decisions made about sample size, the concentration on girls only, selection of the sample, recording method, and interviews of parents and nursery staff. They then describe the process by which they analysed the data and wrote up the research for publication. They also discuss how they tried to ensure that their potentially controversial results were given a fair hearing by the press, but show that misinterpretation was widespread by teachers and by other academics. They discuss some of the academic criticism in detail.

Chapter 3 by Neil Mercer is also concerned with language and communication but in a rather different way. It discusses research on the teaching-learning process that he conducted with Derek Edwards and published in the book *Common Knowledge* (1987). The research is based on a series of video-recorded school lessons with a group of eight- to ten-year-old children. Their analysis of the data leads them to question traditional individualistic psychologies that have underpinned much of present-day educational theory and practice. They argue that even the most 'child centred' education is a process of cognitive socialization under teacher control where 'common knowledge' or shared understandings are created between teacher and pupils. They show the presenting, receiving, sharing, controlling, negotiating, understanding and misunderstanding of knowledge in the classroom to be an intrinsically social communicative process which can be revealed only through a close analysis of joint activity and classroom talk. They show how classroom communications take place against a background of implicit understandings, some of which are never made explicit to the pupils, while there develops during the lessons a context of assumed common knowledge about what has been said, done or understood.

In the chapter here, Neil Mercer takes the reader through the research process which led to the book. He describes the problem that the research was designed to investigate, the way in which the research was planned and the data collection methods used. He points to some of the problems encountered during the research and evaluates the effects of these problems, and of various decisions made throughout the research, on the validity and reliability of the final analysis. He explains why they rejected some existing methods of analysing classroom talk, and describes the method adopted which stressed the social and physical context of interaction as well as the content of the talk. Finally, Mercer describes the methods used in the presentation and dissemination of the research findings, and relates these to the audiences with whom they wished to communicate. He argues that well-chosen and clearly described new technical concepts need not hinder communication with audiences wider than the narrow world of educational researchers.

Chapter 4 is also concerned with communicating findings to the appropriate audience. Here the topic of research is pupils' views on transfer to a comprehensive school which are the subject of *Changing Schools* by Lynda Measor and Peter Woods (1984). The book is based on an ethnographic study which lasted for about a year and a half, and followed one group of pupils in their last term at a middle school and throughout the first year of their lives in a comprehensive school after transfer at age 12. This extensive period of observation and informal interviewing allowed Lynda Measor to live through the detailed day-to-day experiences of these children with them as they transferred from one school to another. The focus of the research was on understanding the informal culture of the pupils, and it investigated pupil expectations and myths about the new school, and how they accomplished the status passage between the two schools. They explored the forms and levels of anxiety experienced by these pupils, their initial encounters in their new school, their adaptations during the first year, and their changes in status and identity as they passed through this transfer process.

In their chapter, Measor and Woods reflect on the variable

8

fortunes and flavour of their research – the stops and starts, false trails and blind alleys, long periods of routine data collection and occasional flashes of excitement, the alternating experiences of obstruction and promotion, and of being deeply involved and almost totally marginalized. They structure their accounts by considering the significance of both blockages and breakthroughs for the direction of the research and the eventual outcome, and pay particular attention to the various decision points throughout the research. Their account takes the reader through all stages of their investigation, from initial conception and funding, through negotiating access, data collection, analysis and writing-up. Particular issues discussed include varying relationships with teachers and pupils, fruitful and unfruitful aspects of the analysis, and features of the writing-up. They give some clear examples of where they were and were not able to free a blockage, and where breakthroughs occurred. An unusual feature of the chapter is that the authors describe the effects of collaborative research and co-authorship on the way in which decisions were made, especially at the analysis and writing-up stages, and given an extended example of how ideas were modified during the writing-up period as a result of the flow of correspondence between the two authors then based at different institutions.

The next chapter by Geoffrey Walford relates to a research study of the first of the new City Technology Colleges (CTCs) that opened in Kingshurst, Solihull in September 1988 (Walford and Miller, 1991). The highly controversial plan for a network of twenty new colleges was made by Kenneth Baker towards the end of 1986. They were to be non-fee-paying private schools to be run by trusts established by sponsoring industrial or commercial companies and to be sited in inner-city areas. They were to offer a curriculum rich in technology, and were to be funded jointly by sponsoring companies and a direct grant from the Department of Education and Science (DES). The major point of dispute was that, although they were to cater for children with a range of abilities, they were to be selective schools serving only a proportion of the children within a large catchment area. Selection was to be on the basis of pupil and parental motivation as well as supposed suitability for a highly technological curriculum.

The chapter here discusses three aspects of the research. First, it looks at the difficulties that were experienced in attempting to gain access to conduct research at the CTC and the process by which an agreement between the CTC and the researcher was eventually accomplished. Access to research sites is frequently a problem for researchers, but the difficulties were amplified here as the research site was a specific, named establishment which was at the centre of political controversy! Second, the chapter examines some of the difficulties of publication that were related to the specific context of the research. In all research, researchers are not free to report everything that they observe, but must take care not to do harm to those who have given them access. The publication of research on the first CTC, where the identity of the research site could not be hidden, had to be circumscribed in several ways to avoid potential harm to individuals. The third aspect of the research to be considered in this chapter is that of interviewing children, where it is argued that researchers need to take children's views more seriously, and consider more carefully the social context in which research with children takes place.

One researcher who has already taken the views of young people very seriously is Máirtín Mac an Ghaill whose book, *Young Gifted and Black* (1988), is the result of two linked ethnographic studies of black youth in an inner city. It gives an account of the school lives of these young men and women, and of teachers' and students' opinions about each other. He describes the variety of staff and student sub-cultures and how and why they build their different survival strategies, concentrating on the three student sub-cultures of the Black Sisters, the Rasta Heads and the Warriors. Mac an Ghaill argues that the major problem in the schooling of black youth is not their culture but the phenomenon of racism, which pervasively structures their social worlds. He emphasizes the importance of a class analysis as racism is mediated through the existing institutional framework that discriminates against working-class youth as well as through race specific mechanisms such as racist stereotyping, which in turn is gender specific. He suggests that teachers are of central causal significance in the problems that these youths encounter.

In Chapter 6, Mac an Ghaill examines the five-year teacher–researcher experience which led to his book. He describes the way in which his initial interest in Irish pupils in English schools was diverted into a research project on Afro-Caribbean and Asian pupils, and how he developed a close relationship with three different groups of black pupils by allowing them to share part of his life. This deep ethnographic experience led to a gradual change in his theoretical framework, from one which implicitly classified black students as a 'problem', to one identifying racism as central to the problems that black students face. He explains the methodological ramifications of such a change in theoretical understanding, and the creative tension that it produced between the roles of teacher and researcher. He outlines a collaborative model of research that he developed with students as a result of his long-term involvement, and indicates the ways in which accidents of biography can have major effects on research relationships. Finally, Mac an Ghaill explores some of the political and ethical issues associated with such research.

Young people's experience is also the subject of Chapter 7 by Bell and Raffe which discusses the Edinburgh University evaluation of TVEI (Technical and Vocational Education Initiative), which was funded by the MSC (Manpower Services Commission) from August 1986 to July 1988. This was one of the two Scotland-wide evaluations of the TVEI pilot project which started a year later in Scotland than in England and Wales. With the other Scotland-wide evaluation carried out by the Scottish Council for Research in Education, they parallel the roughly equivalent evaluations of TVEI by Leeds University and the NFER (National Foundation for Educational Research) for England and Wales.

The Edinburgh evaluation was centred on the themes of liaison and articulation with industry, and was based around two main activities – fieldwork in the TVEI projects, and enhancement of the sample of the 1987 Scottish Young People's Survey, with a specially designed questionnaire for young people from TVEI schools. The report, *Liaisons Dangereuses?* (Bell *et al*,. 1988), drew attention to a variety of issues in education-industry liaison (for example, the need to specify a clear role for industrialists, logistical problems, issues arising from the low levels of 'enterprise' actually demanded by local employers, problems of TVEI–YTS (Youth Training Scheme) articulation). It reported on the problems of delivering TVEI at 16-plus, and of using TVEI to counter sex-stereotyping. It found little evidence of a TVEI effect on relatively tangible outcomes such as staying-on rates or employment, but it did find some attitudinal differences between TVEI and non-TVEI students. Overall the reactions of TVEI students were positive, but there were differences among projects and among types of students. The original evaluation finished at the end of July 1988, but the Centre for Educational Sociology (CES) was funded by the Training Agency to include TVEI students within a follow up survey in autumn 1989, at age 19. The ESRC (Economic and Social Research Council) also funded a reanalysis of the 1987 data, a replication of the TVEI enhancement on another year group two years later, in Spring 1989, and a further one-year study which aims to examine the changing 'effect' of TVEI over time.

The chapter here examines the technical, political and social issues that surrounded the TVEI pilot 'experiments' and their evaluation. They discuss both the qualitative and quantitative aspects of the evaluation and the relationship between them, the conflicts between the quasi-experimental design of the pilot programme and elements of action research which developed, the tension between the demands for formative and summative evaluation and the relationship between researchers and sponsors.

Chapter 8 moves from research with pupils and young people to research with teachers. *Primary Teachers Talking* by Jennifer Nias (1989) is another recently published account which is likely to become obligatory reading in its field. It is a detailed study of the personal and professional experience of primary teachers in England and Wales, and is based upon interviews with teachers conducted during their first decade of work, and again ten years later. In the book Nias discusses the importance attached to the ways in which primary teachers see themselves and the main dimensions of that self-image. She also examines the subjective experience of 'being a primary teacher', looking at the main factors which contribute to job satisfaction and dissatisfaction, and at teachers' relationships with their colleagues. In her chapter in this volume, Nias describes the way in which this long-term research project developed as the result of accident and opportunity. An initial idea to explore the strengths and weakness of a particular teacher training course, with a small group of teachers who had formerly been her students, eventually led to an investigation of teachers' lives which spanned more than 15 years. Nias explains her developing research strategy, describes the decisions made at each stage, and analyses the implications of those decisions for the validity, reliability and generalizability of the findings. She also describes some of the mistakes and difficulties that occurred during the research, and how the progress of the research related to her own personal circumstances. She argues that the length of time that she spent working with her data gave her the opportunity to think about the work a great deal, and to test her ideas against the perceptions and professional insights of other academics and teachers, leading to fully 'grounded' conclusions.

Stephen Ball's book *The Micropolitics of the School* (1987) is also concerned with teachers, and is one that has already achieved the status of a classic. Methodologically, it is very unusual, for it draws upon data from a variety of ethnographic case study projects with which the author was involved over the late 1970s and 1980s. These include his previous study of *Beachside Comprehensive* (Ball, 1981), which focused on an examination of the debates and struggles which lay behind the introduction of mixed ability teaching to replace banding, his separate study of an amalgamation of three schools to form a new comprehensive, and a jointly conducted series of case studies within institutions piloting the introduction of the Certificate of Pre-Vocational Education (CPVE). However, Ball also used data from various case studies conducted by his students, from other researcher's published ethnographic studies and many of his own interviews in a variety of other schools.

In his book, Ball weaves this material into a discussion of the interpersonal influences, compromises and behind-the-scenes negotiations which he argues are central to schools as organizations. He describes many of the micro-political aspects of school organization, looking in particular at leadership, the influence of age and gender, and the politics of teachers' careers, and develops a new theory of organization which is in contrast with traditional bureaucratic models.

In Chapter 9 of this book, Ball describes the way that *Micropolitics* fits into his own personal and political interests, and growing desire to elaborate a political sociology of education. He discusses the problems and potential of this sort of analysis based on a wide variety of data sources, and gives a detailed description of the procedures he used in his analysis of the data. This part of the account provides valuable information on a central part of the research process which usually goes totally undiscussed in methods textbooks. He describes the low-tech physical process by which he gained familiarity with the data, the development of categories and concepts, the breakthroughs that can occur through re-reading the academic literature, and the grouping of categories such that a chapter structure emerged. Finally, Ball discusses the status of *Micropolitics* as theory, and the way in which theory is developed from ethnographic work.

Chapter 10, by David Reynolds, and 11, by Peter Mortimore, are both concerned with school effectiveness research. David Reynolds has been conducting research on school effectiveness in South

Wales for nearly two decades. Although there have been several different research projects conducted during this time, there has been a large element of longitudinal research as well, for the work has all been conducted within the same community of schools – given the pseudoynm Treliw. His most well-known and controversial book, *The Comprehensive Experiment* (with Michael Sullivan and Stephen Murgatroyd – Reynolds 1987) took advantage of the fact that this area of South Wales reorganized its secondary schools in the mid-1970s such that about two-thirds of the children attended comprehensive schools, while the other one-third remained within a selective system of grammar and secondary modern schools. After an extensive study of the academic and social differences between the two groups of pupils at the end of their school careers, the authors argued that the comprehensives had failed many of their pupils. They found that the comprehensive school pupils did badly academically and socially in comparison to the other group. However, this difference was due to the schools' failure with their middle and lower ability children – the high ability pupils were catered for nearly as well as in the selective system. The book goes on further to list a host of problems including: poor management, lack of pupil involvement, inadequate pastoral care provision, distant relations with parents and over-emphasis on academic attainment at the expense of social development.

Such results were political dynamite, and the publication of the book was accompanied by fierce controversy both in the educational and popular press. Those on the political Right took the message of the book as being that the comprehensive experiment had 'failed', and the research results were used to propagate the view that there should be a return to selective education. In practice, the authors' own conclusions were in contrast to this idea, for they argued that the main problem was that the schools were only pseudo-comprehensives. They saw a need for universal comprehensive schools, but with a selective 'top-up' of special provision for pupils according to their differing abilities and needs.

Neither the results nor the ensuing political controversy were likely to endear the author to the headteachers, teachers and local authority officials with whom he continued to work in South Wales. In his chapter in this book, Reynolds describes and discusses his research experiences, and the reactions of teacher and others to the research reports. It is a particularly revealing chapter about the personal side of research relationships and the tensions that critical results can engender. Reynolds writes with humour and honesty on his exposed position as an independent researcher within a tightly knit community.

Peter Mortimore was co-author of two highly influential quantitative studies of school effectiveness – *Fifteen Thousand Hours* (with Rutter *et al.*, 1979) and *School Matters* (with Sammons, Stoll, Lewis and Ecob, 1988). Both of these reports received a great deal of press coverage and fired an extensive academic debate, for they presented results which many did not wish to believe. *Fifteen Thousand Hours* was a follow-up study of a sample of 14-year-old Inner London children who had originally been studied when they were 10 and in primary school. The research team gathered extensive data on twelve of the secondary schools which these children attended by way of interviews with teachers, classroom observation, questionnaires from the pupils, police records and public examination results, and argued that these secondary schools had varied social and academic effects even after taking into account the differences in intakes. More importantly, they found that certain characteristics of the schools were strongly and systematically associated with outcomes.

The *School Matters* research followed from this earlier study, and followed a cohort of 2000 Inner London pupils though the whole of their four years of junior schooling. Again, a wide range of data were collected, and it was shown that schools varied considerably in their effectiveness, with some schools appearing to enhance pupils' cognitive and non-cognitive progress and development far more than others. The research also found that the effective schools benefited all groups of pupils rather than just some, though not necessarily to the same degree.

In Chapter 11, Mortimore examines these two examples as case studies. The first case study explains the aims of *Fifteen Thousand Hours,* briefly details its methods and main findings and then reflects on the impact of publication, particularly looking at press coverage in the daily newspapers. Mortimore then examines several critiques by other researchers and the replies and reposts written by the authors. The second case study similarly explains the aims of *School Matters,* and briefly details its research methods and main findings. Mortimore deals with the reactions to the reporting of the study to the Inner London Education Authority in 1986 and, subsequently, to the publication of the book in 1988. The chapter draws upon these two case studies to raise a number of issues arising from press and journal comment. These are discussed and a set of ten practical recommendations for researchers are proposed. These range from things to do before starting the research to preparation for the press conference at the end.

The various autobiographical accounts given in this book concentrate on different aspects of the research process: from the conception of the initial research topic, through gaining access to the research site of subjects, conducting the observations, interviews or surveys, to the analysis of data, preparation of research reports and the reception given to the work by the public and other researchers. All of the chapters emphasize the constant decision-making that accompanies research and the practical and personal aspects of the process. Whether it is Stephen Ball sitting on his living room floor surrounded by mounds of paper, gradually moving some choice snippet from one pile to another, or Jennifer Nias scrabbling over a municipal rubbish tip to recover cardboard boxes of her notes which had been thrown out by an over-zealous cleaner, or Lynda Measor sitting guiltily at the back of a humanities class about the Arctic watching pupils imitate penguins while the teacher's back was turned – all of the authors allow the reader to appreciate the personal reality of Doing Educational Research.

REFERENCES

Adelman, Clem (1984) (ed.) *The Politics and Ethics of Evaluation*, Beckenham, Croom Helm.

Ball, Stephen J. (1981) *Beachside Comprehensive*, Cambridge, Cambridge University Press.

Ball, Stephen J. (1987) *The Micro-Politics of the School. Towards a Theory of School Organization*, London, Methuen.

Bell, Colin and Newby, Howard (1977) (eds) *Doing Sociological Research*, London, Allen & Unwin.

Bell, Colin and Roberts, Helen (1984) (eds) *Social Researching. Politics, Problems and Practice*, London, Routledge & Kegan Paul.

Bell, Colin, Howieson, Cathy, King, Kenneth and Raffe, David (1988) *Liaisons Dangereuses? Education-Industry Relationships in the First Scottish TVEI Projects: An Evaluation Report*, Sheffield, Training Agency.

Burgess, Robert G. (1984) (ed.) *The Research Process in Education Settings: Ten Case Studies*, Lewes, Falmer.

Burgess, Robert G. (1985a) (ed.) *Field Methods in the Study of Education*, Lewes, Falmer.

Burgess, Robert G. (1985b) (ed.) *Strategies of Educational Research. Qualitative Methods*, Lewes, Falmer.

Burgess, Robert G. (1985c) (ed.) *Issues in Educational Research. Qualitative Methods,* Lewes, Falmer.

Burgess, Robert G. (1989) (ed.) *The Ethics of Educational Research,* Lewes, Falmer.

Cohen, Louis and Manion, Lawrence (1980) *Research Methods in Education,* London, Croom Helm.

Crick, Francis (1989) *What Mad Pursuit,* London, Weidenfeld & Nicolson.

Edwards, Derek and Mercer, Neil (1987) *Common Knowledge. The Development of Understanding in the Classroom,* London, Methuen.

Hoinville, Gerald, Jowell, Roger and associates (1978) *Survey Research Practice,* London, Heinemann.

Latour, Bruno and Woolgar, Steve (1979) *Laboratory Life. The Social Construction of Scientific Facts,* London, Sage.

Mac an Ghaill, Máirtín (1988) *Young, Gifted and Black. Student-Teacher Relations in the Schooling of Black Youth,* Milton Keynes, Open University Press.

Measor, Lynda and Woods, Peter (1984) *Changing Schools: Pupil Views on Transfer to a Comprehensive,* Milton Keynes, Open University Press.

Medawar, Peter (1963) 'Is the scientific paper a fraud?', *Listener,* 12 September.

Mortimore, P., Sammons, P., Stoll, L., Lewis, D. and Ecob, R. (1988) *School Matters: the Junior Years,* Wells, Open Books.

Moser, C A, and Kalton, Graham (1982) *Survey Methods and Social Investigation,* London, Heinemann.

Nias, Jennifer (1989) *Primary Teachers Talking. A Study of Teaching as Work,* London, Routledge.

Punch, Maurice (1986) *The Politics and Ethics of Fieldwork. Muddy Books and Grubby Hands,* Beverly Hills, Sage.

Reynolds, David and Sullivan, Michael (with Murgatroyd, Stephen) (1987) *The Comprehensive Experiment,* Lewes, Falmer.

Roberts, Helen (1981) (ed.) *Doing Feminist Research,* London, Routledge and Kegan Paul.

Rutter, M., Maughan, B., Mortimore, P. and Ouston, J. (1979) *Fifteen Thousand Hours,* London, Open Books.

Shipman, Marten (1976) *The Organisation and Impact of Social Research,* London, Routledge & Kegan Paul.

Smetherham, David (1981) (ed.) *Practising Evaluation,* Driffield, Nafferton.

Tizard, Barbara and Hughes, Martin (1984) *Young Children Learning. Talking and Thinking at Home and School,* London, Fontana.

Walford, Geoffrey (1987) (ed.) *Doing Sociology of Education,* Lewes, Falmer.

Walford, Geoffrey and Miller, Henry (1991) *City Technology College,* Milton Keynes, Open University Press.

Watson, James D. (1968) *The Double Helix,* London, Weidenfield & Nicolson.

Wax, R. (1971) *Doing Fieldwork: Warnings and Advice,* Chicago, Chicago University Press.
Whyte, William F (1955) *Street Corner Society,* 2nd edn, Chicago, Chicago University Press.

2

REFLECTIONS ON
YOUNG CHILDREN LEARNING

Barbara Tizard and Martin Hughes

INTRODUCTION

This chapter discusses a project we carried out with our colleagues Gill Pinkerton and Helen Carmichael in which we studied a group of 30 four-year-old girls at home and at nursery school. The study focussed in particular on the conversations which took place between the girls and their mothers at home, and between the girls and their nursery teachers at school. Our findings were originally published in a series of articles in the late 1970s and early 1980s (Hughes *et al.,* 1979; Tizard *et al.,* 1980, 1983a, 1983b), and in a book entitled *Young Children Learning* (Tizard and Hughes, 1984). In this chapter we look back on how the project was conceived, carried out, analysed and written up; in addition, we discuss how the findings have been received by teachers and by other academics.

ORIGINS OF THE PROJECT

Although our findings did not start to appear until the early 1980s, the project was conceived some years earlier, during the mid-1970s. Inevitably, the issues which we chose to address reflected some of the main theoretical and educational concerns of that period. Three of these concerns were particularly salient for us – namely, the value and content of pre-school education, the relationship between language and social class, and the role of context in children's language and thinking.

The intense interest in preschool education which characterized the 1970s was no doubt inspired in part by the massive American Headstart programme instigated in 1964 by President Lyndon

Johnson, on a wave of optimism about the potential of preschool education to eradicate inequality and poverty. In Britain, a more immediate impetus was the Plowden Report's recommendation (1967) that positive discrimination, including the provision of nursery schooling, was required in deprived areas to raise educational standards to the national average. By the mid-1970s doubts were beginning to surface. Systematic attempts to evaluate both the British and American programmes suggested that preschool education by itself was unlikely to influence later school attainment, and thus have the far-reaching effect on educational inequality which had been hoped for[1]. Attention began to turn to the content of what went on in preschool centres. In particular, the question was being raised as to whether the traditional British approach to nursery education, which rested strongly on ideas of child centredness and free play, was appropriate for those children whose background was considered to be in someway 'deprived' and who seemed destined for future educational failure, or whether a more structured educational programme should be introduced.

This concern about the educational underachievement of children from poorer homes was related to a second prominent issue in the 1970s – that of language and social class. At the time our project was conceived there was widespread support for a 'language deficit' position, as exemplified in the Bullock Report of 1975. The essential elements of such a position were that children from working-class homes are exposed to inferior or inadequate models of language from their parents, and that they thus came to school inadequately prepared to cope with the linguistic demands of the classroom. This view led to the development of compensatory language programmes, such as those of Blank (1973) in the USA, and Tough (1977) in England. At a theoretical level, these views had been challenged by a few educationalists and linguists, such as Rosen (1972) and Labov (1969), who claimed that lower-class children grow up in a rich verbal culture, and hence that the cause of their educational deficiencies must be sought in the schools, not the homes. In Britain, however, such alternative views had not made much headway, and the prevailing belief among teachers and educationalists was that young working-class children were seriously deprived of linguistic stimulation – a view summed up by the oft-repeated comment that 'no one talks to these children at home'.

The third issue which was starting to emerge in the mid-1970s was the role of context in children's thinking and language. British developmental psychologists such as Bryant (1974) and Donaldson (1978) were looking closely at the tasks which had been used by Piaget to assess children's thinking and development. Their work seemed to indicate that children were very sensitive to small changes in the way these tasks were presented, and that it was important to take full account of the context in which children were being assessed: this included the study of children's competences in naturalistic situations as well as looking at the experimental situation as an interactive context in its own right. Similarly, researchers interested in the way young children acquired language were moving away from studying formal features of language, such as the acquisition of syntactic structures, and were starting to look more closely at the situations in which young children actually learn and use language; inevitably, this meant an increasing interest in looking at young children interacting with their mothers at home (e.g. Bruner, 1975; Wells, 1978). Starting from a different discipline and different perspectives, Labov also stressed the role of context in language production, arguing that the social situation is the most important determinant of verbal behaviour. Thus, in a situation which children perceive as threatening, as when being questioned by a teacher or psychologist, they will become monosyllabic, although when more at ease they may be able to express themselves very well.

THE PROPOSAL

These three issues were brought together in a proposal entitled *The Characteristics and Contexts of Adult-Child Dialogue at Home and at School* which one of us (BT) submitted to the Social Science Research Council in 1975. The immediate impetus to the proposal was a recently concluded project which had found, like others, that children's language development seemed unaffected by attendance at ordinary British nursery schools or playgroups (Tizard, Philps and Plewis, 1976). Listening to the staff–child conversations that took place in many of these pre-school centres, one could not help being struck by their limitations. They seemed to be less child-initated and sustained, shorter, and more stereotyped than parent–child dialogues at home. It seemed likely that this might be because of the lack of shared activity and experience between adult and child at school, and because language was being used for different purposes and in different contexts in the two settings.

The obvious next step was to test this hypothesis by observing the same children at home and at school. Although there were some ongoing studies of children's language at home, notably that of Wells (1978), no-one appeared to have followed them into pre-school settings. Our hypotheses, therefore, as stated in the proposal, were 'that there are important differences in the quality of parent–child and teacher–child dialogues, and that certain important characteristics of the dialogue are related to the nature of the ongoing activity of the adults and children'. Although testing these hypotheses did, in fact, form the major part of the study, we became increasingly interested in issues which we had not foreseen at the time of the application, and which became the main focus of the subsequent qualitative analysis (see later). Of these, the most notable were the potential of the home as a learning environment, the role of curiosity in the child's learning, and the role of the adult in facilitating this learning.

It is proposed in the application that the study would be in two main stages. In Stage 1, to last two years, adult–child conversations would be collected and analysed from the homes and nursery schools of a sample of sixty children. Both middle-class and working-class children would be studied, and there would be equal numbers of boys and girls. If, as hypothesized, the study revealed that some contexts were more conducive to longer dialogues ranging over a wider variety of topics than others, we thought that the implications of these findings should be discussed with nursery school teachers. Consequently, we proposed that in Stage 2 (the third year) the research team would return to the schools where the data had been collected and discuss the findings with the staff; in addition, it was hoped to work out with the teachers in at least two nursery schools alterations in educational practice suggested by the study, and to assess the effect of these alterations on the nature of staff-child conversations.

In the event, probably reasoning that research money should not be committed for the dissemination of findings which might not prove to be significant, the Social Science Research Council (SSRC) did not fund Stage 2. In some ways, this decision was unfortunate. The findings did have significance for practice, and it may well have greatly increased the project's impact on schools if they could have been worked through for a year with nursery teachers. The grant of £25,783 which we were given by the SSRC covered salary costs for two years (1976–8) for the project director (BT) and a full-time research assistant (HC), as well as secretarial and equipment costs. But the project was only feasible because two other researchers (GP and MH) were able to work on the project on a part-time basis, supported by general DHSS funds to the Thomas Coram Research Unit. Even so, it proved impossible to complete the analysis and write up the study within the two-year period.

DESIGN OF THE STUDY

The design of our study followed in a relatively straightforward manner from our hypotheses and intentions. We wanted to compare the same children at home and at nursery school. We wanted to compare children from a working-class background with children from a middle-class background. We wanted to have enough children in each category so that we could use statistical tests to compare the groups. We also wanted, initially, to have equal numbers of boys and girls in each group, and to look at gender differences in our data. Consequently, in our proposal to the SSRC we proposed a sample of 60 children, 30 of whom would be working class and 30 would be middle class, and all of whom would be observed at school and at home. Within each group of 30, half the children would be boys and half would be girls.

When we tried to put this design into practice, we soon realized that we would have to reduce the size of this sample. Our pilot studies made it very clear that the process of recording and transcribing children's conversations was much more time-consuming than we had anticipated. Clearly, the social class dimension was crucial to the aims of the study, so the only way to restrict the sample size was to omit boys.

There were two main justifications for the decision. First, at this age, girls tend to talk more and articulate more clearly than boys – using only girls would thus make the task of transcribing the conversations less difficult. Second, it reflected our wider concern with general issues – in a society dominated by men, there was something attractive about the idea of studying girls, their mothers, and their female nursery teachers.

In the event, we came to realize how much we might have lost by this decision, as an increasing amount of research began to suggest that from an early age mothers interact with their sons differently from their daughters. McGuire (1988) for example, found that mothers were more controlling and critical with daughters than

23

sons, while girls sought more attention from their mothers and stayed closer to them than boys. We were not, therefore, necessarily studying 'Young children learning' but perhaps 'Young girls learning'. Nevertheless, given the limited resources, and the fact that the educational agenda at that time was much more geared to social class than gender issues, our decision still seems to us correct. Thus we finally observed 30 girls, 15 from middle-class homes and 15 from working-class homes, talking to their mothers at home and to their teachers at nursery school.Although the sample size was very small, we believed that it would be large enough to reveal any really significant effects.

SELECTION OF CHILDREN

In order to make valid comparisons between the two groups, it was important that the children's circumstances should be as alike as possible in every way except social class. Thus we decided to select children from within a fairly narrow age band – three months either side of their fourth birthday. We wanted to observe children at nursery school in the morning and at home in the afternoon, so this ruled out children who attended full-time school, or whose parents were out at work all day. We also excluded families where the father was at home during the day, as this would have introduced a major variation into the home setting. In addition, we had to exclude families where English was not the main language spoken. We also excluded single-parent families, and families with more than three children, on the grounds that they may function differently from other families (at the time of the study less than 10 per cent of British under-fives lived in such families). We did not, however, exclude black children.

Because of the exigencies of the design, our sample did not include the most disadvantaged working-class children, who were more likely to be at home all day, or attending a full day nursery, or at a childminder's, than at a part-time nursery school. This inevitably limited the validity of any generalizations we could make about social class, although we would argue that our sample was representative of the majority of working-class children, and certainly of those attending nursery school.

We then approached a number of local authority nursery schools and nursery classes in London (where the project was based) and in Brighton (where HC lived), and asked for their assistance. No schools refused. We chose schools which we knew had a fair proportion of children from both middle-class and working-class families, so that we could select an equal number of children from each social class in each school that we used. We randomly selected two – or in some cases four – children from each school from both working and middle class families, who met all our criteria, using information about both the mother's educational level and the father's occupation to assign children to the different social class groups. None of the mothers approached refused to take part in the study.

RECORDING METHOD

Because of our interest in the quality of language, some form of electronic recording was essential. We ruled out video recording because it would be costly, cumbersome and intrusive in natural settings where the child should be able to move around freely. Audio recording, with small radio-microphones like those used in TV interviews, seemed likely to avoid these problems. At the time of our study the use of radio-microphones by researchers was relatively unusual, and we visited Gordon Wells, the only British researcher who seemed to be currently using them, to get some practical advice. Each microphone must be connected by a lead to a small transmitter, which must also be worn by the child; the transmitter sends out a signal to a receiver, which in turn feeds it into a tape-recorder. Once attached to the child, the radio-microphone allows the child to wander freely within a range of around one hundred metres of the receiver; it records everything the child says and everything which is said to the child, within a radius of about 5 metres.

Our main technical problem was to find a way to fix the microphone and transmitter to a small child in an unobtrusive and acceptable manner. First, we took the transmitter to pieces and rebuilt it to make it lighter. We then adapted an attractive sleeveless dress from 'Mothercare' which could be worn by itself or as a tunic on top of other clothes. The manufacturer kindly gave us eight dresses of different sizes and colours. The microphone was sewn into a padded pocket on the front of the dress, about 15–20 centimetres from the child's mouth. The lead from the microphone was sewn into the lining of the dress, and ended up at the transmitter, which was in another padded pocket at the back of the dress. After unsuccessful attempts by the researchers and teachers to put the dress on the children at school, we gave them to the mothers and asked them to put them on the child in the morning. In this context, the children accepted and even liked the 'special dress', as it came to be known, although two children who refused to wear it had to be dropped from the study.

At the same time as we were developing the recording method we were also grappling with another methodological issue – the effect of having an observer present when the recordings were made. Because of our interest in the context of the conversations, an observer was essential. In the initial recordings we made without an observer it was almost impossible to work out what the child was doing, and who was talking to whom. But this decision opened up the further question of whether the presence of the observer would have a major distorting effect on what was being observed, especially in the homes.

We decided, therefore, to carry out a pilot study, involving nine children, whom we recorded over four days at home and at school. We also used this study to help us select the time of day in which to make the home recordings. Initially, we had planned to record from the time the children got home from morning school until they went to bed, but this proved to be far too fatiguing for the observers. We therefore decided to confine the recording to a period of two or two and a half hours, and to use the pilot study to compare recordings that began at 12.30 pm, 2.30pm and 4.30pm. We then analysed whether there were any major changes over the four days, or in the different times of day, in the amount and type of child–adult talk, and in the amount the children approached the observer, or talked about her.

We found, unexpectedly, that the recording process seemed to have more impact on the teachers than the mothers. On the first day the staff seemed to ignore the target child. On the second day they talked to her a lot, while on the third and fourth day the amount of talk declined. At home, there was little difference in the amount and kind of mother–child interaction over four days. This could have meant that the observer had no impact, or that it would have taken more than four days for the impact to decline.

To throw light on this issue, we interviewed the mothers some weeks after the recordings had taken place and asked them how they believed that their behaviour and talk had been affected by the presence of an observer. Eighteen of the thirty mothers said that they had been affected. Typically, they had felt 'a bit ill at ease, not

26

quite natural'. Nevertheless, the observers believed that the effect of their presence was relatively slight. The mothers did not seem ill at ease, and family behaviour seemed very normal. Tempers were lost, children sometimes sworn at and slapped, mothers washed their hair, read the papers, phoned their friends. Probably mothers did modify their behaviour in the direction they thought represented 'good mothering', but we doubted whether the modification was a major one. So far as the children were concerned, their talk to and about the observer was greatest on the first day in both settings, and they did appear largely to ignore the observer after this visit.

Time of day differences in the amount and type of adult and child talk proved not to be significant; probably they vary from one family to another. There was, however, a trend for the late afternoon period to be more chaotic, with older children returning from school, and husbands from work, so we adopted the most convenient arrangement for us and the mothers, which was to return home with the mother and child from morning school, and remain for two or two and a half hours. This covered the period of the midday meal, or snack, and the afternoon until it was time to fetch an older child from school.

In order to reduce the 'observer effect', we decided to record for three successive mornings at school but only to use the second and third days, while at home we recorded on two days but used only the second. The school recordings lasted from the moment the child arrived in the morning until she left at midday – usually around two and a half hours. The recordings took place over a fifteen-month period between summer 1976 and autumn 1977. On the whole, the recording process was unproblematic, although we had to be able to carry out occasional technical repairs and maintenance to the equipment at short notice. Because we thought that a male observer in the home might be problematic, MH observed only in the schools.

TRANSCRIPTION OF THE TAPES

The recorded tapes and observers' notes were handed over to a team of transcribers, who for reasons of economy were not professionals, although able to type. The transcripts were then checked by the observers, who corrected any mistakes or misinterpretations, and added detailed notes (and, where necessary, drawings) about the context. All this proved to be a very time-consuming exercise. Because of the problems of understanding young children's voices, and distinguishing between them, each hour of a school tape had to be replayed many times, and took nine hours to transcribe. The researchers took a further three hours to check and add context notes. Each hour of a home tape (where there was much more talk) took twelve hours to transcribe, and a further five hours to check and add context. We estimated that approximately 4000 hours had been spent in collecting the data, transcribing, and checking the tapes before the analysis could even begin. If word-processors and transcribing machines had been used by skilled secretaries this time could have been reduced, but the task of transcribing natural dialogue involving young children in noisy situations is inevitably very time-consuming. Persistent replaying of the tapes and use of the detailed context notes reduced unintelligible utterances by both adults and children to 1.8 per cent or below.

ANALYSIS OF THE DATA

Two main phases can be identified during this period. In the first phase we worked in an essentially quantitative style, coding the transcripts according to reliably determined criteria and carrying out statistical tests on the results. These analyses were mostly carried out between 1977 and the end of 1978, when the research team dispersed. The second, more qualitative, phase began around 1982, when the two of us started working on *Young Children Learning*.

The most time-consuming aspect of the quantitative phase was the process of working up a coding system which could be reliably used by four coders. The codes themselves were mainly chosen in order to test our hypotheses. For example, we developed a code on 'Complex uses of language' from Joan Tough's writings in order to test her hypotheses about social class differences in language usage. All the team would start by coding parts of the transcripts according to a fledgling coding system: we would then compare our preliminary codings. Typically, this threw up two kinds of problem. First, there might be passages which could not be dealt with by the coding system as it stood, and the number of codes would have to be expanded accordingly. Second there might be large discrepancies between our different interpretations of the coding system: this was particularly likely to happen in the early stages of working up a system. We would then alter our definitions, and try again on a new set of extracts. This process of reworking the coding, trying it out, comparing notes, and reworking yet again would frequently pass through several cycles until we had reached a satisfactory level of agreement – usually a figure of around 80–90 per cent inter-coder agreement. Having reached the final version of the coding system we would then code all the transcripts according to this system. Since there were, on average, eighty pages of typed A4 transcripts for each child, and many separate codes were developed, the coding stage was lengthy and laborious.

The process can be illustrated by the first and simplest analysis carried out, which focused on the amount of talk taking place in each location. It was clear from simply glancing at the transcripts that there was much more adult–child dialogue at home than at school: the average transcript of a two-and-a-half-hour session at home was about sixty typed A4 pages, while that for a school session of the same length came to about ten pages. In order to compare the amount of talk in different contexts and on different topics, we decided to start by dividing the transcripts up into *conversations*, which were essentially episodes of talk on a particular topic.

The task of dividing up a continuous stream of talk into discrete conversations may sound easy, but proved somewhat tricky. One problem lay in reaching agreement as to when the subject had changed to a new topic, or whether it was simply the continuation of the same topic. We also had problems when the same topic was subsequently returned to after some intervening activity or discussion of a different topic – as happened quite frequently at home. We finally decided that a conversation had ended if there was a distinct change of topic, or if one of the participants moved out of earshot. This second criterion sometimes required a reexamination of the observer's original notes to work out whether the adult and child could still be considered 'within earshot'. Assessing the amount of talk in each conversation was more straightforward, as we simply counted the number of *turns* contributed by each of the participants.

Our quantitative analyses provided substantial support for the first part of our original hypothesis – that there are important differences in the quality of parent–child and teacher–child dialogues'. We also attempted to test the second part of the hypothesis – 'that certain important characteristics of the dialogue are related to the nature of the ongoing activity of the adults and children'. Each conversation which lasted for seven turns or more was coded as 'joint activity' if it occurred in the course of, or interrupted, a joint adult–child activity such as playing together, watching TV together, or discussing a book. Such episodes of joint activity were much more frequent at home than at school, with few social class differences; moreover, they tended to be associated with longer conversations. However, there were no clear-cut associations between other features of the conversations and these periods of joint activity thus providing only limited support for the second part of our hypothesis. We were, however, somewhat dissatisfied with these findings, feeling that our codes were insufficiently sensitive to bring out the relationship which we felt existed between the kind of activity and the quality of talk.

The dissatisfaction was one of the factors which, as we began to think about how to write a book about our study, decided us to make a qualitative analysis of some of the conversations. Another factor was our increasing interest in issues which we had not foreseen at the start of the study, such as the potential of the home as a learning environment, the role of curiosity in children's learning, and the adult's role in facilitating this learning. These issues were often highlighted by particular conversations which provided a graphic example of some particular point, but whose essential quality was not being captured by the quantitative analysis. Moreover, in talking about our findings more widely among groups of practitioners, it was clear that the presentation of illustrative conversations helped considerably in communicating the quantitative findings; at the same time, discussion of particular conversations with groups of teachers often increased our understanding of the issues and drew attention to hitherto unnoticed features of the conversations.

Some time after the conclusion of the quantitative analysis, then, we decided to look more closely at individual conversations, focusing in particular on what the children might be learning and how this related to the ongoing activity. Much of our attention was now on the home as a learning environment. Analysis of individual conversations between mothers and their children made us increasingly aware of their potential for learning, irrespective of social background. Many of these conversations took place in contexts which have been traditionally thought of as beneficial for learning – for example, fantasy play, or during games with rules, or while the mother was reading a story to the child. But others occurred in contexts which are often ignored as potential learning environments, for example in the course of arguments between mother and child, or while the two of them were simply spending time together, talking. In *Young Children Learning* we quote a series of conversations which took place while one girl, Pauline, and her mother were discussing what items they needed to get from the shops.

Mother. No, I haven't got enough to get my shopping. All of it.

Child. Not all of it?

Mother. Irene's just taken five pounds. She'll bring some change back. If she's got some, she'll bring some change back. It's not enough to get all that. Is it? (*Points to the shopping list*)

Child. No.

Mother. See? So when Daddy gets paid I'll get some more money and then I'll go and get the rest.

Child. Yeah. That's nice, isn't it, Mum?

Mother. Mm. . . I got one, two three, four, five six, seven, eight, nine, ten, eleven, twelve (*counts items on list*).

Child. (*Joins in counting*) Nine, ten, eleven.

Mother. Fourteen, fifteen, sixteen, seventeen, eighteen bits.

Child. Mum, let's have a look! (*Mother shows child the list*) Do it again.

Mother. We gotta get rice, tea, braising steak, cheese, pickle, carrots, fish, chicken, bread, eggs, bacon, beefburgers, beans. . .Oh, Irene's gone to get them (*crosses off beans*) . . . peas, ham, corned beef.

Our analysis of this conversation suggested that in the course of it Pauline might be learning a good deal about such important matters as that the amount that can be bought has to be balanced against the money available, and this in turn depends on whether the wage earner has been paid that week. She might also be learning about the role of a written list in planning and organizing oneself, and the role of friends and neighbours in helping each other, as well as some basic counting skills. Yet these conversations were triggered by an activity which is not usually recommended as having great educational value.

Analysis of this kind did not lend itself to quantitative comparisons. Instead, it allowed us to examine in a detailed way the learning opportunities that developed during a conversation. It also enabled us to gain insights into the role of questioning in clarifying children's understanding, by looking closely at particular episodes

31

in which children engaged in a sequence of questions around a particular topic. We were particularly struck by what we came to call *passages of intellectual search*, in which the children struggled to understand something which was puzzling them, showing no small degree of logic and persistence in the process.

WRITING UP

The process of writing up the project mirrored the process of analysis, in that it took place over a long period of time and consisted of two main stages. In the first stage, we wrote up the main quantitative findings in a series of five papers for an academic audience. We considered it our first duty as researchers to report our methodology and detailed findings in peer reviewed journals, and in any case we considered the findings, especially those about the relation between context and language usage, of theoretical relevance. As is often the case, the two years of project funding was insufficient to allow time for much writing up. By the end of the funding period only one article had been written. Two of the team then left academic life, GP to train as a teacher, and HC to have a baby and subsequently teach. A third researcher, MH, also left the Unit, but continued as researcher on an SSRC post-doctoral fellowship. The subsequent writing up was therefore done only by MH and BT.

All but one of the five papers were published in the *Journal of Child Psychology and Psychiatry* between 1979 and 1983. With hindsight, the research might have made more impact on academics if we had published in a wider range of journals, particularly American journals such as *Child Development* or *Developmental Psychology*. We were influenced by a desire to support British journals, and unfortunately, at that time, no British developmental psychology journal existed.

The second phase of the writing up process began in 1982. We had always intended to produce a book for a non-academic audience, since our findings were clearly relevant to the ongoing debate about the value of preschool education, and would be of intrinsic interest to parents. (We were encouraged in the latter belief by the fact that our teenage children and adult friends found the transcripts fascinating.) With the five papers finished, we finally started on the book. Our first plan was to follow the format of the papers and present our findings in an essentially quantitative manner, focusing in turn on the topics which made up the academic papers. However, we soon realized that this was not doing justice to our material. Instead, we decided to give more emphasis to issues such as what children were learning at home and the role of curiosity in learning, and adopt a more qualitative approach. With both authors heavily committed to other research, the book was not finished until early 1984. Because we wanted to reach a wide audience, we looked for a publisher who would produce the book cheaply, and market it effectively. Fortunately, Fontana liked the manuscript, agreed to sell a paperback edition for £2.95, and published it within six months.

Writing the book was probably one of the least difficult parts of the project, once we had become clear about how to do it. The feeling that we were at last doing full justice to our material, and that we were on the final lap, helped us to bring the project to fruition. There were the inevitable practical difficulties in co-operating when one author was in London and the other in Edinburgh, but we were able to get together for bursts of three or four days of intensive activity and discussion. We also had surprisingly few disagreements about what we were going to say, or how we were going to say it.

On reflection, our main regret about the book is that it took so long to appear. The project, it will be recalled, began in 1976, and all the data was collected by the end of 1977, yet the book was not published until 1984. In all honesty, we cannot see how it could have been otherwise. The project team dispersed in 1978, leaving four articles and a book yet to be written by MH and BT. Both of us were fully occupied with other projects, and virtually the whole of the writing-up process and a good deal of analysis took place in our 'free time', where it had to compete with demands from the rest of our lives. We do not imagine that we are in any way unique in this; indeed, because of the short-term nature of research funding, there are many projects which are never fully written up. In our case, it was only our belief in the value of our material, plus a mule-like determination to finish what we had started, which kept us at it for so long. In the event, there were also some advantages to this delay. We had time to reflect on our findings and our materials, and to discuss them with colleagues and teachers.

REACTION TO THE PROJECT

No account of the project would be complete without giving some attention to the way our findings have been received. There was virtually no reaction to the publication of our findings in academic journals, and it is rare to come across a reference to them in a developmental psychology article or book. This is probably because the research is seen by psychologists as 'applied' rather than discipline-related, although we ourselves think that it has implications for the study of language and thinking in young children. Probably we should have put the findings more clearly in a theoretical framework. And probably we should have published in a developmental psychology journal, rather the *Journal of Child Psychology and Psychiatry* which tends to be read mainly by clinicians. In contrast, our book *Young Children Learning* provoked reactions from many quarters. These reactions can be considered in four phases – the immediate media reaction to the book; the reaction of practitioners; the reaction of academics in critical reviews; and the long-term impact the book has had on the educational world.

When *Young Children Learning* was published in September 1984, we were worried that the 'nursery school lobby' and feminists (both groups we were in sympathy with) would react critically. The finding that young children were participating in richer conversations at home than at school, irrespective of their social background, would inevitably be seen both as attacking nursery schools, and adding to the guilt of mothers who went to work. In fact, although we were critical of many aspects of nursery schools, we certainly thought that they made a valuable and important contribution to the lives of the children attending them, and to their parents. And we were far from believing that children needed to be constantly with their mothers, or that enriching conversations between mother and child needed to, or could, take place all day and every day. Knowing that the media delight in sensational controversy, we tried to anticipate distortion by writing short articles about the book for *New Society* and the *Times Educational Supplement*, and offering interviews to the quality press. The publishers issued a carefully worded press release, and held a press conference on the day of publication, where brief summaries of the book were distributed.

These precautions to some extent paid off. Sympathetic and well-informed reviews of the book appeared in *The Times*, the *Daily Telegraph*, the *Guardian*, and the *New Statesman*, written by their educational correspondents. And whilst reports in the popular press tended to be headlined 'Mum's the word' or 'Mum really does know

3

RESEARCHING
COMMON KNOWLEDGE
Studying the content and context of educational discourse

Neil Mercer

INTRODUCTION

The research I will describe in this chapter was carried out by Derek Edwards, Janet Maybin and myself in 1984–6 as a project funded by the Economic and Social Research Council (Edwards, Mercer and Maybin, 1987). As part of a line of research begun in 1979 and still continuing, it has generated one book (Edwards and Mercer, 1987) and the other publications listed at the end of this chapter. My intention here is to describe what kind of research we did, why we did it, how we did it, and some of the problems we had in doing it.

What was the research meant to find out?

My first real job was teaching psychology in the sociology department of Leicester University. At the regular departmental research seminars, one of the professors of sociology would often stop those presenting the research – postgraduates, lecturers, visiting academics – in their tracks by posing a single question. As they described in detail their rich data, their theoretical framework, their methodological complexities, he would interrupt and ask, irritably, 'Yes, yes, but what is your *problem*?'. By this he meant (I think): what was your research really meant to achieve? What questions were you trying to answer? What, in a nutshell, did you want to know, and why did you want to know it?

My best attempt at an answer to his question here is this. We wanted to understand how people did teaching and learning together. As participants (teachers and learners) in that process, as well as researchers we felt that we knew very little about how it worked, how it went right or wrong. In particular, we were

41

interested in knowledge, and how it was shared. Whatever else education is about, it is about knowledge. Every day in classrooms, knowledge gets constructed, presented, received, rejected, evaluated, understood and misunderstood. A careful examination of this process might well tell us something of psychological interest and practical educational value.

What kind of research did we do?

We knew from the earliest stages of planning the research that we would use observational rather than experimental methods. We had begun this whole line of research in a state of disenchantment with experimental approaches to the study of cognitive development and reasoning (see for example Mercer and Edwards, 1981). Margaret Donaldson (1978) in particular had convinced us that psychological laboratories were very good at constructing experimental artefacts, and we had no desire to create more. It was our view that too many experimenters began by 'modelling' real-life situations which they knew very little about. And (as Desforges, 1985, has pointed out) too many psychologists have pontificated about teaching-and-learning without studying what actually goes on in classrooms. We wanted to know more about what people did when they went about their normal business.

We also knew that we would be making a qualitative, rather than a quantitative, analysis of our observations. We could not pursue our interests by conducting a large-scale, statistical analysis of classroom interactions in which only a relatively superficial consideration of the exchange of meanings would be possible. It was the qualitative nature of classroom talk and its content that interested us most.

Theory

One function of theories is to set agendas for research – to generate certain kinds of questions which the research will attempt to answer. Another function is to provide a 'universe of discourse' within which the discussion and explanation of research findings can take place. The framework within which our 'problem' was defined was strongly influenced by our reading of Vygotsky (e.g. 1978; see also Wertsch, 1985) and Bruner (e.g. 1986), but also very relevant was psychological research which had explored aspects of the cultural basis of the development of knowledge (though not necessarily in school settings) such as Neisser (1976) and Cole and Scribner (1974). The work of some educational researchers (particularly Barnes, 1976) who had studied communication in the classroom also helped define our universe and shape our methodology. There were other psychological and sociological influences (e.g. Walkerdine, 1982; Mehan, 1979): but this is not the place to go into theory in any depth or detail. However, one respect of the relationship between theory and research practice is, I think, relevant and interesting here. It is the influence of previous researchers whose ideas, while dealing with relevant aspects of the phenomena under investigation and being accorded high status in the field of study, are nevertheless rejected as a basis for the theoretical framework. Sometimes the work of such researchers can be at least as significant an influence as more 'positive' sources, not least because it motivates: dissatisfaction may generate curiosity. An example might make this point clearer. It concerns our conception of the role of language in thinking and learning, and our model of the process of teaching and learning. We were familiar with the work of Piaget (e.g. 1971), and recognized its influence on both research into cognitive development and modern 'child-centred' educational practice. However, we had become increasingly dissatisfied by the way that language was marginalized in the Piagetian model of cognitive development, and also by the way that the role of the teacher was represented as that of a provider of 'learning environments' rather than as an active participant or collaborator in the process whereby a child constructs knowledge. In a way that might seem ridiculous to an outsider, our discussion sometimes led us to get *angry* with Piaget and his followers: couldn't they see that there was so much more, a communicative aspect to teaching-and-learning, which they had largely ignored? One of our motives in doing the research, then, was quite simply to try to prove them wrong (see Edwards and Mercer, 1987 Chapters 2 and 8 for more on this).

COLLECTING DATA

In planning our observations, we had a number of considerations to take into account. We needed to collect very detailed data on classroom discourse because of the kinds of issues we wished to investigate, and there was obviously a limit to the amount of such data we could handle. It seemed clear that our interests would be best served by subjecting relatively small samples of classroom discourse and activity (in terms of numbers of teachers and classes) to close, intensive analysis, in the hope of discovering how knowledge is actually built and shared between teacher and particular groups of pupils. We wanted to look at how teachers introduced new topics, and how they followed this up by setting children tasks, checking on their understanding, and helping them draw conclusions from what they had done. We also wanted the classroom activities we observed to be as similar as possible to what teachers would normally do with those pupils in their classrooms, while avoiding the technical difficulties of observing and analysing conversations and interactions between teachers and all the children in a class of more than 25 children (in which, additionally, much time is taken up by organizational and control aspects). From an earlier phase of research (Mercer and Edwards, 1981), we already had videotaped recording of teachers working with whole classes and small groups in four London primary schools. To provide the main source of data for the present (second) phase, we arranged to make video recordings in three local primary schools. As the primary school teachers in these schools followed the usual English practice of organizing children into small groups around communal tables, working together or in parallel on the same task, we decided to set up conditions which would enable us to observe the activities of three such groups of 5–6 pupils aged between 8 and 11, each working with their usual teacher on one specific topic over three consecutive 'lessons' of 40–60 minutes' duration.

All three schools were state primary schools. Initial contact with the schools was made through the headteachers, with whose agreement and assistance we then met teachers who were working with the appropriate age group who were willing to consider participating in the study (see Maybin, 1987, for a more detailed account of how this fieldwork was organized). The research team's project officer then visited each school, and with each teacher negotiated a suitable plan of activity for the three sessions from within the teacher's existing plan of work. The rationale and general purpose of the research was explained to the teachers. A second visit to each school was made one week before the recording of the first session, to check on final arrangements. By this time, each teacher had identified the group of children that they would be working with for the recording, and had also selected the topic which would provide

Table 3.1 Phase 2 schools: classroom topics

	Lesson 1	Lesson 2	Lesson 3
Pendulums	The teacher talked to the group about what a pendulum was, then split the 6 pupils into 3 pairs to investigate whether the angle of swing, the weight of the bob, or the length of the string, respectively, made any difference to the speed of the pendulum. Results were put into matrices, and their significance discussed.	The pupils had plotted the results of their investigations on graphs, using acetate paper. Teacher and pupils discussed these findings, using an overhead projector to study the graphs together.	In the class PE session, their teacher helped the pupils to test out the properties of a 'human pendulum', using the ropes and bars.
Clay pots	Pupils learned how to make a clay thumb-pot, modelling their own pots under the teacher's guidance and demonstration.	Children made a clay hedgehog or pig, with the teacher's guidance.	Children studied pictures of animals, and then made one of them in clay.
Computer graphics	Using the school's new microcomputer, the teacher showed 4 pupils how to instruct it to draw an F shape. Pupils then tried to write a program for a T shape, using forwards, backwards and angle-turning commands. They tried out and discussed these programs with the teacher, who then helped them write one for an equilateral triangle.	Pupils tried out and modified the programs for octagons, isosceles and equilateral triangles which they had written for homework. The teacher helped them write a program to draw a hexagon, and showed them how to use the 'pen off' and 'pen on' commands, and how to store a program.	The four children with their teacher introduced the work they had been doing to two other pupils from the class, and helped them to write and try out (run) programs for various shapes.

Source: Reproduced with permission Maybin, 1987, p.177.

the main theme for the three sessions (see Table 3.1). Teachers were asked about their aims and expectations for these sessions and their responses were recorded by the project officer.

Video recordings were made by one cameraman, assisted by a sound engineer for some sessions. One member of the research team was also present for each recording, and visited the school again one week after the recording sessions, by which time the research team had viewed the recorded material and drawn up questions to use in interviewing the teacher and pupil involved. We had decided that it was important that one of us was present throughout the related sessions so that a researcher would have had direct experience as an observer of the recorded events, and would also be aware of any incidents which immediately preceded or followed the recorded sessions. That person would also conduct the relevant interviews with teachers and pupils.

Each pupil was withdrawn from class for an individual 10–20 minute interview. Interviews with teachers were carried out separately outside school hours. All interviews were tape-recorded and transcribed. These interviews focussed on such matters as (a) participants' understanding of the substantive content of the session, (b) participants' perceptions of the purpose or aims of the activities they had engaged in, and (c) specific enquiries to teachers (and occasionally pupils) about why they had said or done certain things during the sessions. This included discussions with the teachers about the teaching methods they used, as well as some general enquiries about their general teaching style and educational philosophy. All teachers were questioned on certain general issues, of which the following are examples:

How much work had the pupils done on this topic in previous sessions?

Had the teacher assumed any knowledge or experience of the topic from outside the recorded sessions?

What did the teacher want each session to achieve?

How much did the teacher think the pupils had actually learned?

What did the teacher think was the essence of good teaching? Did she try in her teaching to put into practice any particular pedagogic principles?

These questions were adapted to suit the specific content of particular sessions and sequences.

The children were also asked a set of basic questions, supplemented or adapted to cover aspects of the contents of the lessons in which they had engaged. These basic questions covered such things as:

What did they think were the main things they had learnt?

What did they think the teacher wanted them to learn in the session?

Did they know anything about what they had done prior to the session, from other lessons or from outside school?

Had they found anything in the session confusing?

More specific questions dealt with particular concepts, procedures and problems encountered in particular sessions. Children obviously differed in the way they responded to these questions. Notably, some seemed more willing or able than others to reflect on what they had said and done. But we found the content of their responses valuable, especially when set against the teacher's interview responses, and I certainly feel that any researcher with preliminary doubts about the feasibility of interviewing children of this age should be reassured by our experience.

The outcome of our visits to the schools was about 450 minutes of videotaped classroom activity and about 270 minutes of audiotaped interviews.

Some observations on our observations

I would expect the critical reader to ask how far our methods for gathering data were compatible with our aim, stated earlier, of finding out more about what people did when they went about their normal business. We disrupted proceedings by entering classrooms with a video camera, and once there we focused our attention entirely on how the teacher taught one small group of children. There is little doubt that teachers who know that their teaching is going to be recorded and analysed will be more nervous and self-conscious than usual. They may well have spent more time than usual preparing what to teach. Children, too, are not immune to the presence of the camera, and two or three extra adults. In attending to how a teacher dealt with just one group of children, we may have gained an inaccurate impression of the amount of time and attention that the teacher would normally give to such a group. (Primary teachers who have watched the videos we made are sometimes particularly scathing on this matter, with comments to the effect that most other children in the class must have been sedated or bribed into silence.)

I do not, however, believe that any of this creates serious problems for the validity of our research. There was no reason to believe that the children were more than temporarily and superficially affected by the presence of the camera and its operator. The video recordings show that early in the initial sessions, some children are distracted by the camera, but such signs of interest soon diminish and are not apparent at all in the recordings of later sessions. We were not researching classroom management strategies, or quantifying teacher–pupil contact time, so the balance of the teacher's time spent with the target group against that spent with the rest of the class was not a significant consideration. And if the conditions encouraged teachers to do their best, and gave them the opportunity to work in a more intensive manner on one topic with one group of children than would usually be possible, that is a positive feature of our design, not a problem. We wanted to be able to sample teaching-and-learning in a relatively intense form, and so we created conditions under which this was possible.

Only the most naive of researchers would not expect their visible presence as an observer to affect the behaviour of those being observed. Any observation of social interactions which is carried out with the knowledge of the participants may affect what is said and done. The crucial issue is whether or not the observation causes serious distortion of phenomena or creates artefacts. All one can do is (a) try to employ observational techniques which will obtain suitable data with the least possible disruption of the processes under observation, and (b) use participants' own views and those of other informed sources (in this case, other teachers) to help judge the representative quality of what has been observed and recorded. Although the teachers involved were sometimes self-critical about their activities in the recorded sessions, neither they nor any other teachers who have since watched the recording raised issues of 'reality' beyond those of classroom management as mentioned above.

ANALYSIS

Observational analysis

If you are a researcher using videotaped data, one danger is that making recordings can delude you into feeling that the observation has somehow been accomplished, when in fact all you have done is laid in some serious observational work for the days, weeks, or even months ahead. An experienced ethnographic researcher has estimated that the analysis of one hour of classroom interaction on tape will on average take an ethnographer ten hours (Martyn Hammersley, personal communication: but see Hammersley, 1983 for a discussion of relevant methodological issues). The analytic methods we employed were similar to those of ethnography, in that we were similarly concerned with the minutiae of what was said and done; and we were interested in participants' accounts and interpretations of what they said and did. We differed from most classroom ethnographers, I believe, in being less concerned with the sociological themes of 'social order' and 'control' (cf. Young, 1971; Edwards, 1980) and more with the psychological ones of 'knowledge' and 'communication'.

Through preliminary work we had come to realize that other existing methods for analysing classroom discourse were not suitable for our needs. For example, the commonly employed method known as 'interaction analysis' (Flanders, 1970) or 'systematic observation' (Galton, Simon and Croll, 1980) involves all events being assigned by observers to previously defined categories, with the coded results thus obtained providing the data for the next stage of analysis. That is, the discourse itself does not remain accessible to analysts after the observed classroom activity is over, and so the analysis is wholly dependent on the *a priori* adequacy of the category scheme and on the observers' skills in applying it. As our interest lay in the continuous, cumulative processes by which a common knowledge is developed in classrooms, and as we were making full records of all that was said and done, it was clear that our needs would not be served by reducing our data to numerical frequency codings.

On the other hand, the 'discourse analysis' methods which have been used by some linguists to study classroom talk (e.g. Sinclair and Coulthard, 1975; Stubbs, 1981), while not involving the early loss of actual discourse during analysis, were no more suited to our purposes because they had been designed to deal only with the *structure* of discourse, not the *content* of what is said and done. (A critical comparison and evaluation of these, and other, methods of analysing classroom talk can be found in Edwards and Mercer, 1986, pp.176–9 and Edwards and Mercer, 1987, ch. 2). .

The method we employed involved the complete transcription of all the discourse recorded on videotape. Fortunately, the ESRC provided us with a project secretary who transcribed all the tapes. Having checked the accuracy of the typed transcripts against the recordings, one of the researchers then watched the recordings of each of the three-session sequences, writing on the transcripts any information about physical context and non-verbal communication which was necessary to make sense of what was said and done. An example of a transcript at the end of this stage is provided below. It is taken from one of the 'pendulums' sessions described in Table 3.1. (Note: pauses of less than 2 seconds are represented thus /, those of more than 2 seconds //. **Bold type** indicates emphatic speech.)

T: Now he didn't have a watch/but he **had** on **him** something that was a very good timekeeper that he could use to hand straight away/	*T snaps fingers on 'straight away', and looks invitingly at pupils as if posing a question or inviting a response.*
You've got it. I've got it. What is it?// What could we use to count beats? What have **you** got?//	*T points on 'You've' and 'I've'. T beats hand on table slowly, looks around group of pupils, who smile and shrug.*
You can feel it **here**.	*T puts fingers on T's wrist pulse.*
PUPILS: Pulse.	*(In near unison.)*
T: A pulse. Everybody see if you can find it.	*All copy T, feeling for wrist pulses.*

Next, the researchers (together) re-viewed the videorecordings, armed with the transcripts which now included the 'context notes' as a right-hand column of typescript. This was undoubtedly the most important part of the process of analysis; but it is also the one I find the most difficult to describe programmatically. Basically, it involved watching and discussing the videorecordings, stopping and reviewing sequences whenever necessary, and making notes on what took place. One of our aims was to track themes or elements of knowledge – such diverse things as given information, technical terms, ways of doing things, criteria for success, past events and shared experiences invoked by participants – through the lessons, watching for them to emerge, surfacing like dolphins, in the discourse. We wanted to see how participants took them up (if at all) and carried them along, how they were used, how they changed, how they related to each other, and what significance was attached to them. We noticed how *continuity* of experience was established through discourse.

Content, continuity and context

As well as the *content* of discourse, we were concerned with its *context*. Our consistent view has been that educational discourse is never 'context free': the intelligibility of its meanings always depends on the invocation (explicitly or implicitly) by speakers of an educational 'universe of discourse' (see Edwards and Mercer, 1986; Mercer, Edwards and Maybin, 1988; Edwards and Mercer, 1989). At the most obvious level, our concern with context meant that we noticed how the physical 'props' of the classroom – equipment, drawings, texts, computer screen representations – were invoked by speakers to support the discourse. At a more subtle level, we tried to see how certain events and items of knowledge were used to contextualize others: a piece of corrective advice offered by the teacher might, for example, be contextualized by a reference to some past, shared event ('Remember how we did it yesterday'): a child's re-formulation of an answer might reflect a model offered earlier by the teacher. At the deepest – and most uncertain – level of analysis, we were looking for evidence of those 'taken-for-granted' assumptions which, although rarely or never explicitly invoked or discussed by participants, nevertheless define the process of 'doing education'. We have called these kinds of assumptions 'educational ground-rules' (Mercer and Edwards, 1981; Edwards and Mercer, 1987).

To make these analytic procedures clearer and less abstract, I include here an example of the products of this process. It is an extract from one of our research publications (Edwards and Mercer, 1989). In it, we draw on the analysis of two of the three recorded topics 'computer graphics' and 'clay pottery' (see Table 3.1, above) to exemplify matters of discourse content, continuity and context as discussed above.

SEQUENCE 1: Introducing the lesson.

T: Right/this our new computer/the four eighty   (An RML 480Z
zed. You haven't seen this one before. Erm   micro)
when you've used computer programs before/
what's happened is that the words have come up
on the screen/ or the instructions/for you/have   Teacher gestures
come up on the screen/ and you've just an-   with arm toward
swered the questions/ and/ typed in/ what the/   screen.
computer wanted you to do. This program is
different. In this program the computer doesn't
know what to do. You've got to tell it what to
do/ so you have got to instruct the computer.

The teacher began the lesson by introducing the pupils to their new
computer and immediately established a context for it in terms of their
previous experience with computers in the classroom. Lessons
typically began in this manner, with introductions to the work to be
done and continuity links established with what had been done
previously. Thus Lesson 2, recorded a week later, began with a back
reference to where the previous computer lesson had left off.

SEQUENCE 2: Building upon the previous lesson.

T: Now you've got your programs from last
    week have you/ to show me what you're   T reminding
PUPILS: Yes   pupils of
T: (continuing) going to do/ with angles not ninety   instructions she
    degrees./ We had to try something else didn't   gave last week.
    we. What did you find most difficult Susan?
    What's yours?

Besides these opening links, explicit references were also made
during lessons to what had been done and said earlier. Sequence 3
lists the teacher's back references from the last three lessons of
making clay pottery. (This is a different teacher, pupils, and school.)

SEQUENCE 3: Back references to shared experience and talk.

– What did I tell you about thin bits? What happens when they dry?
– What did I tell you about eyes?
– Can you remember what you forgot to do Patricia/ when you put
    that little belt thing around?
– Look when you put its eyes in./ I did tell you this before Lorraine.
– John/ you seem to have forgotten everything you've learned don't
    you?
– Don't forget/ if it's too wide chop it off.

In Sequence 3, the teacher's remarks to John and Lorraine reflect the
fact that constructing a continuity of shared knowledge can be a problematic process. Indeed, all of the cases listed in Sequence 3 occured

in the context of some difficulty arising with regard to the understanding that teacher and pupils had established up to that point in the lesson. That is, the teacher was most likely to point out that knowledge was, in her opinion, shared when pupils were acting as though it were not. When the pupils seemed not to have grasped some significant principle, procedure, or instruction, the teacher would remind them that this matter had, in fact, been dealt with previously.

It has been suggested that this association of explicit references to past shared experience, including previous discourse, with occasions on which the commonality of knowledge appears to be in doubt is a general feature of conversation, not something peculiar to school classrooms. It has been observed in adult conversation in educational and noneducational settings (Edwards & Middleton, 1986; Mercer & Edwards, 1987) and in parent-child conversation during early language learning (Edwards & Goodwin, 1986). In the classroom, however, such explicit appeals to significant aspects of pasts shared experience might have an important pedagogical function. As transactions between child and adult, they occur in Vygotsky's "zone of proximal development", at precisely the points at which common knowledge is being created. It is the teacher's role to draw children's attention to such matters, and so establish knowledge that is both common and communicable. The next sequence illustrates this very clearly.

Sequence 4: Continuity: What have you been doing all along?

T: Now/how are you fixing them on Katie?
Katie: Putting them/ well its (. . .)   Katie mutters
T: Now/what do you think you should do what   hesitantly.
    have you been doing all along every time
    you've joined anything?
Katie: Putting grooves in it.
T: Putting grooves in it/ haven't you and water/
    grooves and water/ the water to fill up the
    grooves/ on both bits of clay./ You must do it/
    otherwise it will dry/ and when it's dry like
    those are dry/ those ears will just be lying on
    the floor/ or on the table. Take them off/oth-   Katie refits the
    erwise you'll be very sad./ You've got to do   ears.
    things the right way round with clay or they
    just don't work.

(Edwards and Mercer, 1989, pp.94–6, reprinted with
the permission of Ablex Publishing Corporation)

Interviews

As mentioned earlier, we felt that the interviews with both teachers and children were useful and informative. It may be relevant here to define the status of the interview data in our analysis. The interviews with teachers before the observed sessions were intended to inform us about what would be going on, and what the teacher's pedagogic aims and expectations were for the children involved. The interviews with teachers and pupils which followed the videotaped sessions were simply an additional source of information about what was said and done. In the research of some ethno-methodologists, conversation analysts or discourse analysts (see, for examples and discussion of such research, Potter and Wetherell, 1987), interview data may be the prime data: the interviews themselves provide the discourse or conversations which are then analysed to explain actions, 'interpretative practices', attitudes or beliefs. In our analysis, however, the interview data had a *supplementary* status: we talked to participants in order to elicit their ideas about the content and purpose of the activities in which they had been observed to engage, and to help us resolve any ambiguities in what had been said during the recorded sessions.

PRESENTATION AND DISSEMINATION

Matters of dissemination – how to write up the research, where to get it published, and so on – usually become a matter for consideration by researchers well before the completion of a project. There are two common problems to be faced. One is identifying the audiences to whom the research is to be disseminated. The second is deciding how best to communicate the findings of the research to those audiences.

In case of our research we identified two main audiences. The first was the academic community – other researchers, teachers in higher education, students. To this audience, we wished to describe a piece of research which could be seen as contributing to the fields of study of psychology, discourse analysis, educational research. For this audience we wrote journal articles, a book, and presented papers at conferences. The other main audience was the professional educational community – teachers, educational policy makers, teacher-trainers – who we hoped would appreciate the benefits of an 'applied' piece of research. For this audience, we wrote articles in the educational press (e.g. Mercer and Edwards, 1988), wrote material for Open University INSET courses and ran INSET sessions for LEAs. We hoped the book (Edwards and Mercer, 1987) would reach this audience also.

Communicating with these audiences was, initially, no easy matter. By the very nature of our involvement in the project, our immersion in the analytic procedures described earlier, we had developed a highly contextualized discourse for discussing, among ourselves, the data, analysis and theory with which we worked. Somewhat to our surprise, we often found that it was difficult to talk about the research to people outside the project, even if they were social scientists or educational researchers. We felt it was necessary to identify and 'highlight' distinctive qualities of what we had done and found.

In attempting to overcome these difficulties, we came to realize that what initially appeared to be a part of communication problem was in fact a resource for its solution. This was our own vocabulary of 'key terms' which had emerged through the analytic process and through our discussions of other relevant research. We had developed a set of terms and concepts in order to talk to each other about the research: we began now to consider how useful they would be for communicating our findings to others. This phase of research had begun with one such term (mentioned earlier) well established: *educational ground rules*. It was not really an original usage on our part (Neisser, 1976 and Bernstein, 1981 both use 'ground rules' to refer to implicit understandings about how educational activities should be carried out), but we had used it in a particular way, to explain particular phenomena we had studied. We also used *context* and *continuity* with specific meanings. In describing teacher-talk we introduced terms like *cued elicitation* (whereby a teacher encourages a particular response from pupils through intonation, gesture or other physical activity). In discussing qualities and kinds of educational knowledge we distinguished between *principled* and *ritual* understanding. The precise meaning of any of these terms is not important here (see Chapter 8 of Edwards and Mercer, 1987); I include them because they figured in our attempts to move from the 'closed', highly contextualized discourse of researchers engaged in doing the research (within which some of these terms had emerged) into a more 'open', explicit form of discourse suitable for communicating with wider audiences. Contrary to some opinions, the introduction of new technical terms does not necessarily hinder communication with wider audiences. If well chosen, and properly explained, key terms can help people perceive the distinctive qualities of a piece of research, and help them take on new perspectives and ideas which the researchers have developed. Readers may judge the success of our efforts by looking at any of our publications listed below.

We spent a lot of time and effort planning our dissemination and writing up the research. Nevertheless, our dissemination plans encountered some hitches. For instance, we hoped for a simultaneous launch of *Common Knowledge* in Britain and the USA, but the combined effects of our publisher's involvement in a corporate merger and the loss of a book manuscript in the international post prevented this: the book first appeared in the USA only as an inaccessably priced hardback. Reviews of the book seemed slow to appear. It emerged that some of the people we most hoped would read and review the book had never even received a review copy. Persistent pressure from us eventually sorted out some of these problems, and the book has now appeared in American paperback and in a Spanish language edition (Edwards and Mercer, 1988). So although fame and fortune on the grand scale still skilfully evade us, we seem to have been reasonably successful so far in reaching the audiences we aimed for. Our papers have been accepted for publication by referenced journals. Our research has been cited in government policy documents (The Kingman Report, 1988) and *Common Knowledge* has been adopted as a set book for postgraduates and is used on in-service courses for teachers. BBC Radio 4's general interest programme *Science Now* even included an item on our research and its implications for teaching and learning (October, 1989). It is of course particularly reassuring to have now met or read of teachers who have found our ideas interesting and useful (e.g. National Oracy Project, 1989a,b) and to find that some of the researchers who we most respect see value in our work too (e.g. Barnes, 1987; Cazden and Mehan, 1989).

REFERENCES

Barnes, D. (1987) 'The nature of signals: an interview with Douglas Barnes', *The English Magazine* 19, Autumn, 4–10.

Barnes, D. (1976) *From Communication to Curriculum*, Harmondsworth, Penguin.

Bernstein, B. (1981) 'Codes, modalities and the process of reproduction: a model', *Language in Society* 10, 327–63.

Bruner, J.S. (1986) *Actual Minds, Possible Worlds*, London, Harvard University Press.

Cazden, C.B. and Mehan, H. (1989) 'Principles of sociology and anthropology: context, code, classroom and culture', in Reynolds, M.C. (ed.) *Knowledge Base for the Beginning Teacher*, New York, Pergammon.

Cole, M. and Scribner, S. (1974) *Culture and Thought*, New York, Wiley.

Desforges, C. (1985) 'Training for the management of learning in the primary school', in Francis, H. (ed.) *Learning to Teach: Psychology in Teacher Training*, Lewis, Falmer Press.

Donaldson, M. (1978) *Children's Minds*, London, Fontana.

Edwards, A.D. (1980) 'Patterns of power and authority in classroom talk', in Woods, P. (ed.) *Teacher Strategies: Explorations in the Sociology of the School*, London, Croom Helm.

Edwards, D. and Goodwin, R.Q. (1986) 'The language of shared attention and visual experience: a functional study of early nomination', *Journal of Pragmatics* 9, 475–93.

Edwards, D. and Mercer, N. (1986) 'Context and continuity: classroom discourse and the development of shared knowledge', in Durkin, K. (ed.) *Language Development in the School Years*, London, Croom Helm.

Edwards, D. and Mercer, N. (1989) *Common Knowledge: The Development of Understanding in the Classroom*, London, Routledge.

Edwards, D. and Mercer, N. (1988) *El conocimiento Compartido: el desarrollo de la comprensión en el aula*, Barcelona: Ediciones Paidós.

Edwards, D. and Mercer, N. (1989) 'Reconstructing context: the conventionalization of classroom knowledge', *Discourse Processes* 12,1 91–104.

Edwards, D., Mercer, N. and Maybin, J. (1987) 'The development of joint understanding in the classroom', *ESRC End of Adwards Report, Award no. C00232236*.

Edwards, D. and Middleton, D. (1986) 'Conversation and remembering: constructing an account of shared experience through conversational discourse', *Discourse Processes* 9, 423–59.

Flanders, N.A (1970) *Analysing Teacher Behaviour*, Reading, Mass., Addison-Wesley.

Galton, M., Simon, B. and Croll, P. (1980) *Inside the Primary Classroom* (the Oracle project), London, Routledge & Kegan Paul.

Hammersley, M. (ed.) (1983) *The Ethnography of Schooling*, Driffield, Nafferton.

The Kingman Report (1988) *Report of the Committee of Inquiry into the Teaching of English Language*, Chairman: Sir John Kingman, London, HMSO.

Maybin, J. (1987) 'Appendix: outline of the research project', in Edwards, D. and Mercer, N. (1987), op.cit.

Mehan, H. (1979) *Learning Lessons: Social Organization in the Classroom*, Cambridge, Mass., Harvard University Press.

Mercer, N. and Edwards, D. (1981) 'Ground-rules for mutal understanding: a social psychological approach to classroom knowledge', in Mercer, N. (ed.) *Language in School and Community*, London, Edward Arnold.

Mercer, N. and Edwards, D. (1987) 'Knowledge development in adult learning groups', *Open Learning* 2, 22–8.

Mercer, N. and Edwards, D. (1988) 'Re-potting primary science', *Times Educational Supplement* 1, January.

Mercer, N., Edwards, D. and Maybin, J. (1988) 'Putting context into oracy: the construction of shared knowledge through classroom discourse', in MacLure, M., Phillips, T. and Wilkinson, A. (eds) *Oracy Matters*, Milton Keynes, Open University Press.

National Oracy Project (1989a) *Oracy Issues* 3, Summer, p.6.

National Oracy Project (1989b) *Talk* 1, Spring, pp 34–6.

Neisser, U. (1976) 'General academic and artificial intelligence', in Resnick, L.B. (ed.) *The Nature of Intelligence*, New York, Lawrence Erlbaum.

Piaget, J. (1971) *Science as Education and the Psychology of the Child*, London, Longman.

Potter, J. and Wetherell, M. (1987) *Discourse and Social Psychology: Beyond Attitudes and Behaviour*, London, Sage.

Sinclair, J. McH. and Coulthard, R.M. (1975) *Towards an Analysis of Discourse: The English used by Teachers and Pupils*, Oxford, Oxford University Press.

Stubbs, M. (1981) 'Scratching the surface: linguistic data in educational research', in Adelman, C. (ed.) *Uttering, Muttering: Collecting, Using and Reporting Talk for Social and Educational Research*, London, Grant MacIntyre.

Vygotsky, L.S. (1978) *Mind in Society: the Development of Higher Psychological Processes*, London, Harvard University Press.

Walkerdine, V. (1982) 'From context to text: a psychosemiotic approach to abstract thought', in Beveridge, M. (ed.) *Children Thinking through Language*, London, Edward Arnold.

Wertsch, J.V. (ed.) (1985) *Culture, Communication and Cognition: Vygotskian Perspectives*, Cambridge, Cambridge University Press.

Wieder, D.L. (1974) 'Telling the code', in Turner, R. (ed.) *Ethnomethodology*, Harmondsworth, Penguin.

Young, M.F.D. (1971) *Knowledge and Control: New Directions for the Sociology of Education*, London, Collier-Macmillan.

4

BREAKTHROUGHS AND BLOCKAGES IN ETHNOGRAPHIC RESEARCH Contrasting experiences during the *Changing Schools* project

Lynda Measor and Peter Woods

INTRODUCTION

Research reports frequently give the appearance of confident, well-organized progress through the lengthy period of research. This probably is rarely the case, and certainly does not apply to our study, which we conducted between 1980–4 (Measor and Woods, 1984a). It was characterized more by stops and starts, false trails and blind alleys. There were long periods of routine data collection – and some flashes of excitement; alternating experiences of being promoted and obstructed, of being deeply involved and almost totally marginalized.

In this article we aim to capture the variable fortunes and flavour of the research, and reflect on their significance. We give special attention to 'decision points' – moments in the research where crucial decisions had to be made. Consideration will thus be given to the way that such decisions are arrived at (with particular reference to co-researching and co-authorship), and reflection on the appropriateness of some of the decisions that were made.

Why is such an account necessary? Often when research is published, and this is equally true of our research, we are given very little background to it, although qualitative research has a better record than most in this respect (see for example, Atkinson, 1976; Hargreaves, 1967; Humphreys, 1967). We are not given a picture of the daily routines of the research. We are given 'antiseptic accounts'. We want to suggest that what is left out is important, this kind of information is important in order for the reader to be able to scrutinize and judge research findings – and therefore assess its virtues, and its value. Sociological thinking suggests that, because of these omissions and silences which occur in the 'antiseptic' account, readers fill in a picture of their own (Atkinson, 1976). In this article, we reflect on some of those aspects of the research which either hindered or promoted the processes involved; had important implications for the outcome; but were not discussed in the original report.

RESEARCH PLANNING AND DESIGN

Two aspects of this were particularly problematic; (a) the degree of specificity required in the early stages of the research, and (b) the search for funding. We shall consider each in turn.

Degree of specificity

Ethnographic projects are by intention and definition open ended; problems are not specified in advance of fieldwork discovering what they are in particular circumstances. Theory is 'grounded' in the material that is unearthed (Glaser and Strauss, 1967). Research design and theory making is ongoing. This stands in contrast with some other sociological approaches.

While not knowing exactly where one is going may be proper ethnographic procedure, there are drawbacks in relation to obtaining funding. Funding agencies quite rightly want to ensure that public money is wisely invested, and therefore require well-worked proposals, with a high degree of specificity. Our strategy for dealing with this was to be as specific as possible at a time of making the proposal, while building in spaces for change and expansion. There were, in fact, a number of progressive research plans (see Woods, 1986), each one drawing more on the data from the research and thus becoming more grounded.

The final research report focused upon 'transition', encapsulating that within the theoretical structure of status passages. However the initial notion of the work scarcely mentioned this aspect. Thinking at this stage was guided most significantly by a process of 'mapping' the omissions which existed at that time in the research literature. Woods (1986) has argued that this frequently characterizes stage one ethnographic work.

There had been for example several detailed studies of older 'deviant' male secondary school children. There was a gap in our knowledge of the lives and views of younger pupils, and of those with a more conformist orientation to school. But our aim was not

60

to provide only a 'mapping out' of what 'life was like' for pupils on entry to secondary schools. We felt that a knowledge of those earlier years was essential for a proper understanding of what came later in pupils' careers. This meant that the data and the theoretical issues raised by work like Hargreaves (1967), Lacey (1970), Furlong (1976), Delamont (1976), Willis (1977), Woods (1979), Hammersley and Turner (1980) held out possible leads at the beginning, which would guide our theoretical sampling and 'progressive focusing' (Hammersley and Atkinson, 1983).

The initial aims therefore were:

1 To improve understanding of the processes through which pupils adapt to secondary school in their early years there.
2 To examine pupil perspectives and school cultures, looking at their intentions, choices, commitments and strategies.
3 To examine the influences of peer groups, and the wider background culture upon pupil adaptations to school.
4 To explore the parent–teacher interface over the period of change to and adaptation to secondary school, and to examine the way it bears upon the pupil.

In addition a notional and rather complex model of these pupil adaptations was sketched out. This drew on previous research in the field, our own previous researches, and interactionist literature. This was the way round the problem of specification. A set of aims, methods and intentions was provided. A theoretical orientation was laid down, and a model for understanding of the main research theme was elucidated. It was highly unlikely that the model would hold this form in a precise way, once the research had started, but the details were *the most likely ones* discernible at the time of making the proposal, going on the best evidence to hand. There were elements written into it that would undoubtedly survive, and the framework, because of its theoretical strength had marks of some permanence.

The point we wish to make is that specificity emerged as the fieldwork gathered pace. There were 'decision points'. Some of the research aims proved unattainable, some proved impractical. We never progressed as far as aim number 4. The research aims clarified when they were informed by knowledge of the particular situation being studied. There was another factor, ethnography is an intensely personal experience. Peter considered it was important to leave space for the individual interests of the research assistant to have some play. At this stage in the research, the assistant had not been appointed.

The search for funding

This research would not have been possible without funding from the Open University and the (then) SSRC, and we are happy to acknowledge our gratitude to them. However there were difficulties. Grants were only made for one year at a time, necessitating three separate applications for what was always conceived of as a three-year project. This meant that a large part of Peter's time was taken up with making out proposals, while Lynda could enjoy neither the security of a three-year post, nor the confidence that she would be able to see the work to fruition. Such is the 'hit and miss' nature of many research proposals.

At it was the research would not have happened at all without funding from the Open University. They offered one year's funding, in the hope that this would launch the project, and external funding would be attracted to complete it. This reasonable model of one-plus-two was ruined by the cut-backs in funding of research which were made in 1979. This extract from the proposal for the third year of the research recounts the history.

1 The Open University funded the project for one year. A research assistant was appointed in February 1979, and fieldwork began in the school.
2 A bid was made to the SSRC for the remaining two years in good time for its April 1979 decision point (at the time the SSRC had decision points in January, April, September.) The proposal was referred back with certain questions.
3 We aimed to submit a revised application taking those questions into account in good time for the September decision point. Unfortunately government economies forced the SSRC in July/August 1979 to alter its schedules:
(a) it abolished its September decision point
(b) it deferred submissions of all applications for sums over £10,000 until January 1980.
4 Since continuity of the research assistant in post could not be guaranteed by any other means, we brought our submission below the £10,000 limit, applying for only one of the two years, in order to qualify for immediate decision.

5 The revised proposal was accepted by the SSRC.

6 Shortly afterwards the SSRC raised the ceiling for proposals qualifying for immediate decision to £20,000, which would have enabled us to bid for two further years.

The research was thus caught up in a time of change and transition for research funding in the UK. It is difficult to chart the exact consequences for the research. It meant insecurity for Lynda, 'proposalitis' for Peter, but also an inability to plan with sureness, and a shortage of time for reflection. Such a hand-to-mouth existence is not good for research. But, although there were special circumstances attending the situation in 1979, we believe that the piecemeal, stop-go, hand-to-mouth experience is not untypical of much educational research.

So far we have looked at the administration of a large research proposal, but we want to suggest that there are some academic or theoretical issues involved too, in terms of the way a research problem is formulated at this stage.

The original research intention had always been to contact groups of pupils before they arrived at secondary school. However, once this contact was made, we rapidly appreciated the centrality of this transition to the pupils, and it became a major issue of the research. Pupils alerted us to the importance of the issue when they were at primary school. The secondary school also guided our attention to the significance of the transition. It placed stress on easing the transition for pupils, and mounted an elaborate induction scheme. Then, later in the year, as we watched the impact of their arrival at the new school, and discerned their adaptational processes, this consolidated the view of the research as being chiefly about transition. 'Status passage' came to the fore, and our sources of literature shifted to those about the issue of school transfer and other status passages as well.

On completion this was certainly the most noted aspect of the book. The title of the book drew attention to the transfer process, and invitations to speak about the research were all to do with this aspect. Yet it had hardly figured in the early proposal.

The central issues of the research were identified slowly. There were major 'decision points'. However that term is in some senses misleading, for it suggests that the decisions were made quickly at one instant – a kind of Damascus road model. This first stage is one of the most difficult and anxiety provoking parts of doing research.

Inevitably there is a feeling of insecurity. Students doing their first ethnographic study can be tempted to hasten through this stage, but it may be at the cost of finding greater confusion later.

ACCESS

The next stage of research is gaining access. By this we mean not only gaining physical access to the research setting, but also the issue of building trust and developing relationships there, which is so crucial in qualitative research. There are both practical and theoretical difficulties involved in an enterprise, in which relationships are seen to be so crucial. It is inevitable that not all relationships will be equal. Some of the relationships in our research significantly fostered the research, and in addition were a source of support. This was particularly true of some relationships with pupils, which at times could bring exhilaration and delight. Other relationships produced despair, embarrassment and despondency, and we will attempt to document this later. There are also ethical difficulties, which we have elaborated elsewhere (Measor and Sikes, forthcoming).

Access and relationships in one of the schools went quite badly wrong, Lynda having substantial difficulties in the middle school that we called 'Hayes' in the research. Some of them stemmed from an incident early on in the research. Lynda spoke of the pupils to the headteacher, and used the term 'kids'. The head said he was deeply insulted by this language, objecting very strongly to the use of the word 'kids'. From that point on he closed up, and was unwilling to be interviewed or to discuss school matters. There are of course a number of possible explanations for the head's reaction, it is difficult to believe he had never come across the term before, nor heard his staff use it. The problem is that because he closed up, there was never any chance to discover if he had more general reasons for not wishing to co-operate, it was not possible to know what his meanings were. This was a blockage in the research, and one which the researchers were unable to free.

This was not the end of the story. The head had agreed to having a researcher in the school without much discussion or consultation with his staff. There were some teachers who made it clear that they objected to the whole enterprise, and who denied Lynda access to their classrooms, and to the children in their care. This resulted in a number of problems and set backs. The researcher was unable to follow up leads and check out a number of stories. In retrospect, we feel that there is little to be done, once a blockage has been created. In terms of the future it is a question of learning to be very careful. It is worth emphasizing how very uncomfortable and responsible for the difficulties the researcher felt. Things were done rather differently in the secondary school. The head offered his staff full consultation and set up a number of meetings with the researcher before she actually entered the school. There were no substantial problems of access there.

Access in the sense of trust only develops slowly in research, as it does in any relationship. Qualitative research asks researchers to document and monitor their own impact on the situation they are researching, as a strategy for elucidation and validation of data. Relationships and access are two of the areas that need especially careful monitoring. One of the crucial questions that the pupils had to be sure of before they could develop relationships was whose side Lynda was on. Would she 'tell the teachers' when infractions occurred. The data which follows is taken from field notes Lynda made early on in the research. There was one lesson, which seemed particularly significant in this context. Perhaps it was a 'decision point' for the pupils.

Mrs Gates is teaching a humanities lesson on the Arctic. The pupils are very bored which is not unusual in her lessons. I realise that I am also bored, and I feel a sense of relief when some deviance begins. The teacher introduces the lesson with an account of Scott's expedition to the Arctic. There is a lot of general noise and shuffling about in the lesson, while the teacher is talking. Then the teacher writes on the blackboard, setting the class work to do on their own. She is writing up some material about penguins. As her back is turned, a few of the kids begin to do penguin imitations, many of the kids turning round to check out what I will do. I do nothing, I even stop writing my field notes, and I maintain a neutral expression.

The next step is orchestrated by Sean Carpenter (ace deviant). As the teacher writes up a longish piece on the blackboard, he gets up out of his seat, and performs an elaborate pantomime dance, full of silly gestures. This has the effect of reducing the rest of the class to hysterical laughter. Again many of the pupils turn to me to check out what I will do. I do nothing – neither does the teacher.

The deviance then swelled in this lesson. A little later the teacher went into the cupboard, which was a walk in type, to get more stationery, Sean Carpenter happened to be out of his seat. He is standing near the cupboard. He switches into stand-up comic mode, and mimics his teacher's gestures and way of speaking, and standing. He finishes up his performance with a clumsy capering about on the spot. It was in fact a very daring thing to do, because the teacher could have reappeared at any moment from the cupboard. The whole class burst out laughing in unison at his performance. This time pupils do not look at me, they know I won't 'tell' or take a discipline role.

This seems to have been a significant point. The fact that Sean was willing to engage in this level of deviance in front of the researcher signals that she has been accepted at one level. It therefore represents a decision point for the pupils, and consequently a turning point in the research. It meant that Lynda was seen to be 'on their side' not one of the teacher tribe.

The pupils engaged in the same process in relation to being interviewed. Early on in the research the pupils were reticent if Lynda asked questions about their attitude to teachers. She always assured them that she would not under any circumstances tell their teachers what had been said. Slowly the pupils began to open up, about how boring Mrs Gates was for example. When they saw that Lynda had kept her word, and had not 'told' on them, then they became more free in what they said. There was a breakthrough in trust.

This kind of incident is important for what it reveals about researcher reactivity. The fact that the researcher has an impact on the research setting is of course well known. We cannot prevent it from happening, but need to take responsibility for monitoring it. In this situation it is clear that the impact the researcher had changed within a few weeks of her being in the school.

Once some of this initial testing out had been done, the relationships did grow. One of the issues which is not usually discussed in research reports is the extraordinary privileged access that the researcher has when working with a group of pupils. Teachers who have read the research report comment on this factor most frequently. For us it was an enormously exciting thing to do. It is the source of much of the delight in research relationships that we discussed earlier.

This is not to say that there were not limits on pupil-researcher relationships. They were in fact very clear:

> Sean told a joke. Every one on his table laughed loudly. I approach, but he blocked my route saying, 'No grown ups are allowed to hear this joke'. (This is in fact an area which we have documented in detail elsewhere, See Measor and Woods 1984b.)

This is another example of a blockage we never freed, and which we would not for ethical reasons have wanted to attempt to free. It indicates the way that children are capable of putting boundaries into their social activities, and constructing a world in which the distinction between what grown ups can and cannot hear is important (Ball, 1984).

We feel that it is essential methodologically to give some details about the researcher. Vidich (see Stubbs and Delamont, 1976) has written, 'The respondent forms an image of the field worker, and uses that image as a basis of response. It does mean that as researchers we have an obligation to identify and document the nature of the image held by the respondent' (Vidich quoted by Stubbs and Delamont, 1976, p.35) In this context, it is important to note the age of the researcher – about thirty – and the fact that she was a woman, which we suggest affected the kind of research relationships that developed. Lynda comments,

> I also question ten years later, whether I would get the same response from the kids now if I went into school in that kind of research role. This year I went into school with a group of six students to do classroom observation and research. I was aware that my students had a far readier rapport with the pupils than I did.

Accounts such as we have just given direct our attention once again to the fact that research is a 'social activity'. Sociological accounts are joint actions produced in a process of interacting with respondents. What the researcher is, and looks as if s/he is, can foster breakthroughs or blockages in the research. Consequently, there are some topics that are difficult to study according to the researcher's gender and age.

COLLABORATIVE RESEARCH

Teamwork

While teamwork in research is often highly recommended (Glaser, 1978; Payne *et al.*, 1981; Hammersley, 1980; Woods, 1986), it can sometimes cause difficulties, and even be counter-productive (Platt, 1976). It can also take the form simply of a strict division of labour with allocation of separate tasks and areas to cover. Our partnership, we think, worked reasonably well and involved real collaboration for the following reasons.

First, we had different knowledge bases. This enabled us to have a wider range for the formulation of ideas and for interpreting material. We were also able to act as a check and a balance on each other's work. Ideas had to be argued out for the other, and this tested them out. This approach we would argue, is a creative formula.

However research projects do not always operate on the high plane of creativity. There are low points, for example if access if blocked, or if complex ethical difficulties arise. There can be periodic concern over where the research is going and exhaustion and worry in the draining slog of writing up. These and other common research ailments are sometimes easier if shared. It is the case of course, that both these functions of creative insight and of support, can be carried out by colleagues, but it cannot be done to the same depth as by someone fully involved in the research.

It was probably important for the health of this research project that we shared certain basic interests, and also values. For example we had similar views of the British education system and saw equality as a crucial issue. We also shared a fascination with pupil cultures and a common interest in qualitative research methods. We have both witnessed the counter-productive confrontations that can frequently, but not inevitably, erupt from clashes between academics with different orientations. No such basic differences in outlook applied here. We also found that we had complementary personalities and that we could work well together in a professional context.

We would argue therefore that collaboration provides a sound basis for creativity, rigour and lucidity. This is not to judge our work on any absolute scale. Rather it is simply to state that we feel our output was better in these respects than if we had been acting and writing alone. However, much depended on the mode of procedure we adopted. This was democratic and open. During the eighteen months of field-work Peter saw his role as one of facilitator and consultant. His tasks were:

1 To find the funding to keep the research going.
2 To assist in negotiating access and formulating contacts with the schools and teachers concerned.
3 To draw up schedules and timetables to give a shape to and maintain progress on the research.
4 To take part in regular discussions with Lynda about the direction and focus of the research. In the early stages there was an emphasis on research methods, and we will deal with this in more detail in the next section.
5 To create opportunities for speaking about the research, and for written articles.
6 To write the research report, and negotiate a contract with a publisher for a book on the subject.

Training issues

The collaboration began with the induction of Lynda into the research project. In a recent book Peter has spoken of the process of 'washing your mind clean' (Woods, 1986, p.34) when doing qualitative research. This is all to do with, 'opening up the mind, inducing a mood of reflection, identifying prejudices'. (p.19). It is a difficult process to achieve on your own. It is also difficult to teach other people how to do it.

We need to participate so as to observe and experience, but we also need to stand apart, so that we can unpack what is going on in that setting. We need simultaneously to know a setting, and to make it unfamiliar. 'Most events in our own society and especially settings with which we are very familiar seem "natural" and "obvious", We have already learned the culture and we find few things problematic' (Hammersley and Atkinson, 1982, p.128). For the purposes of research, however, we need to unlearn and make these things problematic.

Lofland (1971) talks about these issues.

Being a known observer allows one to get close to some people's world. It can then become quite evident to the observer that although he is in that world he is not 'of' it. He is so close that he can deeply empathise with local pains, joys and boredoms, but these are not truly his own pains, joys and boredoms, for he is ultimately an observer. That is to say there can be in the role of the observer the experience of marginality with its attendant feeling of loneliness and anxiety. If it is any consolation it is out of this circumstance of being marginal – the simultaneous insider-outsider – that creative insight is best generated. Marginality stimulates the actual 'seeing' of the setting and its aspects as problematic topics. (Lofland, 1971, p.97)

Our task then is to make the setting anthropologically strange. In the case of this research Lynda had some difficulty initially. Her background was in training teachers, her experience of watching lessons was from the back of a classroom, judging the performance of student teachers. This was something she had to learn to stop doing. She had to 'wash her mind clean' of this and discover what the research was really looking for.

In Lynda's early field notes she would describe the lesson that a particular teacher was doing, then would comment. For example, 'this tactic, of asking pupils questions, works very well. Mr B. got the pupils thinking independently on their own, this was a good lesson.' Peter would then write comments at the end of these passages. 'Still very much on the "good teacher" as versus pupil experiences of that.' Peter would also put notes in the margins of the field notes. Sometimes these would be academic references: for example Lynda took down an incident where there was 'trouble' in a class. Peter's note says, '"trouble" – see Furlong.'

On other occasions it was issues of validation of data and the strategies of triangulation that were specified or suggested. Often there would be suggestions of how to collect more data or more in-depth data on a particular incident or theme. One example reported in Lynda's field notes gave an account of a dispute between two boys. Lynda was making an interpretation on the basis of what one boy had said. Peter wrote in the margin, 'Get the other boy's side of the story first.' If Lynda had recorded something in a class, and then interviewed the participants, Peter would then suggest that she look for school records on the issue. The object was always to get the richest possible tapestry of data.

The main job in training researchers is perhaps to get the researcher able to 'open closures', to question what seems common-sense, and to investigate the taken for granted. One clear example of this occurs in Lynda's field notes, 'I had given a long account of a quarrel between two girls, the culminating point of which came when one girl accused the other of being 'posh'. Peter suggested that Lynda interview the girls who had the quarrel, this being an excellent way to validate data, through the process of triangulation, and interpretations through the process of respondent validation. He also suggested that I open up an investigation into that word 'posh' which is so redolent of the British class system. What did it mean to the girl who had used it, and what did it mean to the girl who had been accused?

Interviewing

We are interested in providing an account of the 'training' process that went on in relation to interviewing as well as participant observation. Lynda's first interview was with the sixth form of the school. They were not the subjects of the research. Lynda interviewed them on what they could remember about starting secondary school. The purpose of this was to provide a practice run at interviewing. It did not in fact matter very much if Lynda made terrible mistakes, or upset the respondents. It was a safe place to learn some of the craft. In the transcript of the interview Peter wrote a number of comments. The first issue that arose was that of asking 'leading questions'.

Interviewer: What is it about school uniform that annoys you?
Pupil: They're all the same aren't they. It's boring isn't it, its UNIFORM.
Interviewer: Do you think that something happens to people when they wear uniform, think about the people in our society who wear uniform?

At this point Lynda thinks that the fact she was used to teaching sociology is clearly revealed, she was struggling to make the change from teacher to researcher.

Pupil: Coppers, magistrates.
Interviewer: Traffic wardens, British Rail bods.

At this point in the margin Peter had written, 'leading question.'

Later in this transcript, there is an interesting example of the importance of trying to open closures in interviewing.

71

Interviewer:	Did you always feel that you would stay on at school?
Pupil:	No, not until the last minute, and I've regretted it ever since.
Interviewer:	Do you feel you are wasting your time?
Pupil:	It's not that I can't do it. It's that I'm bored with it, and sick of it.
Pupil:	It's not what I expected at all.
Other pupils:	No! No!

At this point Peter wrote in the margin, 'What did they expect?' In fact Lynda in the interview then went on to ask some more rather leading questions about the importance of discipline in the school.

Peter's comment there is an important one if in qualitative research we are serious about aiming to get a purchase upon the meanings that individuals construct. We need strategies for probing the subject's meanings, and getting the fullest possible picture of their ideas and their words, their way of constructing a world and seeing it.

In the same interview transcript there is another area of data that seems useful.

Interviewer:	You said something earlier about secondary school seeming much more impersonal than the primary school.
Pupil:	Yes, Yes!
Pupil:	It's the discipline really isn't it.
Interviewer:	So you think the issue is discipline in a secondary school.
Pupil:	Yes.
Interviewer:	Do you all agree?

At this point Peter wrote in the margins, 'get them to explain words, what does "discipline" or "impersonal" mean to them, – and to explore beliefs.' On another occasion Peter wrote, 'get them to give some examples, get them to talk through an actual experience.' This is an important area of qualitative research. It is often difficult for people to discuss the most important things in their lives, values and beliefs for example. If we encourage people to present those beliefs in the form of concrete examples, or in a narrative, then we may be able to facilitate their ability to discuss these areas.

One of the areas of the research in which we found some difficulty was that of non-verbal communication. It is not an easy task to capture the essentially dynamic processes of sub-verbal communications. We were left with a sense of not having done this with any great success. It was an issue of some importance in the research, when we tried to analyse the myths that were generated by the pupils as they transferred schools. There were a number of such myths, which told in a complex way about the realities of life in the secondary school. One of the most important was that, 'You get yer' ead flushed down the loo on yer' birthday in that school' (Measor and Woods, 1983, p.62).

The myths were important at an emotional level to the children involved. Emotions are not so easy to research perhaps as opinions, and yet we fail to give a picture of the individual's world or his reality if we ignore them. Often feelings are communicated non-verbally, and their indications are fleeting, a raised eyebrow, or difficult to interpret, a querulous tone. As people we respond to these tiny signs without being able to slow down the interaction sufficiently to name and identify them.

We were aware that some important emotional issues were involved in the pupils' use of the myths, and we recognised too late the importance of keeping accurate records of non-verbal communication. This seems to be a blockage in qualitative research generally and new developments in this field seem to have come from feminist social science (Sadker and Sadker, 1985; Hall and Sandler, 1982; Duncan and Fiske, 1977; Knapp, 1978; Chaiken *et al.*, 1974).

Writing up – Collaborative research at a distance

One of the problems with research is that not all of it can be accomplished within definite 'start' and 'finish' points. In some ways this is inevitable, especially when one of the outcomes is a book. By the time we had concluded the funded period of this research we had produced a number of articles, given conference papers and written the required research report; and felt that we had satisfied the terms of our contract. But we also wanted to do a book on the research, since it offers the means to present the research to a wider audience in the most comprehensive and integrated way. This was the most rigorous challenge, and it arose at a time when the research funding had ended and Lynda had already taken up other work in

Brighton. The collaboration therefore had to take place at a distance.

We developed a system for collaboration at a distance which seemed to work reasonably well. We had already agreed a structure and outline in the book proposal. The process was a step by step one that probably took its model from the Open University writing in drafts system.

1 Lynda would produce a first, handwritten draft of each chapter. From her mass of materials she would put together a coherent account of the issue with the data already collected.
2 Peter would then construct a second draft, doing some editing and rewriting, perhaps some reorganising, but also sharpening the analysis. He would suggest ideas, work toward relevant concepts and make connections with the literature. This draft would then be typed.
3 Lynda would then comment on this, again moving towards more analysis, but also saying what she liked and what she did not like about what had been done.
4 The final draft was then produced, and comments were sought on these from other colleagues.

This kind of 'research-triangulation' we would argue is very strong. The conditions stated earlier must of course apply, i.e. there is equal, democratic, truly collaborative input; otherwise as the reader will recognize there are plenty of opportunities for conflict. Having said this, we would be the first to admit that the product was not perfect, not as good as it might have been had we been able to continue face to face discussions during the writing up period. Even so, collaboration often, of necessity has to be done at a distance, and we hope we refined some of the techniques.

One of the advantages of 'collaboration at a distance' is that there are written records of some of these interchanges; although of course not of the many long and detailed telephone conversations that were held. Here are some examples of these exchanges:

Note from Lynda to Peter

Questions on section of chapter called 'pupil perceptions of subject status.'

1) I would appreciate any comments you have generally, but my worries centre on two specific areas.

a) I'm not sure I have really explained the central point about the interplay of formal and informal concerns properly. And secondly I'm worried that I have overplayed the argument at the expense of the other point, about pupil perceptions of a status hierarchy in subjects. Have I made the whole thing too complicated? Advice please.

b) Do you think the data on art and design, p. 8 and 9 should come *before* that on music, given that music is a special and more complicated case.

2) Is it 'within the regulations' to get this typed at the OU.

3) Reference of *Pupil Strategies* please.

Peter's response to this draft

Pupil perceptions of subject status

p.1 Introduction. Yes. I think you might make more of how the curriculum is realised by people in social interaction, and is partly a product of meaning constructions (references to Berger, Blumer, Goodson. . . . . etc.) You might also introduce here how pupil meaning constructions may be influenced by a range of pupil cultures – teenage, gender, social class, ethnic, etc. – most containing particular orientations to the world of work and occupations. School subjects are viewed through these perspectives.

p.1 I think you need to be precise about the group of pupils you studied (i.e. it was not the whole of the intake year).

p.2 I think the whole paper needs editing into a more literary style, e.g. line 3 here could read, 'The attitudes expressed resulted in . . .' with no loss of meaning, there is some slang in here.

I'm not sure what you mean by 'basic orientations to school'... (well I do, but it might not be clear to others).

p.3 Top line – another example of repetition.

p.3 Top para. Stephen Ball has a lot to say about subject status, perception of hierarchies etc. in 'Beachside'. See also his paper with Lacey in 'Teacher Strategies' although the latter is more on inter-departmental relationships). I think Beachside at least should be referred to – see especially the threefold classification of subjects.

p.3 I thought Furlong disputed the existence of peer groups?

p.4 'ideal pupils'. Its rather a big jump to this concept, from the data.

p.9 There are a number of references you could call on re pupils' perception of 'work' – Furlong, Delamont, Pollard, even P.W.

Bottom half of page – 'opposition' – did all of these subjects attract 'opposition' (as opposed for example to 'indifference', 'half heartedness', etc.)? As I may have said to you before Lynda, I find your argument on this gender issue to be presented in too extreme terms to ring true. The implication is that *all* girls and *all* boys reacted in the ways you describe, and that those who did 'objected' in the same kind of 'oppositional' way. Given the criticisms that are often made of our approach of 'selecting the data', I think you need to give more justification for the general view. Some reference to other recent work on girls and science would help – Kelly, certainly.

p.16 This does seem clear to me.

p.17–18 The claim that pupils have such instrumental attitudes so early in their school careers may come as a surprise to many teachers. You can bolster it by referring to Ball 1981, and by saying a little about the pupils – age – is important, they are 12 not 11 year olds, and background. Also, it is not clear from the way you present the data that 'instrumentality' has 'emerged' from pupil perspectives, and was not the result of direct or implicit questioning.

Concerning your questions, I think the formal/informal point is clear and so is the status hierarchies. They should gain further clarity from the referencing.

I have no strong feelings about the positioning of music/art and design.

Comments from Lynda on a P.W. draft 2.

Initial Encounters Informal section (Eventually chapter 4 of the book).

1) Peter I'm worried by this introductory sentence, where you refer to the culture of the middle school as 'child' and 'play' dominated. It is different in the secondary school – no doubt about that, but I think this misses a fundamental point. Had the pupils changed schools at 11+ in the traditional way, then yes

their middle school experience would have been of this child-style variety exclusively. But they don't, they transfer at 12+ and this makes for some crucial differences which were clearly observable in middle school. That extra year gave the kids space to develop further into adolescent cultures and interests, that was obvious from the way they dressed, and their interest in music, etc. Then in a sense they got booted back to a previous stage when they entered secondary school – by the institutions demand for uniform, and by the age grading pressures from the older kids. So I think the issue is in fact more complicated than you suggest as a result of the changes in the age of transfer.

2) I think we need a bit more of the 'how' of identities being built here. I tried to make a point that the individual comes into a new class, virtually anonymous, well how does that change, reputation is accumulated, what are the strategies that the individual uses to achieve the reputation, to get the particular identity.

Also a point that I think we really emphasize later has got lost in here somehow, that allegiances and identities are tied up; and the girls at least see their friends as reflecting their own identity. So, for example, Amy breaks her friendship with Rosemary, for she feels she is 'getting a name', i.e. getting an identity she does not want as a result of the simple fact of being seen with Rosemary, of being friends with her.

3) I think it is an interesting paradox, that the factor which really influences the informal culture's groups is the formal culture and the individual pupil's attitude to it. The fact that it is a paradox has got lost in your draft.

4) I'd like to make a critique of Furlong's work here, although I know you might not agree. I do really think that he misses the point, although I don't want to say so quite that publicly. The thing is he only describes one of the kinds of informal groups which exist among the girls in school. Had he recognized what he was doing, i.e. giving a very accurate description of one of the forms of friendship in the informal culture of girls, that would have been fine. But, that's not what he did, he went on to make a whole theoretical assembly on top of what is partial

data, or rather data which presents only a partial picture. He went on the basis of that data to challenge a lot of the work that has been done on groups in classrooms, and on the differentiation into groups and on the basic polarization and hostilities between groups, and the way it connects with questions of orientation to school. I think maybe we ought to try and put that record straight, but maybe you don't agree.

P.W. comments Go Ahead!

4a) I think this point needs to be made more strongly, the basic fact of differentiation, *the* thing that sets off your friends from your interaction set, is 'out of school' activity. It is absolutely crucial, I'd like to underline it. The girls would really perceive a difference in the kind of relationship they had with someone you could borrow a ruler from in the context of the classroom, as opposed to someone you went out to the disco with.

5) I think we have lost some important points in this section.
a) We have lost all references to the myths and I think that needs to come back in. I think we actually provided rather a specualtive analysis of myths. It was well argued and considered, but still speculative, and I think we should bolster it when and where we can. We suggest that one of the things the myths were all about was gender demands. In the case of the boys the issues were about toughness, strength and physicality. Geoffrey is a really nice bit of proof of our analysis. The myths had warned that awful things would happen to those who fail in this 'macho hierarchy.' Geoffrey had failed, and was shunned – that is a dreadful thing to have happen to you.
b) The second point is that the myths had only made it clear that there was danger to you if you failed to cope in the macho hierarchy from the kids older than you. At the school, it became clear that doing well in gender code terms was also important within your own age grade too.
c) At a later stage the issue of testing for strengths *between* the groups in the same class or age grade became an issue, but it wasn't at this stage. At this point the matter at hand was establishing your identity, and your status in the pecking order *within* your group.

6) Again we seem to have lost the direct reference to the myths, am I pushing this too far?

7) Again we have lost a point I thought important. There are tremendous risks in this adolescent sexual activity at first. Pupils need to test out the waters, to find if they are the sort of person who is going to be successful in these adolescent sexual encounters. I've gone into this much further in the 'reflections' chapter. I was trying to make a point earlier about pupils employing strategies which get others to place them in the identity they want. This is a case in point. Amy for example wants involvement in these adolescent sexual encounters, she wants that identity, but that's not just up to her. She has to see if she is acceptable, can achieve it. In this sense her identity is constructed socially by others, by the reflections they give her.

Having gone through this chapter I'm at a bit of a loss to see what can be edited out, apart from the bits of analysis that have jumped ahead of the data, seems like a much tighter, more confident chapter.

CONCLUSIONS

We have looked at some of the 'breakthroughs and blockages' in research as exemplified in our school transfer project. It is, of course, impossible to cover them all. We have said nothing for example about the importance of dissemination. Difficulties here include the ethical problems concerning the release of certain information; the problems involved in addressing different audiences, both orally and in writing; and difficulties in arranging publication. On the credit side, initial papers, seminars and talks led to occasional breakthroughs. They brought us into touch with other research on transfer, and with a number of interesting LEA schemes. This helped both to strengthen our theoretical position and to link our work to policy and practice.

Finally we take the invitation to write this article as the latest 'breakthrough' in this particular research. It has given us the opportunity to reflect further on the processes involved with the benefit of distance and offers the reader more material through which to interpret the study. Our files have been an indispensable resource here, so one major lesson is never to throw anything away!

One cannot always predict how and when breakthroughs will occur, only try to arrange the circumstances that promote them. It all adds to the excitement of doing research.

BIBLIOGRAPHY

Atkinson, P. (1976) 'The clinical experience: an ethnography of medical education', unpublished PhD thesis, University of Edinburgh.

Atkinson, P. (1980) 'Writing ethnography', unpublished article.

Ball, S. (1984) 'Participant observation with pupils', in Burgess, R. (ed.) *Strategies of Educational Research*, Barcombe, Falmer Press.

Burgess, R.G. (1984) 'In the company of teachers: key informants and the study of a comprehensive school', in Burgess, R.G. (ed.) *Strategies of Educational Research*, Barcombe, Falmer Press.

Chaiken, A., Sigler, E. and Derglega, V. (1974) 'Non-verbal mediators of teacher expectancy effects', *Journal of Educational Psychology* 60, 377 – 83.

Delamont, S. (1976) *Interaction in the Classroom*, London, Methuen.

Duncan, S. and Fiske, D.W. (1977) *Face to Face Interaction: Research, Method and Theory*, New York, Wiley.

Furlong, V.J. (1976) 'Interaction sets in the classroom: towards a study of pupil knowledge', in Hammersley, M. and Woods, P. (eds) *The Process of Schooling*, London, Routledge & Kegan Paul.

Glaser, B.G. (1978) *Theoretical Sensitivity: Advances in the Methodology of Grounded Theory*, University of California, Sociological Press.

Glaser, B.G. and Strauss, A.L. (1967) *The Discovery of Grounded Theory*, London, Weidenfeld & Nicolson.

Hall, R.M. and Sandler, B.R. (1982) 'The classroom climate: A chilly one for women?' *Project on the Status and Education of Women*, Association of American Colleges.

Hammersley, M. (1980) 'On interactionist empiricism', in Woods, P. (ed.) *Pupil Strategies*, London, Croom Helm.

Hammersley, M. and Turner, G. (1980) 'Conformist pupils', in Woods, P. (ed.) *Pupil Strategies*, London, Croom Helm.

Hammersley, M. and Atkinson, P. (1982) 'Data collection procedures', Block 4 of course DE 304, *Research Methods in Education*, Milton Keynes, Open University Press.

Hammersley, M. and Atkinson, P. (1983) *Ethnography: Principles in Practice*, London, Tavistock.

Hargreaves, D. (1967) *Social Relations in a Secondary School*, London, Routledge & Kegan Paul.

Humphreys, L. (1970) *Tearoom Trade*, London, Duckworth.

Knapp, M.L. (1978) *Non Verbal Communication in Human Interaction*, New York, Holt, Rinehart and Winston.

Lacey, C. (1970) *Hightown Grammar*, Manchester, Manchester University Press.

Lofland, J. (1971) *Analysing Social Settings*, London, Wadsworth.

Measor, L. and Woods, P. (1983) 'The interpretation of pupil myths', in Hammersley, M. (ed.) *The Ethnography of Schooling*, Driffield, Nafferton.

Measor, L. and Woods, P. (1984a) *Changing Schools*, Milton Keynes, Open University Press.

Measor, L. and Woods, P. (1984b) 'Cultivating the middle ground: teachers and school ethos'; *Research in Education* 31, May.

Measor, L. and Sikes, P (forthcoming) 'Visiting lives, ethics and methodology of life history research', in Ball, S. and Goodson, I (eds) *Life History Research* (exact title unknown), Barcombe, Falmer Press.

Payne, G., Dingwall, R., Payne J. and Carter, M. (1981), *Sociology and Social Research*, London, Routledge & Kegan Paul.

Platt, J. (1976), *Realities of Social Research*, London, University of Sussex Press, Chatto & Windus.

Sadker, M. P. and Sadker, D.M. (1985) 'Sexism in the school of the '80s', *Psychology Today*, March, 54 – 7.

Stubbs, M. and Delamont, S. (1976) *Explorations in Classroom Observation*, Chichester, Wiley.

Thompson, H.S. (1966) *Hell's Angels*, New York, Random House.

Woods, P. (1979) *The Divided School*, London, Routledge & Kegan Paul.

Woods, P. (1986) *Inside Schools: Ethnography in Educational Research*, London, Routledge & Kegan Paul.

Willis, P. (1977) *Learning to Labour*, Farnborough, Saxon House.

5

RESEARCHING THE CITY TECHNOLOGY COLLEGE, KINGSHURST

Geoffrey Walford

THE RESEARCH CONTEXT

In October 1986, Kenneth Baker, then Secretary of State for Education and Science, announced the creation of a pilot network of twenty City Technology Colleges. These new secondary schools were to offer a curriculum strong in technology, science, business studies and practical work and were to be sited in inner-city areas. The intention was to establish a new partnership between government and industry for, while the CTCs were to be government funded, they were also to be non-fee-paying, independent schools run by educational trusts, with private sector business sponsors who were expected to make substantial contributions to costs.

In this chapter I reflect upon three aspects of a research project which was conducted within the first City Technology College at Kingshurst, Solihull and reported in Walford and Miller (1991) and Walford (1991). The three aspects to be considered are the problems of access, the ethics of publication and the process of interviewing children. All have to be seen in the context of the rationale for embarking on the research.

An informed educational observer might be concerned that the CTC initiative seemed to be openly encouraging a process of privatization of education. The Thatcher government had shown its clear support for private education by establishing the Assisted Places Scheme and by its continuing financial and ideological support for private schools (Walford, 1987a, 1990). The CTCs could be interpreted as an indication of possible future intentions. Without any prior consultation with local education authorities, the government planned to introduce new, well-funded and supported independent secondary schools into inner-city areas, where they would compete with local maintained schools for students. I, for one, saw this as privatization with a vengeance!

In February 1987, when the first site was confirmed in Conservative controlled Solihull, I decided to conduct some serious research on CTCs. In addition to my longstanding interest in private schools, I had also published an article on an earlier unsuccessful attempt to re-introduce selective education in Solihull (Walford and Jones, 1986), and Aston University was near to the proposed site. I consulted with a colleague at Aston, Henry Miller, and we decided that we would approach the Economic and Social Research Council to fund a three-year project to look at the national, local and college effects of the CTC policy. A somewhat similar research strategy had been used by Tony Edwards and Geoff Whitty in their ESRC funded study of the Assisted Places Scheme, so I wrote to them to see whether we could use their successful application for that research as a model for our own. It turned out that they already had the same idea as us, and were in the process of applying to the ESRC for funding for research on CTCs. So the final proposal to the ESRC from Tony Edwards and Geoff Whitty included Henry Miller and myself as 'consultants' to their project. The intention was that we would conduct the Kingshurst case study, looking at the two LEAs involved, the local secondary schools in the CTC catchment area and the CTC itself. We planned to write a short, mainly descriptive, book about Kingshurst as rapidly as we could, as well as feeding our data into the national study. We did not then realise some of the practical and ethical problems of this decision: to conduct research on a specific, named school which was the centre of political controversy was very different from any research which either of us had previously undertaken.

GAINING ACCESS

The problem of gaining access to a research site is one which has been written about by many others in their reflexive accounts of the research process (see, for example, the collections by Moyser and Wagstaffe, 1987; Shaffir et al., 1980; and Walford, 1987b), but this situation differed greatly from the norm, for we wished to investigate a specific school and its effect on other nearby schools. In this respect the research was similar to that of Punch (1977, 1986) who experienced considerable difficulties during his investigation and publication of his study of Dartington Hall School. Ideally, we wanted to interview local politicians, LEA administrators, the heads and some teachers from neigbouring schools, industrialists, parents and pupils; and to obtain access to the CTC itself, to conduct a mini-ethographic study. We expected access to those on the political left and to the nearby LEA schools affected to be relatively easy, but anticipated difficulty in obtaining interviews with those on the political right and those within the CTC itself. We knew that the College Principal, Mrs Valerie Bragg, was the primary gatekeeper who had to be prepared to give some degree of help for the project to be fully successful.

My first interview with Valerie Bragg occurred in March 1988, in the unrenovated building of Kingshurst School, which at that time still had its final year of local authority pupils. It had been relatively easy to arrange the meeting a few weeks earlier. I explained what the national and local study might involve and we talked for about an hour. It was made clear that I was far from the first person to ask for help. From the time of her appointment onwards, she had received a stream of people wanting to interview her, film her, conduct research on the college, and so on. Local and national press, television and radio reporters jostled with educational researchers of various descriptions. She argued that the problem was over-exposure, and that the tasks of building a college from scratch and providing an education for the pupils had to be the first priorities. She could not grant all requests from researchers. Why should she help me rather than anyone else? And, more importantly, how could she ensure that her pupils and the college were not disrupted?

Although there were clearly difficulties, in general I felt that the meeting had been friendly and helpful, and that I would, probably, eventually be given some form of access. At her request, I sent a letter giving details of the project and waited for a reply. None came, but in early June, I received an invitation to attend a small ESRC information technology seminar for researchers and policy-makers. I wrote again to the CTC to try to interview someone about its plans for information technology. In the first interview Mrs Bragg had talked of the CTC becoming a 'catalyst for change' within the state maintained sector, and I thought that she might see this as a chance to begin to influence future policy. Again, no reply came to the letter. After eight telephone calls from me intercepted by her secretary, Mrs Bragg returned with the answer that it would not be possible for me to talk to her or any of her current staff about information technology plans, simply because they were all too busy. This answer was one which I could quite understand, for the series of telephone calls had revealed just how busy they were – secretaries often inadvertently give away a great deal of information! I asked vaguely about the possibilities for the general project, and it was made clear that the CTC's first priority was the children who would soon be arriving. Any research would have to wait. I was careful not to give her the chance to reject the project outright, but the discussion verged dangerously close.

While some of this exchange was clearly designed to put me off, I still felt that I would probably be able to obtain some form of access after the school had started. If the CTC was to act as a catalyst for change, then it seemed to me that a balanced, objective account of what the college was doing was needed. Mrs Bragg had made it clear that she would support an independent evaluation of the College in due course, and that she wanted to know the effects of the CTC on the pupils. I decided that the best policy was simply to continue interviewing staff in neighbouring schools and other people involved with the CTC, and to try again later. I was still so optimistic that access would eventually be granted that, towards the end of 1988, Henry Miller and I wrote a proposal for our short book. The Open University Press gave us a contract in March 1989. At this point we had no idea just how important that contract would turn out to be in securing the success of the whole project.

Meanwhile, in addition to conducting interviews with the various external participants, I kept up a gentle stream of reminders to Mrs Bragg that I was still wishing to do research. An article on the CTC in the *Times Educational Supplement* in January (Fisher, 1989), conveniently included a quote from one of the staff which suggested that he would like someone to write about the College's curriculum. I wrote to Mrs Bragg saying that this was exactly one of the things I wanted to do. In February, I wrote volunteering to become one of the 'adults in residence' for a week, which had been advertised in earlier promotional literature on the College. No replies were received, and I was gradually becoming less optimistic about being able to gain access.

An imminent meeting with the ERSC national study team in April put pressure on me to show some progress. Within a two week period I made about 40 telephone calls to the CTC trying to arrange an appointment with Mrs Bragg. Since she controls her own diary, it was necessary to talk directly with her. Again, I found out quite a lot about how busy she was, and was even given a message that she was 'not trying to avoid' me. Eventually, however, I received a message from her personal assistant that she could not see me in the near future. In response, I decided to risk putting on some more explicit pressure and sent a letter to Mrs Bragg explaining that I had been conducting research outside the CTC and had a contract for a book. I enclosed a copy of my *Life in Public Schools* (Walford, 1986) and explained that reviewers of that volume and my *Restructuring Universities* (Walford, 1987c) had remarked on the degree of objectivity that I had shown. I said that I wished to do the same in the book on Kingshurst, but that this would be difficult if I was going to have a rely on second-hand information about what was occurring inside the College. All I asked at this point was for an interview with her, at least on curriculum and organizational matters. By this time I had learned (correctly) not to expect any rapid reply.

By September 1989, a further meeting with the national research team was imminent, which acted as another spur to activity. In the week preceding this meeting I telephoned the college some ten more times to try to make an appointment. The secretaries began to recognize my voice, but I got no nearer to arranging a meeting.

The world of British educational research is a small one. I knew that several other academics had tried to obtain access to the CTC, to conduct research or just to find out what the college was doing. None had got very far. At one academic conference I compared notes with a colleague. I was not doing any worse than him! He though that nobody was going to be allowed in for a few years. I was beginning to fear that this was correct, but, for a variety of reasons, I could not wait that long. First, in the Summer of 1988 I had written a short book in which I had attacked the CTC concept as a stage towards privatization. Although I found it inexplicable that my publishers could take 16 months to publish it, I was somewhat glad of their tardiness as I felt that I would have even less chance of access after publication, due in January 1990. Second, the contract we had for the book on the CTC gave us until April 1990 to get the manuscript to the publishers. I had to make one final 'all or nothing' effort to get a meeting with the Principal.

I decided to try to engineer a meeting with the Principal by attending a British Educational Management and Administration

Society Annual Conference in September 1989, at which Mrs Bragg was due to talk about 'Managing a CTC'. I sat through a rather dull three days of conference in order to hear, and possibly meet again, my primary gatekeeper. Luckily, on the Sunday morning on which Mrs Bragg was due to speak I opted out of the 'Members' Papers' sessions, and was the first person she met on entering the conference building. We talked for about fifteen minutes in the empty conference hall, and agreed to discuss further after what turned out to be a very impressive presentation. Our discussion had been frank, open and friendly. I had already explained my main purpose in attending the conference to some of the organizing committee, so that they were not surprised to find me sitting with them, opposite Mrs Bragg, during the informal lunch. I made it clear that I already had a contract and a great deal of material for a book, and that I wanted to be able to present an objective and balanced account. On the other hand, quite understandably, Mrs Bragg did not want a book written about Kingshurst yet, and argued that if anyone was going to write one, it ought to be her. I agreed with her that she should do so, but that there was also a need for an outsider's account. A possibility of compromise developed, as both of us began to see that one way out might be for the book to include both an insider's and an outsider's account of developments. I suggested that she might write 15,000 words for the book with no editorial control being exercised by me, if she would give me access to the college and help with information. This is what we eventually agreed. In order that I should really understand the college and be able to write about it, she insisted that I attend for about two days each week and that I went to some of the special college events during the following term – exactly what I wanted to do!

Sadly, in the end, the book did not include this contribution by Mrs Bragg. In order for it to be topical and to make a contribution to the debate, the book had to be written quickly, and the period for writing coincided with the time that the college was preparing for its first Post 16 intake. Mrs Bragg decided that developing new courses and planning for a virtual doubling of staff and student numbers were higher priority activities than writing. I guess that by that time she was also more confident that we would be honest and fair in the major part of the book, so the perceived need for her to contribute was lessened.

THE POLITICS AND ETHICS OF ACCESS

I have recounted the long process of gaining access to the CTC, not because I am proud of having been 'successful', or still less that I feel that it is a method to be emulated by others; but because I believe that such a description is necessary to understand the nature of the research and the constraints under which it was subsequently conducted. I am well aware that the account can be read in several different ways, with far from all of them being complimentary. While some readers may see the process in terms of perseverance, others may see it as unwarranted harassment. There were certainly times when I felt that I was engaging in the latter, for it was obvious that Mrs Bragg would have preferred me to have just given up on the research, at least for a few years until the CTC was really established. At several points my own inclination was certainly to give up, for this method of badgering my way into the CTC was far from the ideal of 'informed consent' which I had tried to apply in my earlier research into private schools. Indeed, I felt this to be desirable in practically all research.

My initial reasons for trying to obtain access were innocent – maybe even naive. I had a continuing research interest in private schools and privatization, and I had previously written about Solihull. I was against the idea of selection of children for particular well-funded schools, whether by IQ tests or by motivation and aptitude, simply because I feared the effect of such selection on rejected pupils and other nearby schools. But I was genuinely interested to know how pupils' experiences in a CTC would differ from those of pupils in other maintained schools. It was an example of the simple 'nosiness' of the sociologist about how organizations structure themselves, and how these different structures affect the lives of those within them. I expected that there would be an interesting story to tell about the CTC, which many would wish to read. I recognised that Kingshurst, being the first CTC, was particularly in the public eye, and that the whole scheme was highly controversial politically, but I only came to appreciate the full implications of this highly exposed position as I tried to obtain access and, more directly, once I was in.

I recognized, of course, that it was politically important to the Secretary of State, and to the Conservative Government, that some CTCs came into operation quickly. Industry had not responded as generously as had been hoped and there was pressure from the

Labour party and many others to abandon the scheme in the face of rising predicted costs to the Exchequer. What was less obvious to me at the time was that Kingshurst was the first school which the DES had ever directly funded from its start – those involved in establishing the college had little previous experience of setting up any school, let alone a CTC. It only opened on time in September 1988 by an army-like campaign and a tremendous amount of work by a small number of people at Kingshurst itself. All of the design and building for the college had been conducted within very strict time limits but, even then, the builders were still working in the college for the first few weeks of its existence, and amongst the teachers first tasks was that of unwrapping the many boxes of equipment, most of which they had not themselves ordered. Only a few of the staff had been appointed more than a couple of months earlier, and there had been little time to plan details of the curriculum.

In any other newly established school it would be expected that 'teething problems' would occur and that these would be gradually overcome in the first few years, but Kingshurst was expected to be a showcase from the very first day. Newspaper and television reporters demanded to see what the college was doing, industrial sponsors wanted to get their money's worth in advertising, and the Government wanted to receive publicity and praise for its new venture. From the very first day, through the official opening by Kenneth Baker in November and onwards into 1989, a constant stream of VIPs of one description or another visited the CTC. In many of these cases their visits were clearly of benefit to the CTC and their presence welcomed, but a visit of an hour or two, which might mean a discussion with the Principal followed by a tour of the college, is very different from allowing an outsider open access for a term. A researcher staying for such a long period inevitably finds the problems as well the strengths of any school, and while these problems would not be newsworthy in most schools, they certainly would be for Kingshurst.

Once I was inside the CTC, I recognized the total unreasonableness of my desire to conduct any ethnographic research. The risk to the college of allowing me to sit and watch teaching and to talk to students and staff was enormous – not necessarily because anything startling was taking place, but because I could have exaggerated any incident of disruption, misdemeanour or sexism into something 'newsworthy'. Activities common in any school could have been presented in a highly potentially damaging way. Moreover, the college would have found it difficult to defend itself against any possible published comments. I had simply not recognized the risks that I was asking the CTC to take.

The Principal's reluctance to allow a researcher into the CTC was compounded by several previous bad experiences with the media. For example, in one particular television documentary an 'industrial tutor' was shown teaching a class of children who looked bored and mystified by what he was saying. In fact, he was not an 'industrial tutor', and the shot of the children was engineered by the programme-makers by telling the children to look sad. While I was at the CTC I witnessed several other media misrepresentations. As articles appeared about the college in the national press, Xerox copies were circulated in the staff room, and I watched as teachers checked off the errors. It made me recognize even more clearly the need for a balanced account, but also made clear why it had been so difficult to gain access.

Yet, before gaining access, it had seemed to me that there was some public 'right to know' what the CTC was doing (Barnes, 1979; Pring, 1984). It was at the centre of a political controversy where there was little unbiased evidence, and where the taxpayer was paying far more towards the costs of the college than anyone had anticipated. Surely there was some 'right to know' which was more important than the problems that any research would cause the college? I recognized that such a right was not absolute, and that it had to be conditional on not causing 'too much' harm to individuals involved, but it seemed to me that the potential gain to public interest in this case was great. There would be some intrusion into the private lives of those involved, but this could be justified in research on such an important policy issue as CTCs. Having done the research, I am now less happy with this justification than I was originally.

In the end, one of the major factors which led me to continue to harass (or persevere) to obtain access was simply that I knew *no* researcher was being allowed in. If anyone else had been allowed to do *something* I might well have given up.

BURROWING DEEPER

The time to be spent at the CTC had to interweave with my existing teaching and administrative responsibilities at Aston University, so I eventually spent about 225 hours spread over 29 days at the college, including two staff development days from October until Christmas. I like to think of this as 'compressed ethnography', although there are many who would argue that it is inappropriate to use the term ethnography for such a short period (Lutz, 1981).

Negotiating my way past the primary gatekeeper to the CTC was only the start of a long process of access to people and information which was to last throughout the term. In true independent school fashion, my presence at the college had not been discussed with any of the staff. I arrived at 8.00 am on Monday morning, in good time for the daily 'briefing' at 8.10 am, to find that none of the staff seemed to know I was coming. They were surprisingly friendly, and those I talked to appeared unconcerned that I would be there for a good part of the term. At that first briefing meeting I wanted to make a short announcement to staff about what I was doing. Unfortunately, in introducing me, Mrs Bragg stated that I was going to be doing 'an evaluation' of the college, a term with which I was most unhappy. In the few seconds I had to decide, I chose to risk antagonizing Mrs Bragg by seeming to correct her, and to say that I actually thought of what I was doing as a 'study' rather than an 'evaluation'. I added that I thought it was rather too early to be thinking about a real evaluation – important though that was. An awkward moment!

I knew that for the first few weeks I would have to be careful not to antagonize anyone, and to try to become part of the background. For the first half of term I thus wanted to adopt the standard technique of following teachers and pupils in their daily tasks. For the first few days I felt very effectively 'managed', for I was assigned to be with only 'safe' and highly trusted teachers. We were all testing the water, but as the weeks passed and I showed myself to be trustworthy, I was able to negotiate with individual teachers to watch their classes. Towards the end, there were days when I was left to fend for myself completely. All of the teachers asked agreed to allow me into their classes and most were only asked on the same day as being observed (some with only a few minutes warning).

In the classrooms I usually found myself a seat as out of the way as possible and simply watched. I took very few notes in the classrooms, but recollected at length using a tape recorder at the end of each day. I tried to describe what I had seen in each of the lessons, noting anything which struck me as being routine, unusual, or of special interest. I also noted my conversations with staff and students, and my feelings about how the research was going.

Description, hunches, problems and even tentative hypotheses were all jumbled onto the innumerable tapes.

To describe what the college was doing, I had to try to understand how it was experienced by the different groups involved. To me, the most important group was the pupils (who are called students at the college). No general announcement was made to students about my presence, and I did not ask for such a statement, fearing that it might be accompanied by a demand to be always on best behaviour when I was around. Instead I relied on the student grapevine to spread the news and, in practice, it was some days before any but a tiny few knew who I was. It was four days into the study before any of the teachers in whose classrooms I was observing asked me if I would like to explain to the students what I was doing, and students did not at first ask me individually.

A problem which I had not anticipated was that both teachers and students were reasonably used to having visitors in the college, many of whom would tour the classrooms and ask both staff and students questions. These visitors might be industrialists, sponsors, governors, reporters, politicians and so on and, while teachers were usually given some warning that specific visitors would be around the college, the students generally were not. Indeed, so common were visitors that students identified them as a separate category of participants in the college and it was as if unwritten 'visitors rules' applied when they were present. Students were often told of the importance of creating a good impression for the college at all times, but especially when visitors were present. It was only after a few days that they began to realize that my own position in the college was different, and began to ask me what I was doing. I always explained that I was independent of the college, that I was writing a book about it, and that I wanted to find out what it was like for them to be there. I tried to make it clear that I would not be reporting back anything to teachers and that (generally against their wishes) no students would be named in the book. As the weeks passed, students whom I did not know would check who I was and ask me if I was really writing a book about them. The student 'bush telegraph' obviously worked, but more slowly than I expected: probably because I was simply not particularly interesting compared with the other things that were going on. A man sitting at the back of classes and asking a few questions was a poor second to the excesses of several BBC and independent television crews, or a forthcoming visit by HRH Prince Philip!

The problem with the semi-official status of 'visitor' was that I had to fight to try to indicate that I was *not* to be treated as a visitor. I was there to observe the college warts and all, and not to be the recipient of image management. This took a long time. It was four weeks before I saw more than the most minor rowdiness or misbehaviour in classrooms. Before that, the presence of a 'visitor' had been such that individuals within groups would sometimes chastise other students, by giving a look in my direction. They wanted to maintain the college's reputation if they possibly could. However, eventually, I sat in wonder as a group of boys behaved as 12 year olds do – hitting each other, moving from chair to chair, mock wrestling, and then becoming innocent and busy workers at the approach the teacher. Again I became amazed at the ability of children convincingly to change their topic of conversation mid-sentence as a teacher comes within earshot. The teacher knew little of what was going on behind his back.

Pupils tested me, and came to recognize that I could be trusted not to interfere and to keep whatever I saw to myself. Doors were less often opened for me and I began to have to ease my way down crowded corridors, instead of the waves parting as mysteriously as the Red Sea. Pupils began to talk to me instead of my always having to make the running. But he process of becoming accepted was slow, and I certainly would not claim that it went very deep. As late as the seventh week of research, a boy in front of me in the queue for lunch handed me a tray and cutlery in true 'visitor' form. I cursed him under my breath as I tactfully thanked him. I tried to negotiate a 'special' independent role for myself with the CTC, but it would be foolish to pretend that it was fully successful. Although I saw more of some groups than others, there was insufficient time to develop the sort of close relationships which have characterized the major studies of ethnographers such as Ball (1981), Measor and Woods (1984), Mac an Ghaill (1988) or Aggleton (1987). I retained the status of adult throughout, never approaching honorary studenthood, and thus never being privy to the secret world of childhood. However, I do feel that I approached a desirable 'insignificant other' status with most of the students. They recognized that I existed, knew why I was there, and assumed that I would do nothing to try to affect them. The status attained was very similar to that of most adults waiting at a bus stop with children who have just been released from school. The children will ignore the adult and continue to push and shove, shout and scream, in the assumption that the adult will do nothing about it. The wise adult will stay on the sidelines and not become involved unless one of the children is seriously threatened. But adult status will allow the 'insignificant other' status to be overthrown if the adult so desires. At any point during the research I felt I could easily have acted 'as a teacher' and the students would have acquiesced to this assumed authority.

PROBLEMS IN PUBLISHING

As I sat in lessons and talked to staff, I began to recognize further difficulties of conducting research in the CTC that I had not thought through earlier. At the time I was there, only 27 teachers were spread across all the subject areas. Many fellow educationists, teachers, politicians, parents and others would be fascinated by an account of the effectiveness of various teaching styles and strategies within each of these subject areas. How much technology was used in various subject lessons? How was it used? How did students respond? These were very important questions, but ones that I increasingly recognized I could not fully answer in print. The problem was that with only two or three people teaching each subject, it was impossible to write about individual lessons without identifying the teacher. Had it been possible to restrict the possibility of identification only to those directly involved within the college, it might have been possible to write about specific lessons, but even this would have been ethically dubious. I certainly did not see my role as that of inspector reporting back on teaching to the Principal and others. Some sociologists have delayed the publication of their books until it was judged that disclosure could not do any harm to those involved. For example, Burgess (1983,1985,1987) published his often critical study of a comprehensive school ten years after that research had ben conducted, in part because he feared that the head might use information available in the accounts against the staff involved. In the case of the CTC, if the study was to have an impact and be widely read, there was no possibility of delaying publication. More importantly, because the college was named, any identification of individuals could be made by those outside as well as inside. The fact that staff have continuing careers which might be affected by inappropriate and unverifiable comment made it unthinkable that I should discuss lessons in any but the broadest terms. That I might wish to stress positive aspects of particular lessons rather than negative features does not fundamentally alter the situation. In the end, I did not feel it appropriate to include in the book anything other than a few 'cameos' of partially reconstructed lessons which were intended to give a general indication of the culture of the college.

Ethical problems surrounding the publication of research have been quite widely discussed in the literature (see, for example, Becker, 1964; Burgess, 1989). I had encountered similar problems with my previous research on private schools (Walford, 1987d) where an initial interest in the influence of private school teachers on national curriculum development had to be shelved as the data could not be published without identifying individuals. In the case of the CTC, the problems of possible identification of staff also led to self-censorship of whole areas of interest, some of which were of major importance. For example, one topic area where this self-censorship was at work was that of gender and sexism. One of the requirements of the CTC plan is to provide a balance of provision for boys and girls, and The City Technology College, Kingshurst takes this objective seriously. As in many aware schools, all lessons are taught in mixed sex groups including PE and CDT. There are attempts to balance the gender mix of student chosen 'enrichments' which include a range of sporting, cultural and physical activities. Some girls play five-a-side football alongside boys, while a few boys take part in aerobics. There was an equal opportunities working party dealing specifically with gender issues in the college.

Yet, as in all other schools, this does not mean that sexism and sex stereotyping have been overcome. Children, teachers and, in this case, visiting industrialists and others, bring their existing sexist assumptions into the college. Girls are praised for being pretty, boys are encouraged to be strong, classroom and social activities unintentionally (or sometimes intentionally) re-enforce gender inequalities. In my tape recorded notes made at the end of each day I have several powerful examples of such language and activities, yet I am unable to report them in detail as they would identify individual people. My concern with this issue does not mean that the CTC is particularly bad – I am sure that gender issues are taken far more seriously there than in the majority of schools – but gender equality is one criterion by which the success of the CTC will be evaluated. If too many of the girls eventually choose to become highly skilled wordprocessing secretaries, then the college will surely have failed. Yet, this whole issue is hardly touched upon in the research reports, because individual teachers might have been identifiable.

INTERVIEWING CHILDREN

Although much of the detailed observation of teaching could not be written up, I believe time spent observing was not wasted. Indeed, without it I would not have been able to have obtained the depth of information that I later gained from both students and staff. In addition, as the identities of individual children can be much more easily concealed than those of teachers, it was also still possible to use data obtained from observation of children in classrooms in the final reports.

Toward the end of the term I interviewed a sample of pupils about their experience of the college. I prepared an outline interview schedule based on that used by Edwards *et al.* (1989) in their study of the Assisted Places Scheme, and interviewed a sample of forty-five children drawn from three of the mixed-ability classes. Most of the children interviewed were very open in their interviews, and were happy to have them tape-recorded. I told them that the idea was for them to natter about what it was like for them to be at the CTC, and many of them took me at my word! It was particularly interesting to compare these interviews with similar ones I conducted with children in neighbouring LEA schools. Both groups of children spanned the ability range, and lived in the same area, but the difference was sometimes stunning. Most of the CTC children talked at length about the CTC, the process of choosing it, and what they liked and disliked about it. In contrast, with some notable exceptions, the LEA children were much less talkative. They were prepared to answer purely factual questions, but were very reluctant to expose any emotion or make evaluative comments about their own schools. Part of the difference was undoubtedly due to the emphasis that the CTC places on building self-confidence, and most of the students are surprisingly articulate and confident with adults. But I believe that my time spent in classrooms observing contributed vitally to the willingness of the CTC children to talk openly with me – without it I would have just been another 'visitor' for whom 'special rules' of conversation operated.

Classroom observation was also essential to assessing the validity of the CTC children's answers. As explained previously, all pupils knew that they were generally expected to put forward positive views to 'visitors'. They were not expected to lie, but they did not need to be told that some comments were more appropriate than others. Their keenness about the college was such that most of them would automatically try to protect the college's reputation. I feel that an outside researcher coming in to quickly interview children in that first intake of the first CTC would have obtained data of doubtful validity. For example, I do not believe it would have been possible for any visiting researcher to have probed beyond the responses of 'there's nothing I dislike about it' which I initially obtained from many of the pupils. In contrast, I spent many hours with all of them in classes. I could probe what they meant by 'the classes are always interesting' or 'the teachers are nice' to a far greater degree than someone who had not been with them during a dressing down or a dull lesson. When the majority gave positive responses I knew that their behaviour in class usually backed up what they said, but when particular pupils said that they worked really hard during project week, I could also lightly remind them that I had been at the CTC at the time!

This is nothing revelatory, of course. It is the essence of ethnographic method that the quality and validity of any interviews are likely to be higher when they are part of a longer-term involvement, but I believe that this is particularly pertinent when attempting to obtain information on children's (rather than adults') thoughts and experiences. First, it is far easier to explain confidentiality and the purpose of research to adults than it is to children. But, second, children also have less reason than adults for believing that an interviewer is going to be honest with them, and they are often correct in being cautious about claims from adults about confidentiality. For example, in a previous interview study with which I was involved, a co-researcher, who had promised confidentiality to children being interviewed, was within an hour unthinkingly passing on information to their teachers. He was treating what the children said as essentially unimportant, and thus open to being passed on at whim to others. It is an interesting indication of the way many adults view promises to children, and reflects a common lack of respect for children's rights as individuals. Children experience similar infringements of their rights daily, and are wise to treat all adults with care.

What was particularly interesting in the CTC research was that it was possible to directly compare the quality of the interviews obtained in two contrasting situations. In contrast to the CTC interviews, the children interviewed in nearby schools had no time to get to know the interviewers. Although my colleagues and I were able to give a brief introduction, senior teachers were present when the arrangements were made, and children were simply 'wheeled in' one after another. For the study of the CTC itself, the children had good reason to believe that I could be trusted, while for the interviews conducted in other schools they had every right to be suspicious.

Interviewing children is perhaps the most challenging problem of access. It is relatively easy to arrange interviews with them once assess to a school has been achieved, but access to children's understandings is far more difficult. As Fine and Sandstrom (1988) argue, because all adults have passed through childhood it is tempting to assume that we have greater knowledge of children's culture than we actually do. Even where we are able to obtain adequate answers to our questions, we usually interpret what children say on the basis of adult expectations, which may differ markedly from those of children. Uncovering 'kid society' (Glassner, 1976) is a major challenge, and a necessity if we are to understand schools. The published study of Kingshurst CTC hardly scratches the surface of those children's understandings, but the experience of observing and interviewing them reminded me of what a great privilege it is to be allowed to discover something of their world. It left me with the desire to try just that bit harder next time.

ACKNOWLEDGEMENTS

My sincere thanks to to Mrs Valerie Bragg and the staff and students of the City Technology College, Kingshurst, for allowing me to enter their world and to experience their kindness and hospitality. Although this project could not have been completed without their generous help, the responsibility for the contents of this chapter is mine alone.

REFERENCES

Aggleton, Peter (1987) *Rebels Without a Cause*, Lewes, Falmer.
Ball, Stephen J. (1981) *Beachside Comprehensive: A Case Study of Comprehensive Schooling*, Cambridge, Cambridge University Press.

Barnes, John A. (1979) *Who Should Know What?*, Harmondsworth, Penguin.

Becker, Howard, S. (1964) 'Problems in the publication of field studies', in Vidich, A.J., Bensman, J. and Stein, M. (eds) *Reflections on Community Studies*, New York, Harper & Row.

Burgess, Robert G. (1983) *Experiencing Comprehensive Education: A Study of Bishop McGregor School*, London, Methuen.

Burgess, Robert G. (1985) 'Some ethical problems of research in a comprehensive school', in Burgess, Robert G. (ed.) *Field Methods in the Study of Education*, Lewes, Falmer.

Burgess, Robert G. (1987) 'Studying and restudying Bishop McGregor School', in Walford, G. (ed.) *Doing Sociology of Education*, Lewes, Falmer.

Burgess, Robert G. (ed.) (1989) *The Ethics of Educational Research*, Lewes, Falmer.

Edwards, Tony, Fitz, John and Whitty, Geoff (1989) *The State and Private Education. An Evaluation of the Assisted Places Scheme*, Lewes, Falmer.

Fine, Gary A. and Sandstrom, Kent L. (1988) *Knowing Children Participant Observation with Minors*, Beverly Hills, Sage.

Fisher, Paul, (1989) 'Getting down to business', *Times Educational Supplement*, 13 January, p.35.

Glassner, Barry (1976) 'Kid society', *Urban Education* 11, pp.5–22.

Lutz, F.W. (1981) 'Ethnography: The holistic approach to understanding schooling', in Green, J. and Wallat, C. (eds) *Ethnography and Language in Educational Settings*, New York, Ablex.

Mac an Ghaill, Máirtín (1988) *Young, Gifted and Black*, Milton Keynes, Open University Press.

Measor, Lynda and Woods, Peter (1984) *Changing Schools: Pupil Perspectives on Transfer to a Comprehensive*, Milton Keynes, Open University Press.

Moyser, George and Wagstaffe, Margaret (1987) *Research Methods for Elite Studies*, London, Allen & Unwin.

Pring, Richard (1984) 'Confidentiality and the right to know', in Adelman, C. (ed.) *The Politics and Ethics of Evaluation*, London, Croom Helm.

Punch, Maurice (1977) *Progressive Retreat*, Cambridge, Cambridge University Press.

Punch, Maurice (1986) *The Politics and Ethics of Fieldwork*, London, Sage.

Shaffir, William B., Stebbins, Robert A. and Turowetz, Allan (eds) (1980) *Fieldwork Experience*, New York, St Martin's Press.

Walford, Geoffrey, (1986) *Life in Public Schools*, London, Methuen.

Walford, Geoffrey, (1987a) 'How dependent is the independent sector?', *Oxford Reveiw of Education* 13, 3, pp.275–96.

Walford, Geoffrey (ed.) (1987b) *Doing Sociology of Education*, Lewes, Falmer.

Walford, Geoffrey, (1987c) *Restructuring Universities: Politics and Power in the Managment of Change*, London, Croom Helm.

Walford, Geoffrey (1987d) 'Research role conflicts and compromises in

Walford, Geoffrey (1987d) 'Research role conflicts and compromises in public schools', in Walford, G. (ed.) *Doing Sociology of Education*, Lewes, Falmer.

Walford, Geoffrey (1990) *Privatization and Privilege in Education*, London, Routledge.

Walford, Geoffrey, (1991) 'City Technology Colleges: A private magnetism?' in Walford, G. (ed.) *Private Schooling: Tradition, Change and Diversity*, London, Paul Chapman.

Walford, Geoffrey and Jones, Sian (1986) 'The Solihull adventure: an attempt to reintroduce selective schooling', *Journal of Education Policy* 1, 3, pp. 239–53.

Walford, Geoffrey and Miller, Henry (1991) *City Technology College*, Milton Keynes, Open University Press.

6

YOUNG, GIFTED AND BLACK
Methodological reflections of a teacher/researcher

Máirtín Mac an Ghaill

INTRODUCTION

I entered or anyway I encountered the white world. Now this white world that I was encountering was, just the same, one of the forces that had been controlling me from the time I opened my eyes on the world. For it is important to ask, I think, where did these people I'm talking about come from and where did they get their peculiar school of ethics? What was its origin? What did it mean to them? What did it come out of? What function did it serve and why was it happening here? And why were they living where they were living and what was it doing to them? All these things that sociologists think that they can find out and haven't managed to do. . .(Baldwin, 1965, p. 121)

I will try to show the ways in which 'doing sociological research' is just a method of making sense of the world; as well as the fact that 'doing research' changes the way in which the researcher sees the world; a different way of understanding emerges from the research. (Corrigan, 1983, p.6)

One of the major reasons why social scientists have failed to answer the black American novelist James Baldwin's questions is because they have not asked these questions, concerning the American or English white social world. Rather, white social science research has made problematic dominated social groups, such as the black community.[1] Furthermore, the researchers have used their cultural power to define the dominated groups' social worlds.

In the educational research tradition of Lacey, 1976, Moore, 1977, Ball, 1984, and Pollard, 1985, I wish to reflect on and discuss some of the processes and issues involved in the methodology of my study *Young, Gifted and Black*. This includes a reflection as a teacher/researcher on a methodological and political apprenticeship. There are three main areas. The central significance of qualitative methodology for theoretical and conceptual development, my relationship with the students and the political and ethical issues involved in a white male researching black female and male students. A main theme that links these areas is, as Corrigan indicates above, that methodology enables us to alter our understanding of how we see and engage in the social world. Hopefully, a more adequate picture emerges of English schooling as a social system described from a number of participants' perspectives. In using this approach, the methodology pointed to and allowed a critical examination of the dominant assumptions of the white social world.

I carried out two ethnographic studies in the institutions in which I worked. The first study looks at the relations between white teachers and two groups of anti-school male students – the Asian Warriors and the Afro-Caribbean Rasta Heads – at an inner-city comprehensive school (Kilby), in a black population area in an English city during 1980–2. The second study looks at a group of black female students, of Afro-Caribbean and Asian parentage, called the Black Sisters, who responded positively to education, at an inner-city sixth form college (Connolly), in the same city during 1983–5.

FORMULATING THE RESEARCH CONCERN

All educational ethnographies have a hidden history; a narrative of what really happened while 'doing educational research'. This is illustrated, for example, in relation to my choice of PhD thesis, on which *Young, Gifted and Black* is partly based. I had orginally intended to study the experience of Irish students in the English school system. However, I was informed that no tutors were available to supervise such a thesis. I was recommended to examine Afro-Caribbean or Asian students' schooling. At this time I was not fully aware of how my research concern with black students was being chosen for me.

Historically the Irish have been the largest immigrant group in England. At present they consititute the largest ethnic minority group. But the arrival of black workers has served to displace the visibility of the ethnic status that the Irish experience in England. Empirically it can be shown that the Irish continue to experience racism, at personal, cultural and structural levels (Curtis, 1985). However, they continue to be under-researched. One of the main reasons for this is because social science researchers have tended to collude in the ideological construction of the dominant images of black and white migrants and their children in England. For example, white ethnic groups were and continue to remain invisible to the educational research community, policy makers and teachers because they are not seen as constituting a problem for schools. I now realized that this racialization of school life should be the starting point of any critical educational research. It was not my starting point.

My concern with the study of racism in schools arose as a result of my teaching in Kilby, which in the early 1970s was officially regarded as one of Britain's main black 'problem' areas. The careers teacher at Kilby School, an 11–16 boys comprehensive, where I taught English as a Second Language, informed me of the high proportion of Afro-Carribbean students who were achieving poor examination results and their resulting high level of unemployment. I chose to look at their transition from school to work and to examine the relationship between the Afro-Caribbean and Asian students' responses to schooling and their future destiny in the labour market. Thus, hoping to establish possible causal links.

At this time the 'race-relations' ethnic explanation of black students' educational performance was dominant (Ballard and Driver, 1977). This culturalist perspective focuses upon the black students' distinctive cultural attributes and suggests that social behaviour is to be understood primarily in terms of culture. Adopting a discourse of deficit, the main social images constructed by this approach portray the black community as a 'problem' (John, 1981 and Solomos, 1988). Ethnicity is assumed to be a handicap for their integration into British society, resulting in their relative social subordination.

As reported in an earlier paper (Mac an Ghaill, 1989, p. 176), my initial research design implicitly shared the white norm of classifying black students as a 'problem'. The substantive issues focused upon the deviant students and methodological and data techniques were employed to meet the culturalist assumptions of this theoretical approach. This reductionist perspective juxtaposes Afro-Caribbean youths' assumed underachievement with Asian youths' assumed linguistic difficulties, who are seen to be 'caught between two cultures' (Community Relations Commission, 1976; and see Lawrence, 1982 for a critique). At this stage of my research I became preoccupied with the question of why the Afro-Caribbean students appeared to be rejecting school in contrast to the Asian students' academic conformity. I was aware of racial discrimination within the school but concentrated on the apparent student differential response to it.

REFORMULATING THE RESEARCH CONCERN

Williams (1988, p. 133) in his ethnographic study of racism in the youth service argues that;

> The choice of methodology should also be based on sound theoretical foundations. Frank Burton (1978) argues cogently that Participant Observation as a sociological method is particularly appropriate to analysing a 'mediated social reality' . . . given that I was concerned to see how black young men were responding and coping with the racism and discrimination they met in their daily lives, how their 'subculture' relates to their parent culture and how the latter relates to white hegemonic culture, the study falls into the category of 'meditated social reality'.

Similarly, for me the core methodology of my studies of Kilby School and Connolly College was participant observation (McCall and Simmons, 1969). Methodology was of vital significance in the generation of theory. The use of the methodological imagination, that acknowledges the relative autonomy of methodology (Meyenn, 1979) from inter-related theoretical and substantive issues and the dialectical relationship between these elements, was the major breakthrough in the research. This approach prevented the study from simply reproducing inadequate data of the 'race relations' ethnic approach.

Intensive participant observation of the anti-school Rasta Heads led me to shift my theoretical perspective, identifying racism rather than the students themselves as the main problem in their schooling. This was a significant shift, involving role conflict, albeit creative, between my position as a teacher and that of researcher. As a teacher, I interpreted the Rasta Heads' negative responses to their schooling as the primary cause of their academic under-achievement. At the same time, I was committed to helping them to overcome these self-erected barriers, that unintentionally served to reproduce their subordinated place in the labour market.

What was missing from this analysis was an understanding of the material conditions, both within the school and the wider society, that created what I came to see as their collective coping strategies. At this stage the field-work became a narrative of black student survival. They explained to me the forms of racism that they experienced in relation to, *inter alia*, English immigration laws, the education, labour and housing markets, welfare institutions, inner-city policing and media presentation. Adopting a black perspective, that is, the view that the black community experience the social world in a systematically different way to whites, was vital here. It enabled me to reinterpret the students' subcultural responses, not as primarily causal of their academic underachievement but as symptoms of their coping with a racially structured institution. My methodological concern with attempting to understand the Rasta Heads' lived culture directed me towards re-examining the effects of school processes, such as ' "gateways", streaming, banding, setting, suspensions and remedial units,' that worked disproportionately against their interests (Wright, 1985).

The creative dynamic of participant observation in developing my analysis of student–teacher interaction was highlighted in relation to the discovery of the institutional structure of the teachers' stereo- typing of the black students. The anti-school students informed me of the system of racist stereotyping that operated at Kilby School. The teachers juxtaposed the 'troublesome, underachieving' Afro- Caribbean students with the 'conformist, academically successful' Asians. This served to make invisible the Asian students' resistance to schooling, which in turn served to highlight the visibility of the Afro-Caribbeans' behaviour.

Getting to know the social structure of the students' peer group networks, helped to demystify the dominant teacher perceptions of and responses to the students, on the basis of ascribed ethnic characteristics. For example, I identified the Asian Warriors, as a main anti-school group. As the anti-school students pointed out, it was not a question of the Afro-Caribbean students actually being intrinsically more deviant than the Asian students but rather that the teachers tended to see it that way.

By this time I realized that my examination of the students' transition from school to work was too ambitious a plan, though I continued to collect data on their first six months post-school experience. As a result of the methodological concern with the students' perspective of teacher–student relations, new substantive

105

questions emerged. First, what was the response of the teachers to the schooling of black students? And, second, what was the meaning of the students' responses to schooling? In attempting to answer these questions and offer a critique of the 'race-relations' culturalist explanation of black students' response to schooling, a theoretical framework was developed, which takes account of both economic and sociological explanations (Sivanandan, 1978; and Rex and Tomlinson, 1979). Other work that explicity acknowledges a black perspective, including Bourne and Sivanandan (1980) and the Institute of Race Relations (1982), has emphasized the need for an analysis of the black community's social location in a racially and class stratified society. Most significantly for the research, this theoretical perspective led me to see how racism was mediated both through the existing institiutional school framework that discriminates against all working-class youth (Williams, 1986), and through the operation of 'race' specific mechanisms, such as, the non-representation of black culture and the system of racist stereotyping.

I had not intended to carry out a study of black female students. In fact it would be more accurate to say that they chose me. In early 1983 I met a small group of black female students, of Asian and Afro-Caribbean parentage, at a sixth form college, where I was teaching Sociology. I discussed the study of the Rasta Heads and the Warriors with the Black Sisters. They were enthusiastic about the findings but were critical of the absence of the discussion of gender relations, serving to reinforce the male norm in academic research (Griffin, 1986). I became particularly interested in carrying out an ethnographic study of the Black Sisters, who as a group of academically successful students, challenge the stereotype of black underachievement. This investigation included an examination of the student-teacher relations that the young women and I were involved in. My professional teaching skills were of much more significance to them than to the anti-school Warriors or the Rasta Heads. At one level, as Hameeda indicates below, the Black Sisters exchanged participation in the study for my support of them as a teacher.

Hameeda: It wasn't thought out like this but I think we probably did think, we'll help you with the study because you were helping us. Your being a teacher was really important. People from the working-class, black and white, don't know the hidden rules of schools, like how to act with teachers, study skills, examination techniques and university applications. But in terms of our motivation for taking part in the study, its hard to separate from other reasons. Like our shared political views, which I think became the most important. It was and still is exciting the way we discuss and share ideas and the way we feel about things that really matter.

Like Whyte (1943) I found that the insights, hypotheses and the kinds of questions to ask were developed in the actual process of investigation. For example, in interviews the Black Sisters frequently returned to the question of racist stereotypes, their origin and the power of whites to implement them within particular social practices (Mac an Ghaill, 1988a, pp. 16-17).

Nihla: I think that all the teachers had these stereotypes. Like they'll say for the blacks, yes, they're stupid, for the Asians, yes, they're sly and the women have to stay in the house all day and do the housework, and yes, they have to get married when they're sixteen and yes, they have to have all these kids. And there are no stereotypes for white people.

Wendy: No stated ones.

Judith: There are stereotypes but its unstated. In a sense its not what you say but what you don't say. You can have positive stereotypes, that's for whites, superior compared to us. They measure us against what they assume they are.

Nihla: You don't find blacks making up stereotypes about white people.

Wendy: The haven't got the power really. Even if they do, they can't make them stick, make them affect whites.

Most importantly the Kilby School and Connolly College students helped me to shift my understanding of stereotyping in the psychological sense, with its focus on individuals' attitudes, such as prejudice, to the sociological view, that locates stereotypes within the wider context of the society and the ideological function they serve in reproducing the dominant power relations (see Barrat, 1986). In other words, I came to see how an idealist analysis which reduces racial stereotyping to a question of teacher prejudice creating black student deviants is insufficient to explain the complex social interaction of white teachers and black students. Rather, the process of racism involves concrete practices linked to the objective material conditions and expectations both within the institution and the wider society. Throughout the book I attempted to understand how specific racist stereotypes were grounded in the social relations of the school and the college.

Like Corrigan (1979, p.16) getting to know the students' experience of schooling directed me to the use of the historical method. I began to examine how the black community were first 'incorporated' into Britain. More specifically, I examined the history of multicultural/anti-racist policy at national and local authority levels (Arnot, 1986 and see Dale, 1989). This became specially important, in order to understand the specificity of how racism operates in English schools in the 1980s. As Gilroy (1981, p.208) points out: 'different racisms are found in different social formations and historical circumstances'.

In this re-evaluation of the central value of methodology, that I had under-valued at the planning stage of the Kilby School study, I found of particular significance the employment of different methods. Following the logic of the conventional 'race relations' perspective, I had initially concentrated on students' behaviour and had not intended to include the teachers as part of the study. In shifting my research concern to include teacher ideologies and practices, I identified them as part of the problem. The methodological concern with studying the teacher–student relations as a whole process rather than concentrating on student responses resulted in the use of different methodologies and data collection techniques. Thus, producing different types of data. In the early part of the research, there had been a tendency to concentrate exclusively on the quantitative material. For example, in trying to establish links between the Afro-Caribbean and Asian students' attitudes to school and the resulting academic outcomes, I collected data on school absences, lateness, suspensions, the ethnic composition of students in academic/non-academic teaching groups and examination results. But as the study developed there was an attempt to combine and integrate observations and interview transcripts with the quantitative data (Lacey, 1976). This helped to develop a practice of reflexivity, enabling me to make alternative readings of the empirical material gathered from the use of different methods.

In examining the complex nature of the teacher's response to the schooling of black students and, the students' sub-cultural responses to schooling, the use of different methodologies provided an invaluable means of cross-checking. This was of particular help in relation to the vast amount of material that I had collected from observation, with the potential dangers involved in this method of inferring meaning from understanding the context by participation in the teacher and anti-school groups. So, for example, in attempting to identify the operation of racist mechanisms within the school, observations were checked against students' and teachers' views and these further checked by reference to information in the school, careers service and local newspapers. The different methodologies informing each other, hopefully have led to a more accurate and complete account of the social processes involved in the interaction between the teachers and the students.

RELATIONSHIP WITH STUDENTS:
A COLLABORATIVE MODEL

Researcher's autobiography

It is suggested in the literature on social science methodology that one of the main disadvantages of qualitative research is the amount of time required to carry it out. I found participant observation to be very time consuming and demanding of my full commitment during the field-work. Just as the art of teaching is regarded by experienced practitioners, 'as caught rather than taught', so also the success of this craft depends upon the researcher's ability to establish relationships with the subjects of his or her study. The establishing and maintaining of these relationships will largely determine the quality of the data collected.

Rather surprisingly, an element that I had not seen as important at the planning stage of the Kilby School research, was of central importance in the initial encounter and maintaining of relationships with the students. Absent from much of the social science research literature was the question of the significance of the personal and autobiographical characteristics of the researcher. The students frequently positively commented on the fact that I was one of the two teachers at the school who chose to live in the local area. My living in Kilby gave them the opportuntiy to see me outside of my teaching role. We bumped into each other in local shops, Asian restaurants and in the swimming baths. By accident I had attained a certain 'street credibility' before starting my research, that aided my access to their social world.

Living in Kilby also made me accessible to the students. My home provided a mutually relaxed atmosphere, in which we gained a 'clear first hand picture' of each other's lives, on our own grounds and in our own terms (Liebow, 1967, p. 11). Over the research periods the Rasta Heads, the Warriors and the Black Sisters visited my home regularly. The experience of talking, eating, dancing and listening to music together helped to break down the potential social barriers of the teacher/researcher role that may have been assigned to me and my seeing them as students with the accompanying status perception. Socially much of my time was taken up either in such informal activities, or the more formal occasions, such as attendance at temples, mosques and churches for religious festivities, marriages and funerals. In a review of the Kilby School study, Kevin, a Rasta Head, explains the students' perception of the positive response to my role as a teacher/researcher.

Kevin: You know me better than my family. I told you more things than even my friends. And you told us everything about you. We've (the students) spent more time here with you in the last couple of years than with anyone else, haven't we? I wouldn't ever believe that I would trust a teacher. But really people are for us or against us. You always proved to be on our side. You came to see how our lives really are and you explained things to us about our lives that made more sense than we could have thought of.

The Rasta Heads and the Warriors also identified with the fact that I was younger than many of the teaching staff at Kilby School. It was assumed that I was interested in young people's social world. Hence, they would often initiate conversations about their girlfriends, music or football. Talking to young female teachers made clear to me that gender was also of significance here. These male students assumed that this was male discourse and excluded the female teachers from such informal talk.

Such biographical details were perceived by the students as of central significance to my roles as a researcher and a teacher, that at times were in conflict and at other times mutually supportive. Kilby School was typical of many secondary schools, in that its authoritarianism was expressed in 'macho' terms. 'Being tough' was a social attribute that had high status for male teachers and students in classroom interaction. Each group assumed it was a necessity as a survival strategy. Partly as a result of my being small in height, I was assumed not to be 'tough' and hence I was not seen as a physical threat. This had advantages for my role as a researcher, in helping to build rapport with the students. However, in the classroom I had the usual problems of maintaining order. My research reinforced my liberal teaching style, of trying to create new coping strategies within lessons, such as trying to win the students' consent to be taught by someone who was sympathetic to them. 'They in turn redefined my behaviour and did not adopt the traditional student strategy of interpreting a more liberal teaching response as an indication of a 'soft teacher', who was an easy target for classroom interuption. We created a fragile alliance that broke down from time to time, resulting in further re-negotiation' (Mac an Ghaill, 1988b p. 220). Khalid, a Warrior, indicates how the students resolved the conflict of my teacher/researcher role.

Khalid: The kids always treated you as a different kind of teacher. OK you had to act as a teacher in the school but even there we knew you were on our side. There was a way in which we felt that we should protect you from the other teachers. OK you were doing your study but you were really one of us. You always defended us, you always told us the truth. And in class you treated us with respect, even when the other teachers didn't like it.

One of the most enjoyable parts of the Kilby field-work were the trips to such places as Wales, London and Donegal. Both members of the Warriors and the Rasta Heads complained before going that they were not interested in what they ridiculed as 'school camping trips'. But such occasions were enjoyed by all and talked about for weeks after. These trips reminded me of camping holidays with Northern Irish young people. They shared similar material and social conditions, projected tough images and similarly protested about being treated like school children. However, away from the social pressures and constraints of their respective local areas, I felt the freedom and youthfulness that they expressed as they spent hours, talking, quietly fishing, climbing mountains or swimming. Also, whether driving back to Derry or Kilby, I felt return the dominant social response that they adopted on their 'home ground'.

What was of particular significance about these events was that they were a useful reminder of the limitations of this type of research, which does not and cannot record the total complexity of the social behaviour of groups. That the students' behaviour away from Kilby took me by surprise served as a necessary qualification of my feeling that the intensive participant observation had led me to 'really know the lads'.

When I came to carry out the second ethnographic study at Connolly College, obviously I was aware of the importance of personal details for the research. But I was not aware of the particular personal dynamics of my relationship, as a white man researching a group of young black females. Again unexpectedly, our common biographical experience of shared class origins and potential social mobility through education was often referred to by the Black Sisters, as an indicator of my assumed understanding of their situation within the college. While acknowledging the power relations that existed between us, they tended to emphasize what we had in common. Most importantly, they made a feminist reading of our personal interaction as political. With different members of the Black Sisters I shared a similar sense of humour, enjoyed similar books and music or simply enjoyed 'doing nothing' (Corrigan, 1979). The young women informed me that at another level, they felt that such personal interaction was evidence of my political identification and support for them in a racially and gender structured institution and society.

Perhaps most unexpectedly of all my Irish origins helped to facilitate my entry into the students' social world. They tended to identify positively with my being Irish. For example, on some occasions when their friends were suspicious of my presence among them, the students claimed that I was 'Irish not white', which acted as a code, suggesting that I could be trusted. For the Black Sisters, my being Irish had political and cultural implications, as Smita pointed out;

Smita: I think your being Irish is very important. You see you are the first white teacher who hasn't selected and caricatured cultural aspects of our lives, like arranged marriages as the only thing that happens to Asian women. That was very important to me, when you started talking to me. You seem to know from your own background how these things fit into Asian life. I suppose that is why you don't have the usual racist expectations. You made us feel equal, which we are, of course!

RESEARCH COLLABORATION

As my research developed, I moved to a collaborative model that involved the students, their parents and other members of the black community, in generating empirical data and formulating and validating theory. Our continuing critical discussion was vital to my attempt to ground the theory in the data collected (Glaser and Strauss, 1967). Most of the students and their parents felt that white researchers could not adequately represent their lives. But Joanne's agrument that one should not adopt a reductionist position to the issue of a white male researcher and black female respondents, was representative of the Black Sisters' perception of their involvment in the study. Furthermore they were not mere objects of my research but rather they were actively involved in its construction.

Joanne:　I agree with Judith, you can't show what its like for a black woman in this society and of course we should carry out our own studies but you can't reduce everything to 'race'. We all had black teachers but we felt close to you. It all depends on things like your political position. Like I would agree more with your interpretation of our lives at school and college than a black conservative view or a black man's view that was sexist. Of course I am biased because we contributed so much to the study. You took serious the way that we saw things, you listened. And we probably learnt more about life by being involved than anything else that we've done at school. But as you said, it really was our study not just yours.

An important factor that underpinned my collaboration with the students was my general pedagogical approach. During my professional training, one of the main theoretical influences on me was Freire's work, *Pedagogy for the Oppressed*. Central to his approach is the concept of conscientization, that is, learning to perceive social, political and economic contradictions, and to take action against the oppressive elements of reality. Adopting such a practice informed my making contact with the students' parents and local community groups in Kilby.

Taking part in anti-racist activities enabled me to see, as Gilroy (1981:212) argues, that the quantitative methodology of conventional studies of the political structure of the black community fails to make explicit that:

> Localised struggles over education, racist violence and police practices continually reveal how blacks have made use of notions of the community to organise themselves.

Involvement in local community politics provided an insight into theorising the students' different forms of resistance to racism and authoritarianism with schools, as linked to their parents' survival strategies. They made clear their understanding of their children's critical response to school, as part of the resistance to racism that they have fought since they arrived in England (see Mac an Ghaill, 1988a, pp. 88-9). In wide ranging discussions with the parents, they explained how racism operated to lock them out from involvement in their children's education. I built up trust with the parents partly as a result of acting as a link between them and the school. I was seen by them as both supporting their interests within the school and providing educational advice within the local community.

Mr Baxter: We [the parents and I] work well together. It would be much better for black parents if the teachers were part of the community. That was the main difference with you. You are always there for the kids and us.

POLITICAL AND ETHICAL ISSUES: WHOSE SIDE ARE WE ON?

So really you have to choose whose side you're on and really there is no choice. When the police shoot black people, they try and show how the family were criminals and deserved it. They wouldn't do that to whites. But its easy to do it to blacks because this society sees all black people as criminals. (Judith, Mac an Ghaill, 1988a, p.147)

Williams (1988, p.136) discussing the procedural and ethical dilemmas of carrying out participant observation warns us that:

It could be argued, however, that a more damning criticism could be subsumed under this heading, namely the paternalism entailed in participant observation, and the arrogance of the researcher invading another group's world to get information in order to relay it to the outside world. This criticism is particularly salient when it comes to researching black people. Gus John relates the resentment which black people felt towards his research team: 'We were brought face to face with anger and frustration of black people in England at being the subject of even more surveys, researches, studies and reports' (John, 1981, p. 17).

I was acutely aware of this particular dilemma. There has been a long history of white researchers constructing images of the black community that have served to reinforce hegemonic racist caricatures. I hope that by adopting an analysis of racism developed by black activists and theorists that I have contributed positively to their political struggle. As is evident from the above the actual process of carrying out the research politicized me in relation to the question of 'race' and racism. The students and their parents involved in the studies were remarkably generous in not generalizing from their individual and collective experiences of racism to whites as a whole, thus not excluding me.

During the research period the students were involved in surveys, one of which Arshid discusses below. The more positive involvement of the Kilby School students in my work was decisively aided by Parminder and Gilroy, two key participants, who were respected and trusted by the other students. They became unofficial research assistants, in advising me on the social structure and perspectives of the Warriors and the Rasta Heads (see Mac an Ghaill, 1988a, p. 144).

Arshid: Like when that woman came into the school asking us all those questions about someat. . .we med things up. It was none of her business but we trusted you and anyway we spent so much time together, you knew what we were like. And you let the teachers have their little say, usually its only them that's talking.

The Black Sisters informed me that my anti-racist stance within Connolly College was of primary significance in their deciding to participate in the ethnography. Nevertheless, the study of black females and males by a white male researcher raises methodolgical and political issues. Meyenn (1979), in his study of white girls' peer groups, reports that private areas of their lives were not discussed with him. More importantly, as Lawrence (1981) argues, in the past researchers have failed to take into account how their relationship with black respondents may be informed by racism. It should be added that my interaction with black females also may be informed by sexism. I hope that by adopting a theoretical position, that locates racism and sexism as the major barriers to the schooling of black youth, I have become more sensitive to the question of how social location in a stratified society, including differential power relations influences one's perspective, and that this in turn influences the ethnographic studies of Kilby School and Connolly College.

A problem that remained throughout the research was the feeling of 'ripping off' the students. Asking the students about this, two of the Rasta Heads, Kevin and Leslie, sarcastically suggested that I had probably 'saved them' from other white liberals, such as social workers and government training officials who 'visited Kilby to help them!'.

As I have argued above, most white researchers in their studies of multicultural schooling have followed the logic of the conventional 'race-relations' approach and concentrated on the behaviour of black students. The examination in *Young, Gifted and Black* of the interaction of white teachers and black students, which it is suggested offers a more adequate explanation, raised specific political and ethical dilemmas. Becker (1967) answered his question, whose side are we on?, by suggesting that the researcher must choose between the 'subordinates' and the 'superiors' perspectives (see also Gouldner, 1975; Lather, 1986 and Troyna and Carrington, 1989). In the polarized environment of Kilby School and Connolly College my main problem was not whose side I *was* on but rather whose side I *appeared* to be on.

I found that while observing and participating with both the Kilby School teachers and the anti-school students created tensions of identifying and being assumed to be identifying with groups who were hostile to each other, nevertheless, it was productive for my understanding of what was really going on in the classroom. Equally productive was the conflict of the teacher–researcher role. Educational researchers of dominated social groups appear to find it easy to identify with the students' rejection of authoritarian school structures (see Corrigan, 1979). I found this to be the case. The students assumed that I was on their side. In a review of the studies, their particular concern was whether I identified with the pro-education females or the anti-school males (see Mac an Ghaill, 1988a, p.143).

Leonie:	I think that you prefer them [the males] in a way because you admire their anti-authority.
Arshid:	I don't. Even now you and them [the females] are closer than us, yer all successful, yer more together than us.
Raj:	Yeah. Them. You're always telling us we are sexist and all that. You influenced them more. They followed you. We went our own way.
Judith:	You admire their freedom. We're stuck in the system and so are you.

Many of the Kilby School teachers assumed that I was not on their side but that as a teacher, I should be. One of the most interesting responses came from the liberal teachers, who theoretically held the values of social justice, equality and participatory democracy (see, Troyna and Carrington, 1989); but were critical of my interpretation of their classroom interaction that suggested that their pedagogy contributed to the failure of the school to implement these values in relation to black students. There was heated debate about the implication from my work that all white teachers are potential racists. This arose from my discussion with the teachers, where I argued that if classroom interaction was an arena where systematic inequalities of power between white teachers and black students are acted out, then all those teachers are in a position to exercise this power, albeit in different forms, whether or not they are so inclined.

Such political issues were not resolved. However, my analysis did not serve to isolate me from the liberal teachers, many of who were active in the Labour Party and union politics, and all of whom were opposed to racism. My not being isolated was partly the result of the differing perspectives that the teachers adopted according to the specific contexts that they were in. At Kilby School and Connolly College these varying social contexts included; union meetings, staff meetings and staffroom and classroom situations, in which the contradicitions of holding a multicultural position in a racially structured institution were acted out.

117

CONCLUSION

Pollard (1987, p.117) in conclusion to his reflection on his collaborative study with young children writes that:

> I would draw attention to the fact that in many ways I was attempting to make a virtue out of necessity. I muddled through attempting as I did so to be theoretically aware and trying to be creative in obtaining the best quality data that is possible for me to manage in the circumstances. Perhaps 'doing sociology of education' is often a little like that in practice, particularly for researchers working alone.

Such a conclusion finds much resonance in my own work. My isolation as a researcher working alone was essentially overcome by my status as a teacher/researcher, which provided a 'role which . . . (could). . .credibly be accommodated in the social group. . .being studied' (Ackroyd and Hughes, 1981).

I hope that the above will serve to develop the reader's 'sociological imagination' which 'enables us to grasp history and biography and the relations between the two within society (Mills, 1970, p.12). For Mills, a central task for sociology is the bringing together of 'private troubles' and 'public issues'. Such an approach, for example, in my educational research enabled me to shift from seeing 'getting my group of kids through the examination system' as teacher's 'private classroom problem' to a researcher's 'public issue', involving the historical, socio-economic, political and ethical questions that James Baldwin suggests social scientists have failed to answer. The methodological concern with examining the black students' perspective made it possible for me to shift my focus from a concern with individualistic student 'failure' to the problem of racism.

NOTE

1 Black is used in this chapter in a socio-political sense and includes Asian and Afro-Caribbean people, emphasising their common experience of racism in England. Racism may take different forms for the two social groups and is class and gender specific.

REFERENCES

Ackroyd, S. and Hughes, J.A. (1981) *Data Collection in Context*, London, Longman.

Arnot, M. (1986) *Race, Gender and Education Policy-making*, module 4, Milton Keynes, Open University Press.

Baldwin, J. (1965) *Nobody Knows My Name*, London, Corgi.

Ball, S.J. (1984) 'Beachside reconsidered: reflections on a methodological apprenticeship', in Burgess, R.G. (ed.), *The Research Process in Educational Settings: Ten Case Studies*, Lewes, Falmer Press.

Ballard, R. and Driver, G. (1977) 'The ethnic approach', *New Society* 16 June, pp. 543–5.

Barrat, D. (1986) *Media Sociology*, London, Tavistock.

Becker, H. (1967) 'Whose side are we on?', *Social Problems* 14, 239–47.

Bourne, J. and Sivanandan, A. (1980) 'Cheerleaders and ombudsmen: the sociology of race relations in Britain', *Race and Class* XXI, 4, pp.331–52.

Burton, F. (1978) *The Politics of Legitimacy*, London, Routledge & Kegan Paul.

Community Relations Commission (1976) *Between Two Cultures: A Study of Relationships between Generations in the Asian Community*, London, Community Relations Commission.

Corrigan, P. (1979) *Schooling the Smash Street Kids*, London, Macmillan.

Corrigan, P. (1983) *Schooling the Smash Street Kids*, 2nd edn, London, Macmillan.

Curtis, L. (1985) *Nothing but the Same Old Story: The Roots of Anti-Irish Racism*, London, Information on Ireland.

Dale, R. (1989) *The State and Education Policy*, Milton Keynes, Open University Press.

Freire, P. (1972) *Pedagogy for the Oppressed*, New York, Herder & Herder.

Gilroy, P. (1981) 'You can't fool the youths. . .race and class formation in the 1980s', *Race and Class* 23, 2/3/, 207–22.

Glaser, B. and Strauss, A. (1967) *The Discovery of Grounded Theory: Strategies for Qualitative Research*, London, Weidenfeld & Nicolson.

Gouldner, A. (1975) *For Sociology: Renewal and Critique in Sociology Today*, Harmondsworth, Pelican.

Griffin, C. (1986) 'It's different for girls: the use of qualitative methods in the study of young women's lives', in Beloff, H. (ed.) *Getting Into Life*, London, Methuen.

Institute of Race Relations (1982) *Patterns of Racism*, London, Institute of Race Relations.

John, G. (1981) *In the Service of Black Youth*, London, National Association of Youth Clubs.

Lacey, C. (1976) 'Problems of sociological fieldwork: a review of the methodology of Hightown Grammar', in M. Hammersley and P. Woods (eds) *The Process of Schooling: A Sociological Reader*, London, Routledge & Kegan Paul.

Lather, P. (1986) 'Research as Praxis', *Harvard Educational Review* 56, 3 257–77.

Lawrence, E. (1981) 'White sociology, black struggle', *Multi-racial Education* 9, 3, 43–8.

Lawrence, E. (1982) 'In the abundance of water the fool is thirsty:

sociology and black "pathology" ', in Centre for Contemporary Cultural Studies, *The Empire Strikes Back: Race and Racism in '70s Britain*, London, Hutchinson/CCCS.

Liebow, E. (1967) *Tally's Corner*, London, Routledge & Kegan Paul.

Mac an Ghaill, M. (1988a) *Young, Gifted and Black: Student–Teacher Relations in the Schooling of Black Youth*, Milton Keynes, Open University Press.

Mac an Ghaill, M. (1988b) 'Sociology and teacher practice: a fruitful alliance', in P. Woods and A. Pollard (eds) *Sociology and Teaching: A New Challenge*, London, Croom Helm.

Mac an Ghaill, M. (1989) 'Beyond the white norm: The use of qualitative methods in the study of black youth's schooling', *Qualitative Studies in Education* 2, 2, 175–89.

McCall, G.S. and Simmons, J.L. (eds) (1969) *Issues in Participant Observation: A Text and Reader*, New York, Addison-Wesley

Meyenn, R.J. (1979) 'Peer networks and schools performance', unpublished PhD thesis, Birmingham, University of Aston.

Mills, C.W. (1970) *The Sociological Imagination*, Harmondsworth, Penguin.

Moore, R. (1977) 'Becoming a sociologist in Sparkbrook', in Bell, C. and Newby, H. (eds) *Doing Sociological Research*, London, Allen & Unwin.

Pollard, A. (1985) 'Opportunities and difficulties for a teacher-ethnographer: A personal account', in Burgess, R.G. (ed.) *Field Methods in the Study of Education: Issues and Problems*, Lewes, Falmer Press.

Pollard, A. (1987) 'Studying children's perspectives: a collaborative approach', in Walford, G. (ed.) *Doing Sociology of Education*, Lewes, Falmer Press.

Rex, J. and Tomlinson, S. (1979) *Colonial Immigrants in a British City: A Class Analysis*, London, Routledge & Kegan Paul.

Sivanandan, A. (1978) 'From immigration control to induced repatriation', *Race and Class* 20, 75–82.

Solomos, J. (1988) *Black Youth, Racism and the State*, Cambridge, Cambridge University Press.

Troyna, B. and Carrington, B. (1989) 'Whose side are we on? Ethical dilemmas in research on "race" and education', in R.G. Burgess (ed.) *The Ethics of Educational Research*, Lewes, Falmer Press.

Whyte, W.F. (1943) *Street Corner Society: The Social Structure of an Italian Slum*, Chicago, University of Chicago Press.

Williams, J. (1986) 'Education and race: the racialization of class inequalities?', *British Journal of Sociology of Education* 7, 2, 135–54.

Williams, L. (1988) *Partial Surrender: Race and Resistance in the Youth Service*, Lewes, Falmer.

Wright, C. (1985) 'School processes: an ethnographic study', in S.J. Eggleston, D.K. Dunn and M. Anjali (eds) *The Educational and Vocational Experiences of 15-18 Year Old People of Ethnic Minority Groups*, Warwick, Warwick University.

7

WORKING TOGETHER? RESEARCH, POLICY AND PRACTICE
The experience of the Scottish evaluation of TVEI

Colin Bell and David Raffe

INTRODUCTION

The Technical and Vocational Education Initiative (TVEI) was introduced, as a pilot scheme, in England and Wales in 1983 and in Scotland in 1984. It was explicitly experimental. It aimed 'to explore and test ways of organizing and managing the education of 14–18 year old people across the ability range' in order to strengthen the links between education and 'the world of employment' and to increase the relevance of education to that world. This was to be done in such a way that (among other things): 'the educational lessons learned can be readily applied in other localities and to other groups among the 14–18 year olds;. . .emphasis is placed on careful monitoring and evaluation;. . . the overall conduct, assessment and development of the initiative can be assessed and monitored by the MSC' (MSC, 1984).

Each local authority in Britain was eventually permitted to run a TVEI pilot project – typically based in a small number of schools, in conjunction with a local further education college, and on 'experimental' cohorts of 200/250 pupils drawn from consecutive school year groups. But local diversity was encouraged. These were planned as pilot projects from which education authorities were meant to learn. The emphasis on innovation in TVEI, the scope for schools and projects to try out different approaches, and the distinction (at least in most early projects) between an 'experimental group' of TVEI students and 'control group' of non-TVEI students: all these factors combined with the published aims of TVEI to give the initiative something of the character of a scientific experiment. It was a scientific venture, moreover, on which the three worlds of research, policy and practice worked together.

From 1986–8 we were part of this collective venture. Together with Cathy Howieson and Kenneth King we were members of the Edinburgh University team conducting one of the two Scottish-wide evaluations of TVEI[1]. In this chapter we reflect on that experience.

Seen as a collectively managed scientific experiment, the pilot TVEI raised at least three sets of issues. For simplicity we refer to these as technical, political and social, although they were in fact closely related.

The technical issue can be understood as a problem of research design. What was the key dimension of experimental variation? Did the TVEI experiment seek to learn primarily from the 'cross-sectional' variation between TVEI students and non-TVEI students, and between schools and projects with different approaches to TVEI? Or did it seek to learn primarily from the less systematic variation that was internal to projects, as they developed their own approaches, tried out new ones, and generally learned from their own internal experimentation and from trial and error? The distinction is essentially that between 'testing' and 'exploring', the terms used to define the aims of TVEI. In the former case the design would be a 'quasi-experiment' (Cook and Campbell, 1979); in the latter it would be closer to action-research. In the former, the role of the evaluator/researcher would be more summative; in the latter, it would be more formative. There were clear limitations on the value of TVEI as a cross-sectional, quasi-experimental design. The selection of students to the 'experimental' TVEI cohort and to the non-TVEI control group was anything but random; differences between the two groups might have been due to any of a range of factors, of which TVEI was only one (Fitz-Gibbon, 1989). TVEI schools and projects differed in so many ways that it would be difficult to single out the factors responsible for their relative successes or failures; and their approaches varied over time, but unsystematically, making quasi-experimental inferences ever more difficult. Nevertheless, the action-research design, with its more formative approach to evaluation, also raised awkward questions. What if the TVEI experiment as a whole failed? Or if it consistently encountered problems that mere trial and error could not overcome? Would action-research and formative evaluation be powerful enough to identify the underlying general, and possibly external, sources of these problems?

The second set of issues was political. In a scientific experiment we may distinguish between scientific and operational success (see

Raffe, forthcoming). Operational success is achieved when the null hypothesis is rejected: when the experiment reaches the conclusion that the experimenter hoped to reach. But operational failures (for example null findings) may still be scientific successes, if they contribute to knowledge and help to close off blind alleys. Scientists are often slow to recognize this (how many scientific journals publish null findings?) so it is hardly surprising that policy-makers, too, tend to judge the success of their 'experiments' in operational rather than scientific terms. When the results of a re-analysis of our evaluation data were reported under such headlines as 'TVEI failure in Scotland', the policy world did not stop to ask whether the failure was scientific or operational (THES, 1989). Indeed, policy-makers may invest considerable political capital in the operational success of their experiments. This was certainly the case with TVEI. Before we started our evaluation, in 1986, the government published the White Paper, *Working Together – Education and Training* (DES/DE, 1986), which announced the 'Extension' of TVEI to all schools in all local education authorities. Hitherto the 'replication' of the pilot projects, rather than their Extension, had been the name of the game. The Extension, and by implication the operational success of the pilot TVEI, was announced before the national evaluations were all up and running, let alone producing 'results'. If nothing else, this served to put us researchers in our place.

The third set of issues was social. The practice of science – or research – is embedded in a social infrastructure, and especially in a culture or what we shall describe as a 'normative world' of research (see also Broadfoot, 1988). This tends to value such principles as objectivity, validity, generality, 'basic' or 'fundamental' research and long-term horizons. In practice, of course, researchers may be driven by all the baser motives depicted in countless university novels. But the normative world of research, and the social infrastructure that sustains it, helps to channel this motivation in a direction that, at least on balance, favours the advance of knowledge. However when – as in our evaluation of TVEI – the endeavour is a collective one, and involves the three very different normative worlds of policy, practice and research, tensions may be created between these worlds which raise awkward questions not only for the conduct of research, but also for its purpose.

In this chapter we discuss how these three closely related sets of issues were raised for us during our evaluation of TVEI in Scotland.

THE PILOT TVEI AND THE EVALUATION

TVEI was always controversial (McCulloch, 1986; Chitty, 1986). It was seen variously as an encroachment of 'training' into the territory of 'education', as an elitist attack on comprehensive education (because of its insistence on identifiable cohorts doing TVEI and the channelling of money into 'enclaves'), as a threat to local control of education, and in Scotland as an attempt to anglicize Scottish education (on the latter see especially Bell *et al,* 1989 and Howieson, 1990a and b). This meant that the political context of TVEI, and subsequent research and evaluation on it, were always going to be contentious and contested. This was even more the case given that the essence of TVEI remained contested within the TVEI world itself. A recurring theme of TVEI research has been how, despite the top-down approach implicit in its earmarked 'categorical' funding, there has been enormous local variation, not just in the means of implementing TVEI, but in the interpretation of its aims and objectives (see Harland, 1987 and other contributors to Gleeson, 1987). This variation can be found not just across projects, but across the different participants involved in the same project: MSC officials, project co-ordinators, head teachers, classroom teachers, students and their parents (Fiddy, 1987). In the words of two local evaluators of TVEI:

> Curriculum theorists have sought to tease out the curriculum and professional models implicit in TVEI rationales. But both critics and apologists of TVEI assume at least a loose coupling between the rhetoric of the innovation and its various practices. Our evidence suggests that this may be unwise. So loose or contradictory is the coupling, so extensive the accommodation to institutional norms, or so eccentric the creative moments, that there may be little reason to assume that the philosophies or models embedded in the rhetoric act potently on educational practice. Are our commentaries fantasies about fantasies? (Fiddy and Stronach, 1987, p.113).

The areas served by the first five Scottish projects differed widely: city, small-town, new-town and rural areas; areas of high unemployment and low unemployment, areas with very different social and economic profiles. The approaches to TVEI followed by the five projects also varied. All, however, focused the resources made available through the initiative (some £2million per project) on four successive cohorts of 200/250 students – from the age of 14 through potentially to 18. In the event a majority of TVEI students left at 16.

Pilot TVEI programmes consisted of a core, common to all TVEI students, and options. Together they made up from zero (see below) to 60 per cent of Scottish TVEI pupils' timetables – the modal figure was well below 60. In Scotland the core usually included information technology, personal and social development, careers education, work experience and a residential experience. Options included subjects chosen by students to meet their needs, such as business studies, computing, catering, textiles, control technology, pneumatics and caring. Many established curriculum areas were also 'enhanced' through TVEI funding in the sense of adding to existing subjects by providing resources. Both in these enhanced subjects and in the TVEI core and options there was an attempt to introduce technology across the curriculum. There were equally important changes in the modes of teaching, emphasizing a problem-solving approach, experiential learning and more negotiated, individualized study (Black *et al.*, 1988).

TVEI had been up and running in Scotland for nearly two years by the time the Extension to all schools in Britain was announced. The Extension was to be supported by a much reduced unit level of funding: what we were to refer to as 'barefoot TVEI'. The aims of the Extension were similar to those of the pilot TVEI with one crucial exception: they contained no mention of testing, exploration or experimentation.

Evaluation had always been a part of pilot TVEI. Not less than 1 per cent of funds from each project had to be spent on evaluation locally. In addition there were special studies and initiative-wide or national evaluations. Two such were funded in England and Wales at the National Foundation for Educational Research (NFER) and at Leeds University. In 1985 the MSC, after discussions involving the Scottish Education Department (SED), invited the University of Edinburgh and the Scottish Council for Research in Education (SCRE) to tender for the Scottish-wide evaluation. Within the University, the evaluation was to become a joint activity of the Centre for Educational Sociology (CES) and the Department of Education. After discussions with SCRE we decided that it would not be sensible to plan a joint bid, but we agreed on a division of the evaluation between the two bodies. Edinburgh would focus on the out-of school/college dimension of TVEI, and SCRE would focus on within school/college dimensions. We knew that this distinction would be hard to adhere to strictly but it reflects an emphasis that was maintained. We proposed that:

the central purpose of the Edinburgh University evaluation is to monitor education-industry relationships and their development in the context of TVEI. 'Industry' is understood to cover all sources of employment, both public and private, and to include the primary and service sectors: the term embraces employers and their representative associations, trades unions and other concerned bodies such as ITBs and training associations. Two main aspects of the relationship between education and industry will be examined in relationship to TVEI: the pattern of liaison between education and industry, which may transmit influences in both directions, and the articulation of TVEI with the demands of local employment and with recruitment, selection and training practices in the labour market (and also with further and higher education).

Liaison and articulation were indeed the major organizing themes of our published evaluation report: *Liaisons Dangereuses? Education-Industry Relationships in the First Scottish TVEI Pilot Projects* (Bell *et al.*, 1988). A Steering Group was set up to cover both the Edinburgh and SCRE evaluations. In addition to the project teams and the MSC it included a TVEI project co-ordinator and a representative of the SED. We reported to the MSC's TVEI Unit in London, but the MSC's Scottish Advisers for TVEI were important local contacts. The Edinburgh evaluation was to run for two years, from August 1986 to July 1988.

We had not, however, envisaged at the time of our proposals that the Extension of TVEI would be announced before we had started serious work on evaluating the pilots. It meant that we were pushed to disseminate 'findings', before we were very certain that that was what they were, to two new audiences: those responsible for 'extending' TVEI from the existing projects and those starting TVEI in new education authorities ('new starts'). This was ironical given the stated nature of TVEI as experimental. Although our evaluation had been designed primarily as a 'summative' one, at our first Steering Group meeting we were asked to change our emphasis to a 'formative' one, and given strong encouragement for early dissemination. Inevitably our research design gave us only limited flexibility to switch emphasis in this way. This meant that the fundamental technical, political and social issues about the nature of the TVEI 'experiment' and our role in it were raised for us right at the start of the evaluation.

How though did we go about our work?

NARRATIVE AND METHODS

Our original proposal described our main activities as:

interviews and discussions with key figures on each side of the education-industry relationship in each project; case studies on the themes of liaison and occupational and technical change; and analysis of the 1987 Scottish Young People's Survey (SYPS) with boosted sample numbers of TVEI schools.

Our methods embraced the qualitative and the quantitative. We were going to do fieldwork, to create ethnographies of organizational change (although in contrast to the English and Welsh evaluations we never proposed, nor in fact carried out, much classroom observation); to interview informally 'industrialists' as well as 'educationists'; to talk to pupils, teachers and TVEI administrators. But also we were going to conduct a systematic social survey of the first Scottish TVEI cohorts, by enhancing the sample of the spring 1987 Scottish Young People's Survey (SYPS), part of a well-established series of large-scale multi-purpose postal surveys, conducted by the CES (Raffe, 1988). We would be able to compare those cohorts with their peers and their predecessors (in the same schools, and in the rest of Scotland) to gain a different perspective on the TVEI effect. These data were to support the more 'quasi-experimental' elements of our design.

The spring 1987 SYPS covered a 10 per cent national sample of young people who had been in the fourth year (S4) of secondary school in the (1985/6) session. S4 is the last compulsory school year for a majority of Scottish pupils. As part of the evaluation we boosted this 10 per cent sample to 100 per cent for the 19 schools that comprised the first five Scottish TVEI projects. The sample was boosted both for the TVEI students and for the 'control group of non-TVEI students from the same schools. For this boosted sample – the extra 90 per cent – we needed to design a questionnaire that included questions of specific interest to TVEI, as well as questions asked in the main 10 per cent survey. To match the SYPS timetable we needed to produce our first draft within six weeks of the project being fully staffed. The demands of questionnaire design therefore drove much of our early field-work: a discipline which focused our minds very quickly on the particularities of the TVEI experience.

In the autumn of 1986 we talked to S5 TVEI pupils, individually or in groups, in all projects. This was the year group to be covered by the SYPS. S5 is a notoriously pressurized year in Scottish education: the syllabus of as many as five or six Highers subjects must be covered in little more than two terms. Fitting TVEI into this overcrowded timetable presented, in the words of one project co-ordinator, 'unprecedented management difficulties'. A number of pupils were resisting TVEI in S5, emphatically and aggressively in some cases. Others had voted with their feet and were either refusing to do it or had already left school. In other cases the schools themselves had given up the struggle or the ambition to deliver TVEI in S5 at all. For instance while a school could find S5 pupils who had done TVEI in S3 and S4 for us to talk to (for the purposes of piloting the questionnaire) the school did not pretend still to be delivering TVEI to these pupils; as far as the pupils were concerned TVEI was what they used to do and some thought it was a pity that there was, as they saw it, no TVEI in S5. We were stumbling up against the discrepancy between what the education authorities had contracted to deliver and the reality in Scottish schools. This was to be confirmed by the survey; one third of fifth-year pupils described by the schools as officially on TVEI did not believe they were still doing TVEI (Bell *et al.*, 1988, Appendix 1). Some schools we visited seemed virtually empty and had hardly anybody in school beyond fourth year – and it was claimed that all those who had remained were doing TVEI. Some projects were 'infilling' TVEI places, others were not.

We quickly discovered that TVEI was being delivered in two markedly different ways that had consequences for the way we conducted the field-work. Some had TVEI Centres on which a great deal of TVEI resources had been lavished and into which TVEI staff were seconded. TVEI pupils were often bussed into the Centres for much of their TVEI work. There was a contagious atmosphere or organizational euphoria in the Centres. Elsewhere education had been starved of resources, promotions and career development blocked, pedagogic innovation and experiment inhibited. But amidst the bright primary colours of the TVEI Centres, full of hi-tech gadgetry and young people working through open-learning modules, all was innovation. Staff based in Centres were sometimes distanced from both the reality and the perception of TVEI that prevailed back in the schools. They had got so used to 'selling' TVEI to pupils, parents, staff, employers and us that their judgements were often a little rose-tinted. And of course we started our field-work of necessity, with them. We conducted focused interviews with members of staff responsible for education-industry liaison on the basis of a close reading of their project's proposal documents. They were gatekeepers in every sense of the word (Malcolm, 1988). And like most gatekeepers they could get field-workers very far very fast. But were they pointing us in the right directions? TVEI projects that were less centrally organized provided important correctives. Projects that were more classroom based had proceeded slower, had less to show and yet the classroom teachers were more confident about TVEI and more supportive of it. Co-ordinators in 'decentralized' projects insisted that we talked to classroom teachers to find out what was going on; the centralized project co-ordinators took it on themselves to tell us what was going on.

Having visited all the projects, we wanted to talk to 'their' industrialists. This was a sensitive issue as projects discerned, correctly in some cases, that industrialists were already over-burdened by demands from educationists. We saw most of the industrialists on steering committees, most of those who had been involved in curriculum development (not always recognized as such), and a range of those providing work experience – we found that there was a limit to what you learned after visiting your tenth hairdresser. As many as possible of our interviews were conducted jointly by two members of the research team (usually Colin Bell and Cathy Howieson). Despite projects' protective attitude towards their industrialists virtually none refused to see us. We were met with unfailing courtesy towards ourselves but with some criticism of education and its practices. In retrospect we suspected that TVEI staff who had wanted to protect 'their' industrialists from us had often been projecting *their* unease with us onto the industrialists. We posed no threat to those industrialists – they were courteous but not usually very interested in us. We were more threatening to the educationists, some of whom saw us as a cross between HMIs (who were conducting an inspection of TVEI during the latter part of our project), advisers, and MSC spies. That not all local evaluations had gone smoothly, and that we and our colleagues from SCRE did indeed make demands on their time, meant that we were frequently welcomed less than enthusiastically by TVEI staff. The fact that we ourselves were based in education, but in a relatively 'elite' institution, did not help; nor did the English origins and accents of the two of us (our two colleagues are native Scots). In the west of Scotland University of Glasgow ties were waved at us, 'ordinary' degrees defended and stories were told to frighten us. (But no, our hub-caps were not stolen and offered for sale back by enterprising TVEI youngsters, although we were assured that this has happened to one of the MSC's TVEI Advisers.)

Our central research concerns were not necessarily so central to the projects. Education-Industry Liaison (EIL) was important, in the words of one project co-ordinator 'because the MSC says that it is important'. The fact that the MSC had funded us to evaluate EIL must have reinforced this message. So, if we were not quite putting EIL onto projects' agendas, we were certainly raising its priority. The first projects had had very little planning time before their first cohorts started TVEI, and projects were under constant pressure to keep their planning one step ahead of their students. Given that the most immediate focus of EIL, work experience, was rarely provided for TVEI students in their first TVEI year (S3), little was done about it until the necessity of work experience loomed in S4. Even then, aspects of EIL that were not primarily aimed at providing work experience placements continued to have relatively low priority. When we asked about the role of industrialists, however widely defined, we sometimes created an anxiety about the lack of such a role, and gave it an importance that it had not previously had for the projects. The same was true at a later stage of our field-work when we asked about TVEI's articulation with YTS, the role of the careers service in this articulation and what the careers service would be doing under the Extension of TVEI. A Principal Careers Office told us with admirable frankness that these were the right questions to ask but they had not thought about them yet.

We soon came to realize that our most useful role as formative evaluators was to hold a mirror up to practitioners. At least this was the role that TVEI staff seemed to value most. They wanted a fresh perspective on what they were doing, and the context in which they were doing it. Our function here was not very different from that of illuminative evaluation (Parlett and Hamilton, 1972), with the important rider that quantitative data, especially comparing projects, could provide as much illumination as qualitative data. In consequence the boundary between field-work and dissemination activity became irretrievably blurred. The information we passed on exceeded the normal reciprocity of field-work. We found that by asking questions we helped hard-pressed practitioners to arrive at solutions: 'Have you thought of using school kitchens for catering work experience places?' 'Do you send your project's annual work experience report to work experience providers?' 'Do S3 and S4 pupils have any contact with the Tech?' 'Can you get employers into classrooms to give interview experience?' 'Why don't you certify through Scotvec?' and so on. In attempting to understand ourselves why the projects were the way they were, we necessarily widened the discussion and debate among the TVEI staff. This was clearly closer to action-research than quasi-experimental research. Schools and projects learned both from each other and from their own internal experimentation and trial and error. We were part of the feedback. We were never able to be purely summative evaluators even if we had wished to be.

As researchers we were always going to face the issue of how to put our diverse data sources together. We have already indicated the range of sources and types of data available from our fieldwork. Our interviews had taken the bulk of our research time. We did not record them, but we took detailed notes and wrote lengthy reports on each, preserving the original words of our interviewees where appropriate. These reports filled several box files. They were an important basis for communication within the research team, and provided much of the raw material for our final report. Perhaps inevitably in a project of this kind, the vast majority of these 'data' were never used directly in our report.

The survey questionnaire collected at least three kinds of quantitative data. There were 'objective' questions which asked about students' family backgrounds, their experiences at school (including TVEI), whether or not they had left school, and if they had their subsequent further education, training or (un)-employment. These data enabled us to contextualize TVEI, and also allowed us to compare TVEI students with non-TVEI students from the same or other schools, or from earlier cohorts. (Such analyses found no TVEI effect on attainment, staying-on or employment, but indicated a favourable effect on truancy: Bell *et al.*, 1988; Raffe, 1989.) Second, we asked structured attitudinal questions of a general kind; these allowed us to compare TVEI and non-TVEI students to show, for example, that significantly more of the former felt they had learnt about the world of work and about self-employment (Bell *et al*. 1988); items referring to personal and social development showed smaller differences. Third, we asked attitudinal items specifically about TVEI, often using open-ended questions. These showed, for example, that work experience was the most widely liked aspect of TVEI, but they also revealed significant differences among projects.

In addition to quantitative data the survey yielded more qualitative data, especially from the 'back-page comments' where respondents were prompted to write more expansively about TVEI. We have written these up in detail elsewhere (Bell and Howieson, 1988); the methodological issues in their use as data are discussed by Walford (1988). More than half (54 per cent) of our respondents made back-page comments. We judged 49 per cent to be favourable and 26 per cent hostile; the rest had to be called 'mixed'. The inter-project variation was again wide – from a project getting half hostile comments to another getting two-thirds favourable comments.

When the first survey findings became available those of us with experience of the survey urged most caution in their interpretation while those who had done most of the field-work seized upon the survey data as confirmation of what they thought they 'knew' about the projects. The stereotypes of the 'qualitative' researcher obsessed by problems of validity, and the 'survey' researcher indifferent to them, were reversed. In fact the survey results were being accepted in this apparently uncritical way precisely because they tended to confirm the evidence of our field-work. The variety of our data sources was invaluable for the mutual confirmation they were able to provide. But this process of 'triangulation' tended to be iterative. We were engaging in a continuing series of interpretative conversations among ourselves, with TVEI 'experts' and 'gurus', and with our key informants – including survey respondents. Because of this we had confidence in our 'findings' – exposed as they were continually at all these levels. Our findings also had to be formative, 'helpful' and 'useful'; and to the extent that they were found to be so in formal and informal disseminations we were given further confidence in what we did. But is the fact that research is 'helpful' or 'useful' necessarily an indication that its conclusions are also valid? To consider this we turn our attention to the three normative worlds of research, policy and practice, as they impinged on our work.

Table 7.1 Three normative worlds' views of research

	Research	Policy	Practice
Control	Researcher (on behalf of objectivity, independence, etc.)	Policy-maker (on behalf of public interest)	Independent (must be able to empathise with, and reflect, practitioners' viewpoint)
Main objective	Summative	Varies	Formative
Timetable	Long-term (follows timetable of scientific enquiry)	Unpredictable (follows unpredictable policy-making timetable, financial year)	Short-term (this year's or this term's problem: follows timetable of school year, progression of TVEI cohort, development of TVEI policy)
Agendas	Unbounded, or bounded by discipline or field	Bounded by policy (focus on TVEI)	Pragmatic
Initial audience	Open (includes practitioners and fellow-researchers)	Policy-makers (who control subsequent dissemination to practitioners and public)	Should include practitioners (who can influence representations of their viewpoint)
Good research	Valid, original (contributes to scientific knowledge)	'Helpful' (respects policy constraints and sensitivities)	'Useful' (illuminating, timely, focused, shows empathy)
Bad research	Dishonest, unambitious	Out of control, reckless of consequences	Remote, elitist, out of date, uncomprehending of practical and social realities

THE NORMATIVE WORLDS OF RESEARCH, POLICY AND PRACTICE

Considerably over-simplified, these three normative worlds are summarized in Table 7.1. Our account draws on our own experience with the evaluation of the pilot TVEI in Scotland; other educational research projects may experience these worlds in slightly different ways but the basic contrasts are likely to be similar. (We discuss the typical nature of the worlds we engaged with, especially the policy world, in the next section.) Our account is necessarily a partial one; we inhabit one of these worlds and our accounts of the other two many well be incomplete.

At root the three normative worlds represent different views of the purposes of research and of how (and by whom) it should be controlled. In the normative world of research, control should rest with the researcher, who can both preserve the independence of the research and determine the necessary means to ensure its validity. In the normative world of policy, policy-makers should control research on behalf of the public interest. Practitioners did not (at least in the case of the national TVEI evaluations) assume the right to control research, but they did think it should be independent and capable of representing the views of practitioners. We should stress here that the normative worlds represent different views of how research *should* be controlled and organized. Perceptions of how it actually was controlled and organized were often different. For example, as mentioned above, our actual role was sometimes perceived as being closer to that of inspectors or even the spies of the MSC.

All three normative worlds accepted that a major purpose of the research was to generate knowledge that would inform both policy-makers and practitioners, and to evaluate the success of TVEI in terms of its stated aims and criteria. However, given the varying timescales within which this purpose could be followed, and the relative vagueness of the aims of TVEI, this agreed purpose allowed for widely varying interpretations. The main emphasis of the research world was on summative evaluation, and on basic or fundamental research; it sought to understand the success or failure of TVEI, or of various TVEI policies and approaches, in order to contribute to general understanding of educational change and to inform future policy formation. The normative world of practice put more emphasis on formative evaluation and its contribution to current practice. The normative world of policy potentially embraced both objectives, and was distinctive mainly for its ability to switch between them. The switching of emphasis followed the phases of a cycle of policy formation and implementation which we describe in the next section. But it was also affected by factors that were less predictable and more 'political'. The change of emphasis from summative to formative, following the announcement of the Extension of TVEI, was an example of this. It also illustrates another difference between the normative worlds: their expectations concerning timetables. The research perspective is long-term; research is not only time-consuming but also requires a lengthy planning time (to allow for initial orientation, literature reviews, etc.) and a subsequent period for reflection, scrutiny of data by peers and subjects, and so on. The perspective of practice is more short-term. This was illustrated by the reactions of TVEI projects when we started our field-work; overwhelmed by the urgent need to cater for the first TVEI students to enter S5, project staff found it hard to turn their attention to the problems of education-industry links and work experience. They had already tackled these problems for their first cohort, and usually had several months to go before they had to consider them again. The immense pressures under which TVEI was delivered reinforced this 'short-term' focus. At our dissemination workshops we were disappointed by the reluctance of many of those associated with the 'new start' pilot projects, or with TVEI Extension, to accept that evidence on the earlier experience of TVEI could have any relevance to them. But this clash of long-term research and short-term practitioner perspectives also had its advantages. Co-ordinators of the projects which we directly evaluated could be less defensive about negative findings. They could dismiss them to outsiders as the products of teething troubles that had since been resolved; but within their projects they might recognize the problems we identified, and take steps to address them. The practitioner timetable followed the cycle of the school year, the progression of the TVEI cohorts (especially the first, pioneering, cohort) and the progression of TVEI as an initiative (notably the move from Pilot to Extension). The policy timetable was structured to some extent by the financial year but also, as we have seen, by an unpredictable policy-making schedule.

In the normative world of research, agendas are unbounded, or their bounds are set by the research literature and its demarcation into disciplines and fields of study. The policy world that we encountered was bounded by the policy that we were evaluating; our task was to evaluate TVEI, not to address broader issues. In large part this reflected simple bureaucratic logic: it was the MSC's TVEI Unit after all that funded us. While we ourselves did not find this policy cocoon too restricting, it has wider consequences that we discuss later.

The greatest number of conflicts between research and policy and their respective normative worlds probably concern the dissemination of findings. Our research was no exception. As we have seen the MSC attached high priority to dissemination; but it claimed the right to control and, if necessary, to filter it. The research world by contrast considers wide, and unrestricted, dissemination to be essential. It is necessary, not only for independence and public accountability, but also for its methodological value; researchers' accounts should be exposed for public criticism not only by fellow-researchers but also by the practitioners whose work they described. The viewpoint of the world of practice, while less clearly articulated, is probably closer to that of research than to that of policy. At least it stresses the need for researchers to be independent of government sponsors, and for practitioners to know how the data they helped to generate were being used.

Early in the project we were aware that the particular circumstances of TVEI in Scotland raised a number of issues that appeared to be insufficiently appreciated by the MSC. We discussed these issues in a paper entitled 'The Scottish dimension of TVEI'. We planned to circulate it to an audience largely comprising key TVEI practitioners in Scotland; our main purpose was to test the validity of our analysis, although we were also responding to MSC requests for 'product' at the previous Steering Group meeting. Several practitioners who knew that the paper was being written had also expressed interest in it, and in its circulation. They expected it to confirm points they had already been making in negotiations with the MSC. However when the MSC learnt of our plans their reaction seemed, to us, to border on panic. At a hastily convened meeting we were prevailed upon to restrict circulation of the paper to the Steering Group. (At the same meeting we were able to point out to the MSC that they did not, as they thought, control the publication of evaluation findings. As a matter of principle we had, when the evaluation contract was being negotiated, sought and obtained a licence that gave us control of publication. This had been granted by a relatively junior official and was evidently not in line with general policy. With the MSC even more than with most government departments, the cock-up theory explained much more than the conspiracy theory.) For the sake of good working relationships we agreed to restrict the circulation of the paper although in practice it probably reached most of its intended audience. We were not the only people in Scotland with a photocopier.

Two years later an updated version of the paper was published in the *Scottish Government Yearbook* (Bell *et al.*, 1989). Neither we nor the Training Agency (the MSC's successor) have been overwhelmed by the shock waves; we have not noticed even a ripple.

We had no further conflicts over the dissemination or publication of findings. This was partly because we deliberately drew our horns in after the 'Scottish dimension' episode; we produced fewer papers for circulation, particularly to projects, and those we produced were 'finished' products of the evaluation rather than discussion papers. But it was also because later papers from the evaluation tended to show TVEI in a broadly positive light (e.g. Bell and Howieson, 1988), and were seen as 'helpful' by the MSC. In writing these papers, and our final report, we did not consciously exercise more self-censorship than is implict in any attempt to write for an audience. Nor did the MSC censor our published final report: they asked us to 'beef up' sections on topics that they thought important, but they did not ask us to remove anything or tone down any of our judgements.

Perhaps the best indicators of the differences among the normative worlds are the terms used to describe 'good' and 'bad' research respectively. In the world of research, good research is valid and original; in the world or practice, as we have discussed, it is useful, it is illuminating and shows empathy, but it may also offer timely and relevant practical tips. To the world of policy, good research is 'helpful', an adjective often used by our MSC contacts. It implied that good research was not only useful but that it respected policy constraints and sensitivities; moreover, if you are helping someone it is likely that you agree with what he or she is trying to do.

These differences are illustrated by an issue that recurrently confronted the research: how far should the analysis be based on comparisons between projects? As researchers we thought that comparisons between projects were important, not only for 'quasi-experimental' analysis, but also to help generate grounded theory on the various possibilities within TVEI. (We were, however, subject to ethical constraints and a survey code of practice which protected the confidentiality of data on individuals and schools: see Bell *et al.*, 1988, Appendix 1). Practitioners, somewhat surprisingly, favoured comparisons between projects for their illuminative function, and found them fascinating. These comparisons helped them to see how their projects were doing. Practitioners were naturally sensitive about publishing such comparisons, but probably felt that they could handle any repercussions, if necessary, by attacking the validity, scope or timeliness of our data. The MSC, by contrast, was the most reluctant to see project comparisons pursued, or at any rate published. They appeared to be concerned about the effects on the morale and reputation of TVEI in local projects. Ironically – given projects' initial fears that we were MSC 'spies' – the MSC was generally anxious that we should support local projects and even protect them. Perhaps this reflected the spirit of *TVEI contra mundum* that seemed to animate much of the pilot initiative.

In the research world, 'bad' research is dishonest and unambitious and lacks validity. In the world of practice, bad research is remote from practice. We have discussed the social and educational aspects of this, but it also relates to methods of research. We probably never persuaded some practitioners that a postal survey could ever achieve the level of quality of response needed to reflect the reality of TVEI for their students. To the policy world, bad research is above all reckless and out of control. And in one respect we did quite literally go out of MSC's control. At the end of the MSC-funded evaluation we secured ESRC funding to re-analyse the TVEI survey data (which were held in public data-sets), and to replicate the spring 1987 survey enhancement with respect to a later TVEI cohort, in 1989. At the time of writing a further ESRC project to analyse data from both surveys, in conjunction with earlier SYPS data, is about to begin. While we kept the MSC and its successor, the Training Agency, closely informed of these developments, the publication of the results of the re-analysis may nevertheless have caused it some embarrassment (Raffe, 1989).

RESEARCH AND THE POLICY WORLD OF TVEI

These normative worlds are ideal types. There were wide variations within each of the worlds described, including research; indeed we were conscious that different members of the research team showed varying levels of affinity or empathy with each of the three normative worlds. And within the village-like TVEI community, personalities and micro-political conflicts were at least as important as the more general pressures of the normative worlds. There were also flows of personnel between the worlds. The role of the TVEI advisers, recruited from the world of practice to that of policy, was particularly important. At times we felt we were caught up in a cross-fire of other conflicts between TVEI advisers or between the advisers and the TVEI Unit. But TVEI advisers could potentially display the public zeal of the recent convert, and over-identify with the normative world of policy. It was a TVEI adviser who told a member of the research team: 'If we don't like what our evaluators say, we change our evaluators.' We doubt whether many longer established residents of the policy world would have said this, even had they meant it.

Tensions between different normative worlds affect all applied educational research. However the particular worlds we encountered were atypical. This was clearly the case with practitioners: the funding arrangements for TVEI, together with its missionary style and the suspicion or hostility of its environment, tended to drive its practitioners into 'enclaves' with distinctive interests, outlooks and aspirations (Saunders, 1986). We ourselves were not typical of researchers in the field. In contrast to many other TVEI evaluators, our ties tended to have been stronger with policy than with practice, and our main allegiance was to 'research' rather than 'evaluation'. Much educational evaluation occupies a normative world quite distinct from that of research, one developed partly in response to the tensions of reconciling normative worlds.

Above all, the MSC was not typical of other 'policy-makers', and especially not typical of other educational policy-makers. The MSC was often resented by educationists as an instrusion of training or utilitarianism into education. But it had many admirable qualities, including a concern for the 'consumer' of education and a refusal to regard high educational failure rates as acceptable, that were sadly lacking in much of the educational policy world. Compared with education departments, the MSC approach was fast, programmatic and executive (the 'can-do' style of Lord Young who brought Mrs Thatcher answers, not problems); the approach of education was slow, consultative and deliberative (Bell, 1990). Paradoxically, as the star of the MSC has waned, and as it has been reincorporated (as the Training Agency) within a mainstream government department, so does its capacity for deliberation and reflection appear to have increased.

The implications of the MSC style for our research were intensified by four further contextual factors. The first was the history of TVEI itself. In contrast to other MSC initiatives, notably YTS, TVEI was not the MSC's own brainchild. It was the product of decisions taken at a high level, and was imposed on a more or less willing MSC. The Commission's function was thus to execute policy, not to make it. This top-down approach was much less restricting for local practitioners, given the decentralized delivery of TVEI, and the scope for local reinterpretation of the TVEI aims and content. But this further weakened the MSC's ability to exercise strategic control, since it tended to lack the educational experience and competence needed to win debates over the interpretation of TVEI.

The second factor was the character of vocationalism. In a provocative article Stronach questions the overt rationality of vocationalism in education, and suggests that it owes more to ritual than to rationality. He continues:

> But the point about ritual is its power to make thing come true whether or not they are held to be true on other grounds – that is, to convince. . . . The evaluation process is neither independent nor critical: it is part of an apparently technocratic legitimation of the ritual. . .[T]o the extent that vocationalism is ritual, critical evaluation is blasphemy. (Stronach, 1989, pp.26-7)

The third factor was the Scottish dimension. Throughout its lifetime the MSC consistently failed to develop policy at a Scottish level (Raffe, 1990). It remained resolutely centralized and British in scope, which means its policies mainly addressed English problems and were designed for English circumstances. (At a Steering Group meeting a representative from the London-based TVEI Unit expressed interest in a discussion of the Scottish system, and added 'We in Great Britain. . .I mean England and Wales. . .' Such slips are revealing to Scottish-based researchers.) TVEI had to articulate with an educational system that was significantly different from its English counterpart, particularly at the post-16 stage. The Scottish dimension was therefore a central concern of any Scottish-wide evaluation, but one that the MSC politically and organizationally found hard to accommodate (Bell *et al.*, 1989; Howieson, 1990a; Raffe, 1990).

The fourth factor was the stage of the policy cycle. Earlier CES experience of policy-related research points to at least three phases in the relations of policy to research. In the first phase a problem is perceived as requiring policy change but the outlines of the new policy have not yet emerged. Wide-ranging, critical research is welcomed, because it will help to win support for change. The second phase starts with the crystallization of the new policy, and its early implementation. The government now needs to build up support, not for change in general but for this policy in particular; it must retain the confidence not just of the public but of those charged with carrying out the policy. While research which describes how the policy is being implemented may be welcome, research which calls into question the wisdom of the policy itself or the assumptions on which it was based is not. It is during this phase that the policy world appears most restrictive, and control is tightest. In the third phase, there is a degree of relaxation. The policy is no longer so politically sensitive (it is now the flavour of last month); institutionally the policy has become routinized and is no longer dependent on the charisma and messianic fervour of its key practitioners; critical research findings are less potentially damaging; and research which failed to find any fault with the policy rhetoric would in any case no longer be credible. When our evaluation was planned TVEI was in the second of these phases; by the time we finally reported it had probably entered the third. The question remains, however: why is so little policy-related research commissioned in the first phase of the policy cycle?

As a result of these factors, the MSC's expectations for our research were not only unpredictable, and liable to change at short notice; they were also at the best of times uncertain or ambivalent. On the one hand, TVEI was an experimental initiative, whose very aims embraced scientific as well as practical objectives, and our role as national evaluators was explicitly intended to complement the more formative, practitioner-oriented role of local evaluation. On the other hand, the timing of our research in the policy cycle, the 'policy cocoon' which focused our attention on the single policy of TVEI, the political and national sensitivities of our subject-matter and, above all, the fact that the main parameters of the policy (and by implication the main conclusions from the evaluation) were now fixed: all these things may have discouraged the MSC from perceiving the evaluation and its purposes in the way that we, at least, had orginally understood it. Of the three normative worlds described above we have found the policy world the hardest to delineate; one reason for this may be that the MSC was not in fact the policy-maker in respect of TVEI, but at best the executor of policy decisions. The net result of this uncertainty, or ambivalence, may have been to give us more space within which to pursue a research agenda. We remained more securely rooted in the normative world of research than we might otherwise have been. Tangible evidence of this is the number of 'academic' papers that were at least indirect products of the evaluation.[2]

TVEI is – or was – one of the most intensively evaluated and researched policy initiatives of all time in British education. Yet it is remarkable how little of this evaluation and research has explicitly addressed what is surely the fundamental question underlying the TVEI experiment: the viability of the 'TVEI model' of vocational education compared, for example, with the work-based 'YTS model'. This is even more remarkable given that TVEI and YTS were both funded by the MSC. The research needed to answer this question would have to break out of the TVEI 'policy cocoon,' not only to examine other policies such as YTS, but also to encompass educational history (to account for the relative failure of past attempts at technical education), comparative education, the sociology of schools and the teaching profession, the study of the youth labour market, and so on. In short, fundamental research. Our argument – one which the CES experience provides numerous examples to substantiate – is that the research which is best able to provide short-term, policy-focused answers is often basic research designed to address long-term 'fundamental' questions. Only by drawing on a body of basic knowledge can research ever hope to answer the short-term (and unpredictable) policy questions in time.

What then is the balance sheet for our TVEI evaluation? With respect to the world of practice, we believe we may have provided some immediate practical tips, not least by informing projects of fruitful ideas and practices in other projects. We may have alerted projects to new possibilities and new considerations in the planning and delivery of TVEI. We may have helped them represent their concerns to MSC, and even given them the confidence to believe that their own hopes and fears were reasonable ones. But our main contribution to practitioners, we suspect, was illumination: we helped some practitioners to understand better what they were doing, and the context in which they were doing it. These contributions were appreciated in the main by practitioners who felt least social and educational distance from us, and who were prepared to make the conceptual leap required to perceive the relevance of last year's data to this year's problems.

With respect to the normative world of research, we believe that the TVEI evaluation – together with the secondary analyses and the more reflective writing that followed it – made a modest but worthwhile contribution to scientific knowledge. We are struck by the way in which many of our main conclusions were prefigured by earlier non-TVEI research, including our own. For example, CES research had suggested that reforms of the *content* of education (curricula, pedagogy, and so on) were typically constrained by its *context*, that is its position in relation to differentiation and selection in education and the labour market (Raffe, 1984, 1985). Many of our TVEI evaluation findings were consistent with this perspective (Bell *et al.*,1988): a fact which doubtless partly reflects our ability to influence our agenda. Even more striking is the extent to which our conclusions are relevant to policy debates that are much broader than TVEI, notably the current debates on vocationalism, skills, and post-compulsory education. We believe, in other words, that the main benefit of our research *to policy* has been through its contribution to more 'fundamental' knowledge, even if it was not funded for this purpose.

And what about the policy world? We would not exaggerate our importance – to the TVEI Unit, the Scottish evaluation of TVEI was a fairly distant concern, in more than one sense. Our evaluation report was welcomed – sincerely, we think – and the TVEI Unit supported us in the dissemination of our findings. But we know we were also perceived as difficult, at least on occasions; and the perception that we were prone to go out of control may have been reinforced by our subsequent reanalyses of the survey data and by other published articles (including this one). A senior Training Agency official has since told us that s/he doubted whether the national evaluations of TVEI had been worthwhile – implying that the operational benefits derived from them had not justified the political inconvenience. But this comment was made at a seminar which used our and others' research to inform strategic thinking over a much wider policy field than TVEI alone. In terms of the policy cycle discussed above, this was in the first phase of a possible new cycle. Perhaps this is the true normative world of policy: that of the maker, and not just the executor of policy. It is encouraging that this world is prepared to recognize the broader policy relevance of basic research; it would be even more encouraging if it were prepared to plan and fund research accordingly.

ACKNOWLEDGEMENTS

The research described in this chapter was funded by the Manpower Services Commission (now the Training Agency) and work on this chapter was supported by the Economic and Social Research Council. Cathy Howieson and Kenneth King were our colleagues on the evaluation. We would like to thank all the members of the worlds of TVEI policy and practice whom we encountered in our evaluation; they admirably transcended the normative differences described above and made our work congenial as well as productive. We are grateful to Cathy Howieson, Kenneth King and Andrew McPherson for insightful comments on a draft of this paper.

NOTES

1 We were supported by Ian Morris as consultant, Shona Adie as project secretary, and Andy Furlong, Suzanne Lowden, Nils Tomes and other members of the CES who contributed to the design and conduct of the survey.
2 For example Bell (1990), Bell and Howieson (1989), Bell *et al.* (1989), Howieson (1990a and b), Raffe (1989 and forthcoming). Several other more synoptic papers (e.g. Raffe, 1990) have also drawn on the work of the TVEI evaluation.

REFERENCES

Bell, C. (1990) 'Foreword', in Brown, A. and Fairley, J. (eds) *The MSC in Scotland 1974-1988*, Edinburgh, Edinburgh University Press.
Bell, C. and Howieson, C. (1988) 'The view from the hutch: educational guinea pigs speak about TVEI', in Raffe, D. (ed.) *Education and the Youth Labour Market: Schooling and Scheming*, Lewes, Falmer.
Bell, C., Howieson, C., King, K., and Raffe, D. (1988) *Liaisons Dangereuses? Education-Industry Relationships in the first Scottish TVEI Pilot Projects: An Evaluation Report*, Sheffield, Training Agency.
Bell, C., Howieson, C., King, K. and Raffe, D. (1989) 'The Scottish dimension of TVEI', in Brown, A. and McCrone, D. (eds) *Scottish Government Yearbook 1989*, University of Edinburgh, Unit for the Study of Government in Scotland.
Black, H., Malcolm, H. and Zaklukiewicz, S. (1988) *The TVEI Curriculum in Scotland*, Sheffield, Training Agency.

Broadfoot, P. (1988) 'Educational research: two cultures and three estates', *British Journal of Educational Research* 14 (1), 3–15.

Chitty, C. (1986) 'TVEI: the MSC's trojan horse,' in Benn, C. and Fairley,,J. (eds) *Challenging the MSC on Jobs, Education and Training*, London, Pluto Press.

Cook, T.D and Campbell, D.T. (1979) *Quasi-Experimentation: Design and Analysis Issues for Field Settings*, Chicago, Rand McNally.

Department of Education and Science/Department of Employment (1986) *Working Together: Education and Training*, White Paper, Cmnd 9823, London, HMSO.

Fiddy, R. (1987) 'TVEI: Selling the chameleon curriculum', *British Journal of Education and Work* 1, 3, 149–62.

Fiddy, R. and Stronach, I. (1987) 'Fables and futures: case studies in the management of innovation', in Gleeson, D. (ed.) *TVEI and Secondary Education: A Critical Appraisal*, Milton Keynes, Open University Press.

Fitz-Gibbon, C.T. (1988) 'Learning from unwelcome data: Lessons from the TVEI examination results,' in Hopkins, D. (ed.) *TVEI at the Change of Life*, Clevedon, Multilingual Matters.

Gleeson, D. (ed.) (1987) *TVEI and Secondary Education: A Critical Appraisal*, Milton Keynes, Open University Press.

Harland, J. (1987) 'The TVEI experience: issues of control response and the professional role of teachers', in Gleeson, D. (ed.) *TVEI and Secondary Education: A Critical Appraisal*, Milton Keynes, Open University Press.

Howieson, C. (1990a) 'The impact of the MSC on secondary education', in Brown, A. and Fairley J. (eds) (1990).

Howieson, C. (1990b) 'Beyond the gate: work experience and part-time work among secondary-school pupils in Scotland', *British Journal of Education and Work* 3.

Malcolm, H. (1988) 'The TVEI school co-ordinator', *Scottish Council for Research in Education Newsletter* 40, 8 (reprinted in Bell *et al. Liaisons Dangereuses? Education-Industry Relationships in the first Scottish TVEI Pilot Projects: An Evaluation Report*, Sheffield, Training Agency.

Manpower Services Commission (1984) 'Aims of the New Technical and Vocational Education Initiative,' Annex 2 of *TVEI Operating Manual*, Sheffield, MSC.

McCulloch, G. (1986) 'Policy, politics and education: the technical and Vocational Education Initiative', *Journal of Education Policy* 1, 1, 35–52.

Parlett, M and Hamilton, D. (1972) *Evaluation as Illumination*. Occasional Paper No. 9. University of Edinburgh: Centre for Research in Educational Sciences.

Raffe, D. (ed.) (1984), *Fourteen to Eighteen: The Changing Pattern of Schooling in Scotland*, Aberdeen, Aberdeen University Press.

Raffe, D. (1985) 'Education and training initiatives for 14–18s: content and context', in Watts, A.G. (ed.) *Education and Training 14–18: Policy and Practice*, Cambridge, CRAC/Hobsons.

Raffe, D. (ed.) (1988) *Education and the Youth Labour Market: Schooling and Scheming*, Lewes, Falmer.

Raffe, D. (1989) 'Making the gift horse jump the hurdles: the impact of the TVEI pilot on the first Scottish cohort', *British Journal of Education and Work* 2, 3, 5–15.

Raffe, D. (1990) 'Scotland v England: The place of "home internationals" in comparative research', in Ryan, P. (ed) *International Comparisons of Vocational Education and Training*, Lewes, Falmer.

Raffe, D. (forthcoming) 'Assessing the impact of a decentralised initiative: the British Technical and Vocational Education Initiative,' in Raudenbush, S.W. and Williams, J.D. (eds) *Schools, Classrooms and Pupils: International Studies of Schooling from a Multilevel Perspective*, New York, Academic Press.

Saunders, M. (1986) 'The innovation enclave: unintended effects of TVEI implementation', *TVEI Working Papers* 1, 1–10. University of East Anglia, Centre for Applied Research in Education.

Stronach, I. (1989) 'Education, vocationalism and economic recovery: the case against witchcraft', *British Journal of Education and Work* 3, 1, 5–31.

Times Higher Education Supplement (1989) 'TVEI failure in Scotland', 2 June.

Walford, G. (1988) 'Shouts of joy and cries of pain: investigating young people's comments on leaving school and entering the labour market', in Raffe, D. (ed.) (1988) *Education and the Youth Labour Market: Schooling and Scheming*, Lewes, Falmer.

8

PRIMARY TEACHERS TALKING
A reflexive account of longitudinal research

Jennifer Nias

My research into teachers' lives, life histories and careers has been dominated by accident and opportunity. It started almost by chance growing out of the work in which I was engaged during the 1970s. At that time I was a lecturer at the School of Education at the University of Liverpool, responsible for designing and running a one-year postgraduate Certificate in Education course for graduates who wished to teach children between 7 and 13 years old. Each year there was a substantial cohort of secondary students; the primary group numbered between 12 and 20 and worked in an isolated basement room in a large old building whose upper floors were inhabited by more prestigious courses. The physical conditions under which we all worked were difficult, staffing was limited, the pressure to cover a good deal of professional ground in a short time was intense. As a result, we spent many hours in each other's company and got to know one another well. Once individuals had begun teaching, they would often telephone, call or write, seeking reassurance, support and information from an interested, professionally knowledgeable colleague who did not have the control over their careers which was now vested in their headteachers or inspectors. When, one day, someone who had been teaching for three years returned from many miles away to talk about her experiences in school and, in passing, exclaimed, 'I do wish you could come and see what I am doing now!' I decided to spend a forthcoming sabbatical term visiting past graduates from this course and exploring with them the strengths and weaknesses of their training.

It seemed sensible to limit my enquiries to those who had been teaching for at least two years. By 1974, when I began seriously to listen to 'primary teachers talking', several studies of the probationary year had been published. The early experience of teaching appeared to be similar for all teachers, no matter how long their preparation had been. I was more interested in discovering whether or not students' nine-months PGCE course equipped them to cope with their jobs once they were through the initial traumas of induction than in exploring yet again the apparent inability of any form of training adequately to prepare teachers for the 'reality shock' of classroom life. I also decided to approach those who had left teaching, but not those who, having successfully completed their training, had immediately entered other careers. I reasoned that people who had abandoned the classroom, for whatever reason, might have important things to say about their professional education. Their opinions might be particularly valuable because the views of people who had left teaching had not been solicited by earlier studies of the probationary year.

I contacted by letter or by telephone 37 of my ex-students – 26 were teaching, 11 were not – explaining that I would like to visit them in the following term and talk to them about their experiences in teaching, with particular reference to their PGCE course. I also said that in order to help me understand their circumstances, I would like to spend roughly half a day with them in the classroom. Two (both teaching) said they would prefer me not to visit them, the rest readily agreed. I asked them to make necessary arrangements with their headteachers.

My research was, then, initially conceived as a naive and personal attempt to evaluate the course of which I was tutor, and in particular to discover how ex-students felt that it could be improved. Fortunately, however, while I was waiting for replies to my letters, I conducted two trial visits and interviews with teachers who were working not far from the university. Almost as soon as I began to talk to them I realized that my concerns were of little relevance or importance to them. Instead they wanted to talk to me about what they were doing now and about their pressing memories of earlier encounters with adults in school, not just with their pupils. It did not take me long to realize that there was a mismatch between what they wanted to tell me and what I thought I wanted to know. However, I also realized that they were presenting me with a vivid picture of the lived experience of primary teaching, of a kind and with a richness of detail which I did not think existed in any published form. It would not be impossible, I felt, to listen to what they wanted to tell me and, at the same time, also to acquire some information about the relevance and durability of their professional education.

Accordingly, I reformulated my original aims. My intention became, and remained for the next two years, to capture, as nearly as possible in the words of teachers themselves, a detailed and comprehensive picture of the subjective reality of primary teaching. In the process I hoped also to gain some feedback about the course for which I was responsible, but this was now of secondary importance.

I then approached three more ex-students, with my revised aims in mind and asked them to talk to me about their life in teaching so far. I devised a few very open questions in advance and listed single words on a postcard as an *aide-memoire* which I could use to ensure that at some point in the interview we covered the ground I was interested in. I used these interviews to help me become progressively more aware of areas that teachers themselves felt it important to talk about (e.g. I initially underestimated the salience of the staff group to teachers with all lengths of service and of the head to teachers in their early years in particular; I did not realize how important it was for all teachers to have someone in or outside school to whom they could talk freely about their professional values). These initial discussions also helped me to modify or eliminate questions which appeared to yield little data. I ended up with about twenty topics on which I wanted further information. These ranged from the very broad (e.g. What is it you like about your job? Have you had all the help you felt you needed in each of your jobs? If so, from whom? If not, do you know why?) to the fairly narrow (e.g. Have you ever consciously modelled your teaching on anyone else's? If so, whose?) These areas, represented by single words on a small, unobtrusive piece of card, remained substantially unchanged during the interviews which I conducted over the next two years. Indeed, I used them to re-interview my first five respondents towards the end of this period. Although I was hesitant about approaching them a second time, since I was conscious of how busy they were, none of them appeared to feel that this second conversation was redundant.

In converting areas of interest into questions which I hoped would elicit relevant information, I was guided by three principles. The first was to make the question sound as natural as possible, since I believed the interviews were likely to yield maximum information if they resembled open-ended conversations. So, I altered my wording to suit the circumstances of the individual or the topic under discussion and did my best to introduce my query smoothly into the flow of talk. The second was to seek for concrete rather than abstract responses; for example, I did not ask, 'What has guided your choice of jobs?' but 'Why did you leave that school? Where did you go next? Was that for any particular reason?' And when I received a reply which contained words or phrases capable of many interpretations (e.g. 'unfriendly staff'; 'inspiring headteacher'; 'formal teaching') I asked for examples of behaviours or situations which would illustrate these terms. Third, I approached sensitive areas, and especially ones likely to be associated with strong feelings (e.g. shame, love) with indirect rather than direct questions (What changes in your school would enable you to do better what you're trying to do? Why? Can you give me an example of a really good day? Bad day?). I subsequently discovered Lortie's *Schoolteacher* (1975) and found that he invoked similar principles in collecting data about American teachers' goals and attitudes. His rationale (p.110) proved useful to me in mounting a post-hoc justification for my choice of questions.

While I was redefining my research focus and discovering by trial and error which aspects of primary teachers' lives were likely to yield the most productive data, I was also arranging visits and interview times for the next term. During that term, I visited thirty-five teachers or ex-teachers, in many parts of England from Devon to North Yorkshire. I spent roughly half a day with each of them in their classes, making unstructured observations which I tried to note down before the interview, as a guide to my own understanding of the individual's professional context. However, I was careful never to take notes in the classroom or even to produce a notebook, since I wished to emphasize that I was there as the teacher's guests, and for my own interest, and not in an evaluation or judgemental capacity. I often found this shared experience a useful starting point, especially if it was some years since I had met the teacher; we would talk for some time about the children or their curriculum before we embarked on personal experiences and individual perspectives.

Interviews sometimes started at lunchtime, if teachers said they could not spare much time after school. Generally, however, they took place at the end of the school day and went on for as long as the individual wanted. We talked in their classrooms, until the caretakers shut us out, and then in their own homes, in pubs, cafes, railway stations, parks and on one occasion, in an art gallery. No one talked for less than an hour and a half, some for as long as five hours. Most interviews lasted for three hours. I encouraged people to give long and, if they wished, discursive replies to my questions and I often used probe or supplementary questions.

The hunger that they all showed to reflect upon their professional lives in the presence of a neutral but friendly outsider was almost insatiable, a fact that in itself taught me much about the loneliness of many teachers' working lives. Nor did I find that they talked less, or less openly, in school than they did in other venues. The pleasures, sometimes the release, of talking seemed to override considerations of place or territory. Indeed, in most cases, the largest part of what I did was to listen, seldom interrupting except to prompt or to offer another line of enquiry.

My interviewees' prolixity caused me formidable recording problems. I had no funds for tape-recording or transcription and, in any case, I was uncertain what effect a tape recorder would have upon the teachers' willingness to be frank (as they were in many cases, to the point of indiscretion). So I took rapid notes in a personal shorthand, recording verbatim whenever I could. This proved difficult to do since I was also attempting to create a relaxed conversational atmosphere and so to maintain as much eye-contact as possible. However, it may be that I found these conditions more potentially inhibiting than my interviewees did, as they continued to talk for as long as I was willing to listen.

I also interviewed eight people over the telephone (two were outside England, six were in the UK but too far away for me to visit), having devised a way of holding the mouthpiece which left me free simultaneously to listen and to take notes. Despite being deprived of contextual and non-verbal cues, I found that these interviews yielded a good deal of valuable data. It is possible that some people found it possible to talk more freely because I was not physically present.

As the interviews progressed I began to realize that I had stumbled, almost unawares, upon a rich seam of data which had the potential to illumine an area about which relatively little was apparently known. However, I was also aware that my previous knowledge of, and my relationship to, my interviewees might be having a distorting effect upon what they said or what I heard. Accordingly, as a rudimentary check upon the subjectivity of my data, I decided to interview a similar number of graduates from PGCE courses in other institutions of higher education. I used an opportunity sample of 30 (8 men and 22 women) who between them had attended seven universities, polytechnics or colleges of education. To my surprise, I found these people were as ready to talk openly to me, as a stranger, as were the teachers who I already knew. Over the next eighteen months I also interviewed a further 21 graduates from my own course who had by this time been teaching for two years or who had changed, after at least two year in the classroom, from teaching into other careers (most often, into parenthood). Altogether, I interviewed 99 people (30 men and 69 women), the balance of sexes being roughly the same among those whom I had taught and those whom I had not.

As a further attempt to release myself from the biases which I knew would creep into data collected in this way, I asked members of both groups if they would be prepared to keep a journal, recording significant events and their reactions to them on one day a week for a term. Twenty-two did this and the perspectives they revealed in their accounts were very similar, no matter where their pre-service education had taken place. However, these diaries were much shorter, terser, and less reflective than their writers were in face-to-face conversations and I found them much less informative than the interviews. I now know much more about professional journals as a research tool than I did then (see, in particular, Holly, 1989) and realize that in hoping I would find a rich alternative source of data in journals voluntarily kept by busy teachers who embarked on this task for my ends not theirs, I was expecting too much. Accordingly, I later used the journals to corroborate patterns or trends which I found in the interviews and not as a prime source of evidence.

The desire to move beyond my own perspective also caused me to try to contact – by letter, telephone or visit – all the headteachers of any school in which any of my interviewees were now teaching or had taught. I succeeded in getting in touch with 70 per cent of these, and had brief (at most thirty minutes, usually much less) conversations with them. I used these exchanges to cross-check factual information and sometimes statements of opinion, and to build up my knowledge of the institutional context from and about which teachers spoke, I also solicited headteachers' views about the efficacy of a shorter-than-normal professional training. Almost all the information I derived from headteachers proved of background rather than of direct value and I made little use of it in interpreting the data or writing up. I do however blush when I consider that I did not seek my interviewees' permission for these conversations and that, unless I was visiting a school, I did not tell them I intended to talk to their heads, or about what. I now have a much greater regard for the ethical rights of participants in research than I had then and would approach this kind of data collection more sensitively than I did and only after prior negotiation.

One more point needs to be made about the interviews conducted in 1975–7: in the course of the next eighteen months, after my initial sabbatical term, they had to be fitted in round a demanding teaching load. Sometimes this would be done travelling at weekends, and visiting schools on Mondays or Fridays, at others I used occasions when the university term began later or finished earlier than the school term. When my interviewees worked reasonably locally, I took advantage of any opportunity provided by, for example, an in-service course at a teachers' centre. In general however although visits and interviews were not rushed, they were so spaced out that I had repeatedly to think myself anew into the aims of my enquiry and into the questions I was going to ask.

I had virtually completed interviewing when the whole endeavour nearly came to an end. First, the cardboard boxes in which I kept my notes were inadvertently carted away from my office by over-zealous cleaners and I rescued them from the municipal rubbish tip only after a frantic and unsalubrious search. Second, I took a new job in a different part of the country and for a further two years was too busy and preoccupied to start the task of serious analysis. But I went on thinking about the material and the ideas which had begun to form during the period of data collection gradually became clearer. One day I chanced to talk about them during an unplanned conversation with Rob Walker, then at the University of East Anglia. He asked me to share them with some teachers on a higher degree course, one of whom was a teachers' centre warden. The latter in turn asked me to talk to other teachers on in-service courses and soon I started to receive requests for 'copies of papers'. I began to realize that academics and professionals alike were interested in the issues raised by the teachers who had talked so eagerly to me about their lives, albeit several years before.

Spurred on by this interest, over the next six years, in the intervals of a professional life already heavily committed to my own teaching, I nibbled into, chewed and began to digest the huge quantity of data which I had accumulated. Two things made this a formidable task. To start with, I was overwhelmed by the sheer quantity of data. The open-ended nature of much of the questioning and my search for concrete examples also meant that there were few ready-made categories built into the interview responses. Second, therefore, I was faced with sifting relevant information from conversations about many unrelated topics. I wanted to use 'grounded theory' (Glaser and Strauss, 1967), to allow my ideas to emerge from the data, but this seemed a very daunting task. For example, early on I discerned a developmental sequence in teachers' attitudes to their work (it was this which had formed the basis of my early talks to teachers). However, it was clearly a complex idea and I did not feel capable of developing it in written form without a deeper knowledge of other ideas which might also be present in the data. Yet I seemed to lack the time and the means to explore all my evidence in such a comprehensive way.

In the end I embarked on what I hoped would be a relatively straightforward first attempt at category analysis. While interviewing I had repeatedly noted how often my interviewees mentioned their headteachers and how great an impact these people appeared to have on the job satisfaction or dissatisfaction of individual teachers. So I decided to pull out of the data all references to headteachers and see what I could make of it. Patterns began fairly rapidly to emerge and before long I had the outline of a paper which subsequently appeared in an Open University reader as 'Leadership styles and job satisfaction in primary teachers' (Nias, 1980). The final shape of this paper was itself dictated by serendipity. I had just completed the first draft when I happened to meet someone from the Open University with an interest in educational management. He commented on the lack of empirical studies of primary school management and asked if I knew of any unpublished work. I tentatively offered him my draft, it came back to me with a note saying he liked it, but could I make it more 'theoretical'. A week of the holidays spent in the Institute library enabled me to comply with his request and the article (as it had now become) was on its way to publication.

The swift and unexpected success of this first effort gave me encouragement. As soon as I could, I tackled another 'easy' topic: the word 'commitment' (with a number of denotative analogues) appeared in almost every interview. I decided to see what I could discover about its use and to reflect on what this told me about teachers' perspectives and careers. I was soon able to categorize the meanings which people seemed to attribute to it, using conventional methods to test the validity of the categories. I refined and subdivided them, looked for internal consistency, searched for contradictions and negative instances and went on piling up examples until I was thoroughly convinced that a category was saturated. My next tasks were to consider the significance of these 'grounded' themes to an understanding of the subjective reality of teaching and to explain, if I could, why the same word appeared to have several meanings. Once again, I turned, after I had made a preliminary analysis of the data, to what others had written and, as I moved between my own understandings and those of others, patterns began to form. The first draft of the article which subsequently appeared as '"Commitment" and Motivation in Primary School Teachers' (Nias, 1981a) was completed in the departure lounge of Heathrow Airport at the start of my summer holiday.

As the mention of 'motivation' suggests, it was an easy step from here into job satisfaction and dissatisfaction (Nias, 1981b). In any case these topics were relatively straightforward to tackle because all the interviews had contained questions which bore directly upon them.

By this time three further things had happened. I had encountered Peter Woods' illuminating and seminal work on secondary teachers (especially Woods, 1981), we had exchanged papers and ideas and he had encouraged me to go on thinking and writing. This was timely, because I also knew by now that I was into deeper conceptual waters than I had anticipated; as I had worked on the data I had come to realize that the related notions of 'self' and 'identity' were central to any further understandings that I could reach. Yet it was clear that getting a firm grasp on these slippery concepts was likely to prove difficult and time-consuming. I was also therefore ready, thirdly, for the challenge which was presented by an invitation to present a paper at a conference of educational ethnographers in eight months' time.

Once I had embarked on the time-consuming and complex task of understanding the extent and the nature of primary teachers' self-referentialism I was sustained by a combination of intellectual excitement and tenacity. The former arose because I felt that I was generating fresh insights which were genuinely 'grounded' in the data; it was teachers' constant and persistent use of words like 'I', 'me', 'myself' which had first alerted me to the importance of identity and self-image. The latter was needed for two reasons. One was pressure. I was also involved at this time in doing and writing up another, separate research project into alternative understandings of accountability in secondary schools (Elliott *et al*, 1981). The second was because implicit references to the 'self' and to its salience for primary teachers were scattered through all the data. Analysis was therefore a much slower and more concentrated task than it had been when my attention could be triggered by a few key words or phrases.

I was dimly aware that there were several sub-themes within what I was not certain was a central concept, so I tackled them one by one. However, this was not as straightforward as it appeared. It was clear that to understand any of these sub-themes, I needed to be mentally saturated in the data. Yet I could achieve this only outside term time, since it took between two and four weeks to become immersed in a complex topic, to tease out its implications and to put them into written form. Progress was slow, my friends and family began to complain.

As I wrote this second and more conceptually substantial set of papers I also made deliberate use of a coherent theoretical framework, something which was lacking from my first piecemeal attacks upon the data. I found in symbolic interactionism a productive organizing device and explanatory tool. I would be the first to agree, however, that there are other convincing ways of conceptualizing notions of identity and the self. As I said in the introduction to *Primary Teachers Talking* the choice of theoretical framework is therefore to some extent arbitrary. None the less, I have found this one consistently useful.

In the meantime a decade had passed since my first interviews. At this point the professional interest which the eight published articles had begun to attract, together with my own continuing involvement with the in-service education of teachers, encouraged me to gather some longitudinal data, a development which I had not had in mind when I embarked on the enquiry. I had current or recent addresses for about a sixth of my interviewees, and through them or through previous addresses I contacted over half the original group, asking for their movements to date and whether they would be willing to talk to me again. Fifty-four of them replied, all but three saying they would be ready to meet me (these three were men, still teaching in the same school or neighbourhood in which they had been ten years earlier). I also wrote to fifteen people who had qualified in 1976 or 1977, too late for my original enquiry, but whom I knew were still teaching. Thirteen replied. During 1985, about six months after my original contact with all these people, I conducted a second set of interviews with most of them.

These interviews differed from the first in a number of respects. They took place ten years later in what can loosely be termed 'mid-career' for most of the group. I focused upon a limited number of issues that my experience in in-service education had taught me were likely to be significant: motivation; job satisfaction and dissatisfaction; professional, personal and career development; personal experience of and reflections upon teaching; the place of work in life and future career plans. I also encouraged people to talk freely about any other aspects of their work or career which they felt were important. I did not talk to the headteachers of interviewees, nor, in general, visit their classrooms. Like the first interviews, these were open-ended and loosely structured, but they were shorter; the shortest was about fifty minutes, the longest about three hours. About two-thirds were tape-recorded; for the remaining third I took rapid notes and wrote up a summary as soon as possible thereafter. In both cases, transcripts or summaries were sent to individuals for validation, with the suggestion (of which only three took advantage) that they delete anything they did not want me to use, and with assurances of confidentiality.

The biggest difference of all, however, was that the second group were much more obviously self-selected than the first. I knew by word of mouth what had happened to 29 out of the 45 people who did not reply (4 were in primary schools, 3 were teaching outside primary schools, 13 were raising families, 9 were in other careers including educational psychology), but I did not know why I had not heard from them: did my letter not reach them or were they so disenchanted with me or with their careers that they chose not to reply? Moreover, I had no way of establishing whether the 4 who were still teaching but had not replied, had not done so because they did not receive my letter or because they did not wish to talk about their work, perhaps because they were unhappy in it. By contrast, most of these who answered my letter seemed to be succeeding, in terms of promotion, or were enthusiastically resuming a career after childrearing.

In addition, on this occasion I spoke only to 3 of the 22 people whom I knew had moved to other careers outside teaching (including full-time parenthood). So I do not know whether the 10 married women who indicated an intention to return eventually to teaching had made those plans out of financial necessity or a genuine interest in the work that they had left. Last, during 1975–7 I was in direct or indirect touch for other reasons with many of those whom I interviewed. It is therefore possible that they agreed to my request for information out of courtesy or deference. However, in 1985, only those who were quite happy to be re-interviewed needed to reply to my postal overture.

Thus the second set of evidence on which I drew is heavily biased. With few exceptions it reflects the experience of successful and committed teachers who had been working for between nine and eighteen years (though in the case of married women returners, the years worked varied from five to twelve). What it does not represent is the experiences of those mid-career teachers who may be ready or anxious to change jobs or occupations but are unable to do so. By contrast, the views of such teachers are represented in the first interviews. This difference may be particularly salient because the second interviews were conducted in the spring of 1985, during a period of industrial action for many teachers.

For the second interviews I decided to visit only those who were still working in infant, junior or middle schools. I left the choice of place and time to individuals; 24 chose their place of work, and I met the rest in pubs or in their own homes. The venue did not appear to affect the freedom with which they spoke. However, I also talked to 1 special school teacher (a woman), 3 secondary teachers (2 men and 1 women), 2 adult education tutors (both women), 5 college lecturers (2 men, 3 women), 1 adviser (a woman) and 3 mothers who had recently given up teaching. Altogether, I conducted 50 interviews (2 of them by telephone). I had been PGCE tutor to all but 2 of those who replied to my original letter and several had, intermittently, kept in touch with me. All of the 50 had at some point taught 4 to 13 year olds (the approximate age range for which they trained) and 36 (13 men, 23 women) were still doing so. There were 17 men, 33 women, 5 headteachers (4 men), 7 deputy heads (of whom 5 were women), 8 women doing part-time or supply work.

Notwithstanding its imperfections, I analysed the resulting data in the ways I have already described, with the difference that I was by now aware of (though I had not fully conceptualized) the importance to individual teachers of their self-image. I started my analysis by looking at the main themes which my questions addressed (e.g. motivation, job satisfaction). However, I found that further patterns emerged (e.g. the conflict between personal and professional lives and how this was resolved; subjective meanings of 'career'). Thus the notion of 'feeling like a teacher' was first worked tentatively out as a conference paper (Nias, 1986), but eventually became of central importance in the book (Chapter 9). Indeed, I found that my ideas were growing even after I had completed the manuscript (e.g. Nias, 1989b was written in 1988 at the request of the journal editor and prompted me to extend my thinking about the concept of 'career').

As analysis proceeded, I also faced the problem of how to integrate all the various ideas. Certain themes (e.g. personal development; reference groups) emerged in both sets of interviews, but some appeared more strongly in early than mid-career or vice versa, and a few (e.g. survival concerns) were peculiar to one, not the other. Moreover, it was very difficult to draw valid or reliable comparisons between the two sets of data. Quantitatively, the numbers of potential interviewees had halved during the intervening decade, though the gender balance within each group remained about the same. There were the issues of self-selection and bias which I have already discussed. Further, a very different political climate surrounded education in 1975–7 and 1985. The first interviews took place soon after teachers had received a substantial pay rise and at a time when morale within the professional was relatively high. The second occurred when salaries were very low and when the industrial action of 1984–6, in which almost all my interviewees were involved in one way or another, was well under way. It has proved impossible to estimate accurately the effect of any or all these factors.

Despite the difficulties posed by the task of analysing the final mass of data collected over ten years – hand-written notes, transcripts or validated summaries of interviews, teachers' written accounts – the task was not without its methodological advantages. The main one was the fact that because there was so much material, patterns appeared fairly readily and could be internally checked and validated. I had no shortage of corroborative evidence and, in consequence, have often been able to generalize with some confidence about my findings, as far as they relate to graduates who trained for one year. In absence of further evidence it is a matter of speculation whether they also apply to teachers with a longer pre-service education. Other benefits were the wide range of potential illustrative material and the varied nature of the data which helped to keep me from getting bored.

At the time when I undertook the second set of interviews I had no clear idea of what the final outcome might be. I was motivated by my own interest and by that of others and not by the desire to write a book. However, academics and teachers whose opinions I respected repeatedly encouraged me to bring all my work in this area together in one publication. Eventually a chance meeting with a publisher early in 1986 resulted in the offer of a contract. Even then I resisted; I was by this time directing a funded research project which was obviously going to result in substantial publication, and I had no illusions about the work involved in writing one book, let alone two simultaneously. Furthermore, although the field-work for the research project had been undertaken during a sabbatical year, by mid-1986 I was back at work full-time. Eventually, however, I was persuaded to sign, though the manuscript was not finally completed until March 1988, three months after its contract date. In the intervening eighteen months it had to compete with my job, two accidents, each of which left me one-handed for several months, arranging publication for the research project, co-authoring the resulting book (Nias, Southworth and Yeomans, 1989), and completing three book chapters to which I had committed myself a long time before. It was a period through which I would not willingly live again. Not least, although I tried hard not to let my teaching suffer, I am sure that it did, so the pressures of multiple authorship were compounded by guilt.

Writing was difficult for many reasons. Since I still write longhand, I was dependent on the help of two excellent and long-suffering typists. Had they not been as efficient and as patient as they were and had they not used wordprocessors I do not think the book would ever have been completed. I am a slow and painstaking writer most of whose work goes through four drafts. I do not find writing easy, but I like to do it as well as I can. In consequence, producing a manuscript which I feel is fit for publication is hard and tiresome work, inducing broken nights, bad temper and the kind of preoccupation which it is often difficult to distinguish from utter egocentricity. I can truthfully say that whereas data collection is generally enjoyable and analysis is intellectually rewarding, writing is painful drudgery. I persist in it for only two reasons: I feel I have something to say that I want others to read (this itself is normally dependent on other people telling me that they think it is worth saying); and I take a craft pride in the finished product.

Writing for publication, in whatever form, also presented me with the problem of selecting illustrative examples, especially given the constraints of length and the need to balance against each other the reader's likely interest in abstractions on the one hand and living detail on the other. For the most part, I set myself an arbitrary limit of three or four illustrative comments for any given point and pared these down to essentials. I was painfully aware of all the data I did not, and probably shall never directly use.

The research which resulted in *Primary Teachers Talking: A Study of Teaching as Work* (Nias, 1989a) has never been officially funded. However both my employers directly or indirectly covered the cost of travelling to visit schools, and of postage, and the Cambridge Institute of Education was generous in helping with the cost of tape-recording and transcription. Otherwise I have operated on a self-help basis, staying with friends when I needed to be away from home, squeezing time and resources away from other commitments. I would not however underestimate the importance of institutional backing and I am grateful to have received it. In particular, my colleagues were forbearing and helpful during the tortured months of authorship and I could not have coped without their silent support. The relationships which suffered most obviously during this period were my personal ones.

I have described in detail the sequence of events which has led me more and more deeply over the past fifteen years into a study of primary teachers' lives and careers because this story itself highlights what I feel to be both the weaknesses and the strengths of my research in this area. Among the former I would count: a crude and simplistic methodology; little protection against memory decay over a long period; heavy reliance on one form of data collection; few controls on subjectivity in data collection, recording and analysis; unsophisticated methods for data analysis; lack of attention during the first interviews to the ethical rights of respondents; failure systematically to collect biographical data which might have revealed cohort influences and pointed me towards historical or structural interpretations as well as the socio-psychological one which I finally adopted. In short, judged by most of the accepted canons of qualitative research, my enquiry may be deemed naive, subjective and opportunistic.

Yet it also has its strengths. First, the simplicity of the research design and the relatively uniform format in which the data were presented has freed me to concentrate upon what the teachers themselves had said. My experience as a supervisor and examiner of higher degrees has taught me that operating and justifying complex systems of data collection and analysis can become an end in itself, an excuse not to wrestle with the ideas embedded in the evidence. By contrast, I had to make sense of the testimonies I had collected or abandon the whole enterprise; I could not take refuge in the contemplation of methodological complexities.

Second, the extent and quality of the information I collected challenged me to search for and eventually find connections and relationships between apparently isolated ideas. In seeking not to drown in the data, I found unexpected reefs under my feet.

Third, the fact that I have worked for so long on the material has enabled my ideas to grow slowly, albeit painfully. They have emerged, separated, recombined, been tested against one another and against those of other people, been rejected, refined, re-shaped. I have had the opportunity to *think* a great deal over fifteen years, about the lives and professional biographies of primary teachers and about their experience of teaching as work. My conclusions, though they are in the last resort those of an outsider, are both truly 'grounded' and have had the benefit of slow ripening in a challenging professional climate.

I wish to stress this point. The more research I do, the more important I realize it is to allow oneself the time to think, at every stage from data collection to interpretation. The corollary is that one has to learn not to feel guilty when one is not directly working on the task. I have found that time spent walking, swimming or gardening, activities initially undertaken out of desperation or physical need, can be immensely productive. Time spent thinking about other things can also be valuable; not all cerebral activity takes place at a conscious level and ideas can form while left to 'compost' slowly.

Thinking however seldom takes place in a vacuum. A fourth benefit of returning again and again to the data over such a long period and in pursuit of different themes is that, to continue the gardening metaphor, one rakes it into such a fine tilth that ideas germinate easily. By the end of fifteen years, I knew my data intimately, a fact which facilitated the search for patterns, interconnections and insights.

In this context I would also like to emphasize the value of chaos as a seed bed for creativity. There were many occasions when I felt overwhelmed by the apparent formlessness or the complexity of the material. If the task had been less messy, I would not have needed to struggle so much and might have been satisfied with premature foreclosure. I have repeatedly found that an acutely uncomfortable period of ambiguity and confusion seems to be a necessary condition for the birth of a new idea. My experience in this respect echoes that of Marshall (1981).

Next, in contrast to the largely solitary nature of cogitation, my employment for the past thirteen years as an in-service teacher educator has given me many opportunities to test my thinking against the perceptions and professional insights of academics and of teachers themselves. In particular I have been able to defend and validate my emerging ideas in discussion with practitioners similar in gender, age, status and experience to those whom I interviewed. I am satisfied that, despite its methodological shortcomings, the picture which I have painted reflects the world which teachers themselves inhabit and yet helps them to see it, and themselves within it, in fresh ways. It seems to have fulfilled one of the main purposes of qualitative research, that is, to provide a 'language for speaking about that which is not normally spoken about' (Hargreaves, 1978, p. 19).

Last, another strength of the research has been the way in which I have been able to cross-fertilise it with other ideas. During the past few years I have drawn on my knowledge of psychotherapeutic groups to write a monograph, commissioned as part of distance learning course materials, by Rob Walker, now at Deakin University, Australia (Nias, 1987). In this publication I used some of the same interview material but interpreted it from a different theoretical perspective. In addition, I have also been a participant observer in a primary school (Primary School Staff Relationships Project, funded by the Economic and Social Research Council 1985–7 (see Nias, Southworth and Yeomans, 1989). This project, and its successor (Whole School Curriculum Development and Staff Relationships in Primary Schools, funded by ESRC 1988–90), used ethnographic methods to explore the workings of primary schools as organizations of adults and the relationships of teachers and non-teaching staff as colleagues. Although these last two pieces of research do not focus directly upon teachers' subjective realities, there are obvious areas of overlap. Simultaneous involvement in various pieces of research and writing has enriched them all, sometimes by confirming central ideas such as the importance to teachers and headteachers of their self-image, at others by challenging or extending particular notions (e.g. what are the conditions which make a staff group both affectively satisfying and task-focused?). I have found it immeasurably beneficial to set the picture that teachers gave in interviews of their own behaviour and careers against a backdrop of fine-grained observation of their life in classrooms and schools, and into the context provided by the literature from a different discipline.

In this account of my research, I have tried both to recount its chequered and often opportunistic growth from a naive and misplaced idea to a published book, and to analyse its methodological strengths and weaknesses. The ways in which a small initial enquiry grew in size and scope and eventually became a piece of longitudinal research really were as dominated by chance as I have suggested. Begun and largely pursued for my own interest, it would not have been carefully conceptualized or written up in a published form had it not been for several serendipitous encounters and the encouragement in which they resulted. Although I find that wrestling with data and with ideas and writing are solitary activities, I owe much of the persistence which has characterized this undertaking to the confidence which others have placed in me.

Methodologically, this work is flawed. Nevertheless, I would argue that its long time-span has given me ample opportunity to reflect upon my data and, in the process, to refine, extend and reconceptualize the ideas which have arisen from them. In addition, methodological simplicity has freed me to think about the interpretation rather than the collection of my evidence. I am sharply aware of the limitations of this longitudinal enquiry. Notwithstanding, I am confident both that I have been able to portray teachers' lives and careers in a way that is convincing to them and also that the book contains ideas which others find practically and theoretically useful. I end, therefore, with a claim and a hypothesis. The claim is this: *Primary Teachers Talking* is not the fruit of 'good' educational research, but the prolonged effort of doing it has given me material to think about and the incentive to think, a process which has resulted in some worthwhile ideas. Had I not undertaken and persisted in the research, however imperfect it may be, I would probably not have had the ideas and would certainly not have shared them with others in writing. The hypothesis therefore is this: the value of this enquiry has been the generation of insights which will be validated not by looking back at the research process but by looking forward, to the uses that other educationalists make of them.

REFERENCES

Elliott, J., Bridges, D., Ebbutt, D., Gibson, R. and Nias, J. (1981) *School Accountability*, Oxford, Blackwell.

Glasser, B. and Strauss, A. (1967) *The Discovery of Grounded Theory*, London, Weidenfeld & Nicolson.

Hargreaves, D. (1978) 'Whatever happened to symbolic interactionism?' in Barton, L. and Meighan, R. (eds), *Sociological Interpretations of Schooling and Classrooms*, Diffield, Nafferton.

Holly, M.L. (1989) *Writing to Grow: Keeping a Personal-Professional Diary*, New York, Heinemann.

Lortie, D. (1975) *School Teacher: a Sociological Study*, Chicago, University of Chicago Press.

Marshall, J. (1981) 'Making sense as a personal process', in Reason, P. and Rowan, J. (eds) *Human Inquiry*, Chichester, Wiley.

Nias, J. (1980) 'Leadership styles and job satisfaction in primary schools', in Bush, T., Glatte, R., Goodey, J., and Richer, C. (eds) *Approaches to School Management*, London, Harper & Row.

Nias, J. (1981a) 'Commitment and motivation in primary school teachers', *Educational Review* 33, 181–90.

Nias, J. (1981b) 'Teacher satisfaction and dissatisfaction: Herzberg's "two-factor" hypothesis revisited', *British Journal of Sociology of Education* 2, 235–46.

Nias, J. (1986) 'What is it to "feel like a teacher"', paper presented to Annual Conference of British Educational Research Association, Bristol.

Nias, J. (1987) *Seeing Anew: Teachers' Theories of Action*, Geelong, Deakin University Press.

Nias, J. (1989a) *Primary Teachers Talking: a Study of Teaching as Work*, London, Routledge.

Nias, J. (1989b) 'Subjectively speaking: English primary teachers' careers', *International Journal of Education Research: Research on Teachers' Professional Lives* 13, 4, 392–402.

Nias, J., Southworth, G. and Yeomans, R. (1989), *Staff Relationships in the Primary School: a Study of Organizational Cultures*, London, Cassell.

Woods, P. (1981) 'Strategies, commitment and identity: making and breaking the teacher role', in Barton, L. and Walker, S. (eds) *School, Teachers and Teaching*, Lewes, Falmer Press.

9

POWER, CONFLICT, MICROPOLITICS AND ALL THAT!

Stephen J. Ball

Doing sociological research is not just a matter of having exciting adventures in the field it is also a process of analysis, interpretation, theorizing and writing.

This chapter presents and discusses the conception, methods and writing of *The Micropolitics of the School* (Ball, 1987a). Three aspects of the process of research are dealt with. First, I will place *Micropolitics* in some relationship to my previous (and subsequent) work, both teaching and research. In particular I want to outline my analytical concern with education as a political process and the concomitant empirical interest in those conflicts which occur between groups and individuals who seek to define 'what is to count as education' in their own terms. Second, I will discuss the sorts of data and the methods of collection and analysis employed in the research upon which *Micropolitics* is based. In particular, I want to consider the use of the 'constant comparative' method. Third, in more general terms, I shall explore the role of theory development in ethnography. Specifically, I want to counterpose a model of concept development against a 'theory testing' approach. *Micropolitics* will be reconsidered in these terms.

ORIGINS

The origins of *Micropolitics* lie in two different but related sets of interests, one practical and one theoretical, one based on teaching activities and the other in research activities. In simple terms the origins of *Micropolitics* lie in a sense of frustration. While working at the University of Sussex, for several years I taught a course on 'the school as an organization'. From the outset I found two problems in running the course. The first was the dearth of literature on schools as organizations. The second was the particular nature of what literature there was. Most general texts or papers on schools as organizations were (mid to late 1970s) set within some kind of systems paradigm. Furthermore, many were written in a style and form which seemed to conflate and confuse analysis with prescription. The writers did not seem to be clear in their writing whether they were saying this is how schools are or this is how schools should be. This often, in part, related to the roles occupied by the writers as organizational developers and consultants. Together the theoretical predilections and prescriptive overtones of the available literature combined to make the image of the school they conjured up unrecognizable to me or my students. That is to say, our experience of the way schools worked did not align in any meaningful way with the versions, usually very neat and tidy and unproblematical consensual, produced by the theorists. At this time my involvement in research at *Beachside Comprehensive* (Ball, 1981) provided a major point of reference for my proto-analysis of school organization. My experiences of organizational life at Beachside provided a set of observations which I could not assimilate into the available theoretical models. My ongoing, informal re-thinking of Beachside, as an organization, was to be an important starting point for the fieldwork for *Micropolitics*. (This sort of 'carry over' is an especially important part of the ethnographic process, I believe, ethnographers carry cases, slices of data, concepts around in their heads. Something like the procedures of 'constant comparison' go on informally in work across cases, over time, in different research projects.) As far as the course was concerned I dealt with the literature problems in the first instance by drawing upon other sources of data for the course. In particular, I began to make use of ethnographic accounts of schools and other settings. The point of this was not that these studies focused on the organization per se but often they provided side lights on organizational processes. Texts like Strauss *et al.*, *Psychiatric Ideologies and Institutions* (1961) were immensely valuable. They portrayed the messy realities of life in organizations, usually through the perspective of the organizational actors themselves.

This use of ethnographies was not of course just a matter of looking for data. The ethnographies were, for the most part, based on theoretical premises like symbolic interactionism. They brought with them, often in inchoate form a conception of organization as the product of multiple social interactions. That its 'realities' lay in the things that people did and said and thought, rather than in some kind of abstract system that was somehow greater than the sum of its parts. This meant that the ontological status of 'the organization' was changed. All of this raised interesting matters for discussion in course seminars. As a requirement of the course the students also undertook two weeks of intensive fieldwork in schools, in order to produce their own case study report. I will return to the role of these reports later.

The other motivating factor which lay in the background of my decision to want to write *Micropolitics* was embedded in my continuing involvement in ethnographic research. First, there was my self-initiated study of the amalgamation of three schools to form a new comprehensive (Ball, 1984a and 1985b). This research arose directly out of aspects of Beachside. The centre piece of the Beachside study was an examination of the debates and struggles which lay behind the introduction of mixed ability grouping to replace banding. The analysis had thrown up at least three levels of engagement among the staff in the processes of debate and struggle. First, material interests were at stake. There would be losses and gains associated with the innovation in terms of timetabling, staffing, capitation, etc. Second, there were personal, identity interests involved. Some staff saw mixed ability as a challenge to their substantive professional self-image. Third, there was clearly an ideological dimension. Different people were advocating and defending different, heart-felt conceptions of the comprehensive school. The victory of the pro-mixed-ability lobby seemed to indicate a shift in the ideological centre of the school, as well as a shift in the pattern of influences. Furthermore, the struggles involved in these clashes of interests took a whole variety of interesting forms. Some were straightforward exchanges of views and beliefs in open meetings. Others were less public and less straightforward. Some deals were done, pressure was brought to bear, ruffled feathers were smoothed. My initial contacts with the amalgamated school indicated that the clash of ideologies and beliefs which had been played out at Beachside were occurring in dramatic fashion among and between the staff of the three schools involved. I started work at Casterbridge High. The second study I became involved in around the same time was funded by the SREB (Southern Regional Examinations Board). The board wanted case studies of institutions piloting the introduction of the CPVE (Certificate of Pre-Vocational Education). This I undertook with two colleagues, Dave Burrell and

Hilary Radnor (Radnor, Ball and Burrell, 1989). We did six case studies and I was specifically responsible for one of these. The school which fell to me proved to be a very different kind of organization from either Beachside or Casterbridge High. Ideologies were very much up-front in this school; conflict was fairly normal and not untoward: it was expected, taken for granted. I took the opportunity of visits for the CPVE research to do some interviews with the head and senior staff, to attend school meetings, and shadow the head for periods of time. The head allowed me to sit in on a whole variety of meetings in his office including fairly personal discussions with teachers and some 'heavy' sessions with union representatives. This was in the early stages of the teachers' industrial action (1984–7). The data from the other case studies also provided some interesting insights. In particular the CPVE material offered another view of the processes of change in schools. What happens when innovations disrupt existing patterns of preferment and influence? How are career prospects affected by innovations which do not 'fit' the typical pattern of subject or pastoral care promotion routes? CPVE and TVEI (Technical and Vocational Education Initiative) validated and valued different kinds of expertise. 'Whizz-kid' innovators often experienced 'jet-stream' promotion, especially when pilot schemes offered experience and knowledge not generally available in the education system. All of this was more grist to my conceptual mill. At some point around this time, 1984, I decided that I wanted to write a book about school organization that took all these things into account. A book which would stand over and against the positivist, systems paradigm of school organization and which would express an interactionist, ethnographic perspective on school organization.

Let me try and place this in another way. In an important personal sense the micropolitics study was an extension of established interests and concerns. In particular it represented a development of my substantive interest in the struggle for control and definition of what is to count as education. In my conceptualization of the issues at hand there was also an opportunity for further conceptual and theoretical development of a political conflictual perspective. Essentially what I had in mind was the elaboration of a political sociology of education, a sociology of conflict. A kind of Weberian politics of everyday life. 'Politics is a common activity of human beings, it fills human history' (Freund, 1972, p.218). For the most part Weber emphasizes the development of political institutions and institutionalized politics, where as I am interested more in process, politics as struggle, as contestation. Thus, on the one hand I became specifically concerned with strategies of organizational power and control – domination – and even more specifically with *management* as one such strategy of domination which is burgeoning in contemporary schools. As Freund puts it 'Domination is the practical and empirical expression of power' (p.221). On the other hand, I wanted to explore the ways in which the imposition of organizational forms is resisted, and the participation of varieties of members in the political process; 'politics is the process which ceaselessly aims at framing, developing, obstructing, shifting or overturning the relationship of domination' (Freund, 1972, p.221). This dualistic conceptualization was firmed up in the process of the micropolitics research and was to become fundamental to the construction and writing of the book. In empirical terms the conceptualization of politics in this way pointed to a realist and discursive analysis of micropolitics processes.

As I look back now and attempt to reconstruct the position of the micropolitics research in the longer term perspective of my research activities, I see it fitting into a pursuit of the shifting locus of power in education (see figure 9.1.). As Duverger (1972) puts it, political sociology is 'the science of power'. With *Beachside* the pursuit began in the classroom with the teacher-pupil struggles over what is to count as education. In looking at initial encounters and the different agendas which teachers and pupils brought to bear in the classroom I tried to make sense of outcomes, in terms of curriculum, identities and relationships, as the products of compromise and negotiation. Classroom processes reflect many aspects of larger scale political relationships. And indeed the basis of classroom control – domination – lies in 'the fundamental relationship of command and obedience' (Freund, 1972, p.22). *Beachside* also provided the first foray into organizational politics via the in-school debate and decision-making which took place around the introduction of mixed-ability grouping, as indicated above. *Beachside* also began my interest in departmental politics and in particular the struggles over the definition of subject knowledge, specifically English. (This was pursued in a number of papers and articles Ball 1982a, 1983b, 1984b, 1984c, 1986, 1987b, Ball, Kenny and Gardner 1989.) The subject knowledge and subject communities research took the focus of my work outside the school to a consideration of the 'definitional' work done by subject associations, examination

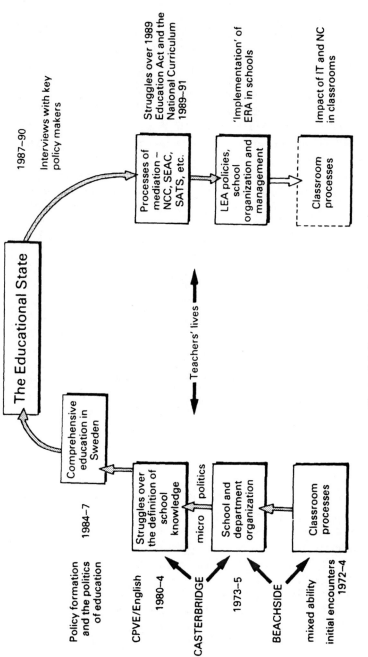

Figure 9.1 Research trajectory

boards, journals, teacher training courses and key committees. This
then articulated nicely with the CVPE study. Here an externally
generated curriculum innovation was traced in terms of its impact in
schools and its origins in the politics of the educational state. This
again led on fairly naturally to work on comprehensive education
policy-making in Sweden (Ball, 1988 and Ball and Larsson, 1989)
and the study and analysis of the policy struggles which led up to
the 1988 Education Reform Act (Ball, 1990). My current work (with
Richard Bowe) moves back towards the processes of 'implementation' (Ball and Bowe, 1989) (particularly of The National
Curriculum and local management of schools (LMS) in schools,
classrooms and local education authorities, and the active interpretation and mediation of educational and organizational change
at these different levels.

DATA AND METHODS

The initial focus for the micropolitical research (although I had not
acquired the term micropolitics at this time – see below) was on
departments. And I began field-work in a school which seemed to
provide the possibility of maximum disputation over subject
knowledge and subject status – Casterbridge High. As indicated
already, Casterbridge was the product of the amalgamation of three
schools: one grammar, one boys' secondary modern and one mixed
secondary modern. It could be argued that it offered a theoretically
significant critical case, in as much that it brought together three
distinct educational traditions and ideologies. In the original outline
for the study I wrote:

> The central focus for the proposed research are three inter-
> connected aspects of the work and social relationships of the
> subject department in the comprehensive school. The first
> aspect is an examination of inter-departmental relationships,
> especially in regard to the negotiation of the curriculum and
> articulation of the perspectives of individual teachers with the
> determination of departmental policy. . .The second aspect is
> the negotiation, conflict and competition taking place
> between departments over the allocation of and their access to
> scarce resources. . .The third aspect is concerned with the
> ways in which individual teachers construct and negotiate

their career, as a subjective process, in and through the school, over time.

As I type this into the word-processor I realize that these three focuses anticipate very directly the threefold division of 'interests' employed in *Micropolitics*. The outlined concluded:

It is intended that this date collection be set against the pattern and flow of a year of activities in the school as these are reflected in the changing demands upon and variations in the role of staff. The majority of the data will be unstructured, in the form of recorded talk from interviews and meetings and observation notes. But the initial analyses of data will be begun while the fieldwork is in progress to enable *constant comparison* and *grounded theorising* (Glaser and Strauss, 1967) and to provide for the *progressive focussing* onto particular areas of data collection.

This was what I did. I spent four terms making field-work visits to Casterbridge and interviewing the teachers there. I visited the school on forty-two separate days with some of these visits condensed into the periods before the beginning and after the end of the university terms. I attended Pastoral and Academic Board meetings, occasional days and public events (plays, speech days, etc.). I spent time sitting in the staffrooms chatting with teachers, I attended departmental meetings and watched a small number of lessons, and I recorded 29 interviews with 24 different members of staff. Thus, I interviewed 28 per cent of all staff and among these all the key figures involved in the amalgamation. Extracts from my field-work diary give some impression of my activities and concerns.

Visit to Casterbridge 12/7/82
A very humid day I arrived at school hot and sticky. The second year drama festival was in progress, each second year form had prepared and rehearsed a play. These were being performed in the hall for the rest of the year group. Several of the English staff are involved. I ask again to talk to Mr Powell and he readily agreed. We covered much of the ground I failed to record last time. He is obviously a central character in the school. I also arranged to talk to Peter Walker: we talked in his hut and he was very forthcoming about his experiences in the pre-and post-merger schools, etc.

A second extract indicates the differences between a straightforward interview study and a participant observation case study. 'Being there' in the school provided data of a type and insights that would not be available in a set of serial, one-to-one interviews. Also the interplay between data collection and analysis and theoretical sampling is evident.

Visit to Casterbridge 24/5/82
I wanted to follow up the redeployment and appointment issues that I confronted on Friday and luckily for once there was space to fit in another quick visit. I arrived at ten and spent most of the time in the east staffroom. I was first able to pursue the situation in History with Maurice. Although this became a public conversation and Kenneth Clarke joined in. (It turns out that he has applied for early retirement.) We talked about history specifically. Three candidates for redeployment were interviewed and Jan Currie was invited to visit Fairview, was offered a scale 2 to be Head of Department there but turned it down. (The LEA must offer two places to redeployees.) Maurice's tone throughout reflected the bad feeling among the staff.

M. Our head's not good at management and a situation like this needs someone that's good at public relations.
KC. Isn't that inexperience though, he's still very green.
M. I don't blame him he's just a cog in a wheel. . . etc.

Once again the question of information about the process of redeployment was raised. Maurice hasn't heard a thing since his interview. He said of the interview, 'we got the pally bit over and then what teaching you do in the school, what responsibilities do you have. Then came the crunch question. Can you justify yourself?. . .' etc.
A young science teacher chipped in, also redeployed. 'I'm a bit apprehensive but I expect it will be better than this place once I settle in.'
There's a massive decline in normative commitment, people don't want to do things for the school. The disintegration of the school as a community. The withdrawal into alienated labour comes closer. The LEA as employer and employment relations (rather than professional work) are much clearer. The head as a cog. 'Labour according to the dictates of those

with authority over them.' * * * The interpretative structure of the school is still redolent with language and imagery harking back to pre-amalgamation.
* * The roles in the school are not occupied by functionaries but are 'made' by the unique personality of the incumbent. Deputy headship and year tutorship differs according to individual 'definitions'.
* * There are still ambiguities, and commitments differ and are complex. The head however has little room for manoeuvre. He can neither reward staff with internal promotions because of over-staffing nor achieve change by reorganizing the distribution of points. The 'stability' of the staff prevents both. The redeployment situation is coming together from the news and gossip and information in staffroom conversations, the direct questioning of informants, key actors and interested parties (i.e. the union rep.).

I began to analyse the data and organize subsequent data collection using the technique of constant comparison (more of which later). But as the research developed I became aware that I had crucial decisions to make about how and towards what end I would write up the Casterbridge study. One option would have been another case-study report, a single institution study like *Beachside*. Another was to extend the substantive and theoretical interests driving along the Casterbridge study and to write up the research as the basis for a substantively focused book on school organization. As outlined above this brought together my teaching and research interests in a neat but powerful way.

I decided on the latter course but realised that in order to proceed I would need a larger, more general data base. I remained committed to producing a 'grounded' theory of school organization *à la* Glaser and Strauss (1967), although in the final writing up I did allow myself some degree of conceptual elaboration.

As it turned out, the book eventually drew upon four sources of data:

1 My own case study material from Beachside, Casterbridge High and the CPVE case study school.
2 Data from published ethnographic studies of schools.
3 The data from various student case studies.
4 My own free-floating interview data from teachers in a variety of schools.

This combination of sources of data clearly raises a series of issues; about the handling and integrating of primary and secondary data from various sources (1); and the integration and interpretation of secondary ethnographic data (2+3). I will address these below. I also want to say something about the organization and conduct of the free-floating interviews (4). I also have to say something about how the various ideas, concepts and materials I was playing with became *micropolitics*.

I have written elsewhere both about the conduct of *Beachside* and the techniques employed to try an ensure rigour in that study (Ball, 1984d) and about the technicalities of maintaining rigour generally in qualitative research (Ball, 1982b and c, 1983a, 1985a). Although different in focus and more modest in scope the general strategy of the Casterbridge field-work was the same as Beachside. What begins to be a little unusual in *Micropolitics* is the use of very different case study material within a single analytical project. The Beachside data were collected intensively over a three year period and there was a considerable body of unused (or not directly reported) data related to the conduct of the school in organizational terms. And the data on the introduction of mixed ability seemed to be open to a micropolitical re-analysis. The assiduous reader can get some sense of what was involved in this by comparing the account in *Beachside* with that in *Micropolitics*. Furthermore, the relationships between this material and that from Casterbridge and the CPVE schools appeared conceptually unproblematical. There were clear parallels in terms of categories of data like career patterns, forms of decision-making, collegial relationships, the position of women, the role of heads. But also and equally importantly there were comparable differences within these categories of action. For instance, I was quickly aware that the conduct and methods of the Beachside and Casterbridge headteachers differed markedly, despite a common basis of strong commitment to comprehensive education. The Beachside head was a deal-maker, both in public and private. But most issues were worked out behind his closed door. Basically he operated out of his office and his day consisted of appointments and meetings. The Casterbridge head was less assertive in deal-making and was often on the defensive over issues raised by staff defending interests forged in their previous school. The head of my CPVE case study school was verbal and confrontational, he liked to take his staff on in open, knockabout argument, friend and foe alike. From these examples I began to form the idea of headship as a style constructed out of interactions with subordinates. Heads would make a claim for a particular sort of working relationship which would have to be asserted, or not, in relation to counter-claims made by others. However, I clearly needed a lot more cases to work on if I were to pursue and refine this kind of analysis. This is one way in which the secondary sources came into play. None the less, by comparing cases it was possible to begin to establish a typology of headship. I tried several versions and variations before I was confident that I could defend a particular typology in relation to all the data I had. That is there was a place for all the cases, and enough sub-criteria in each category to defend the allocation of each case in some detail.

Clearly, working from secondary sources meant that I could be less confident about the full adequacy of each new case. I was having to read off my secondary analysis from the surface features of illustrative data, I did not have access to complete data sets and I lacked the background knowledge and tacit understanding that ethnographers build up about their own 'tribe'. I took heart from the fact that new data did not just fit unproblematically into my existing conceptualizations. Rather new issues and problems were raised. The use of this material was part of a process, which I tried to operate as systematically as possible, of 'constant comparison'. My aim was always to treat each piece of data in its own right and independently from existing interpretations. Only quotations from raw data were employed. Over time my third data source was integrated into this process. The third source being individual interviews mostly conducted on a one-off basis but in some cases clustered in one school. This material obviously brought with it strengths and weaknesses. The strengths being that I was able to 'sample' a wider variety of types of schools (primary/secondary/ sixth form college, coed/single sex, large/small, old/new, grammar/ secondary modern/comprehensive). The weaknesses being that I had to rely upon single respondent views of the life of the organiza- tion. (I had a very limited set of questions as the basis for these interviews but they were invariably long and wide ranging.) Thus, I was playing off the number and variety of cases against depth and sophistication. But there was another particular aspect of these interviews that some reviewers of *Micropolitics* have criticized. Two critical questions have been raised: first, is the 'sample' representative, second, is it big enough? The first implies that variations in micropolitical 'form' are related to structural aspects of schools – size, type, location, etc. This was clearly in my mind in the early stages of the broader data collection exercise but I could find no clear evidence of systematic variations of this kind. Other factors to do with history, ethos, style and ideology were far more important and significant. One key aspect of the constant comparative process is that some categories, interpretations and concepts which may have some initial common-sense appeal, are exploded and discarded along the way. Understandably researchers do not spend much time in published texts discussing their discards. The second question suggests that if I had had more data I might have found new or different things. Things that some reviewers thought I ought to have found. But again a fundamental principle of constant comparison and induction is that you go on collecting data until you no longer see different things – theoretical saturation. My data collection went through four main cycles: initial case-study work and interviewing; the collection and extraction of material from secondary sources; the main interviewing phase in a range of settings; and a second interview phase to 'test' the adequacy of the emergent form of the analysis. Between each phase partial analysis of data led to a refinement of issues for the next phase and some bases for theoretical sampling. It was in these on-going analyses that many propositions and possibilities and categories for data were abandoned and others emerged as important – progressive focusing. The last cycle of interviewing continued even when I had begun the final write-up of material. Certainly it is a precept of this kind of inductive method that the analysis is always 'not quite finished', 'not quite adequate'. There is always the possibility of new, surprising data, and the context is always changing. But eventually perfection and closure must be measured against practicality.

There is another peculiarity (inadequacy some might say) of the free-floating interviews. In the majority of cases the interviewees were known to me directly or were personally recommended to me. I believed that the sorts of questions I wanted to ask and the topics I wanted to address, what Eric Hoyle calls the 'organizational underworld' (Hoyle, 1982, p.87) could not be dealt with by a cold calling interview technique. I needed a degree of trust from my respondents. I needed them to take me into their confidence. I wanted to share their folk-knowledge of their institution with me. In some respects I was operating close to the level of gossip and personal criticism – the informal aspects of organization which are ritually referred to but rarely analysed in organizational theory. Not surprisingly the better I knew my interviewee the more candid the disclosures tended to be, although this was not always the case; I did find others who were willing to be indiscreet with little encouragement. The interviews were long and rambling; they contained many diversions and are full of anecdotes. My approach to interviewing was based on an attempt to minimize 'topic' questions and maximize 'cue' questions. Thus, to pass over as much control over the substance of the interview as possible to the respondent. The following extract from an interview with a woman deputy-head is fairly typical:

S. How do you get on with your Head?

C: Yeah, I mean, it's only recently that he's started to call me Carol, you know, and when I started and he didn't, I invited him to because I thought perhaps he was waiting for me to invite him. But he said, 'Oh', you know, 'No'. So I said 'Well, if and when you feel that your want to, then do', you know. So anyway, I thought that – that the staff had to come to him. I couldn't – I mean, it was – it's much easier now than it was. When I started, there was what I termed 'ritual intransigence'. You know, they really were in knotty little pockets. And if Humanities wanted to do something and Maths wanted to do something and it clashed with English time or something, they would in a ritualistic way say 'No', you know, and they never actually ever came together.

S: Where did that come from? I mean, it must have started somewhere.

C: Well, I've got a feeling – I mean, it is to do with territory, it is to do with geography and it is to do with the fact that there are long wings and it takes a long time to – it's about a quarter of a mile round the building, you know. So in fact I'm at a disadvantage here because if I have to go to the office, it's a long way – a long walk from here. I've got a feeling that the Head encouraged it because I don't think he wanted the staff to come together at the beginning of his time, you know. Also, as I say, he's totally formal and doesn't – doesn't come to any parties, no alcohol and things like that and I think he sees it as a – you know, it's a sort of deliberate advantage. . .

S: What do you mean, divide and rule?

179

C: Yeah, and – well, possibly that. Also I think he just wanted people around because I think the place was so, you know – it was suffering this trauma and I think he thought people around the place would supervise it better. And so I've kind of made a little – you know, made a point of trying to encourage more social interaction.

S: He doesn't like this?

C: Oh, not at all, not all.

S: It's quite hysterical, this – this. . .

C: Oh, it's dreadful, yeah, yeah. In fact, we thought we in a way – I mean obviously as these things always do – you, you know, you come together more against a common enemy. You know, there are some obvious people that haven't involved themselves at all in it but, generally speaking, the staff has been at one over the issues. So that's been quite interesting.

S: But I still couldn't – I couldn't still grasp this them and us thing.

C: I dunno because when I think about it, there's tons of them and us-es. You know, there's the power things, there's the man and woman thing. . .

S: Tell me about the man and woman.

C: Well, what they mean is, if you look at all the things that are going on, like – things like the multicultural working party, it's all women who volunteer and women who sustain it and women who regularly attend. We had some workshops for special provision work. Mostly it's women who come, you know and who commit themselves to things like that.

Buried in this extract are several of the basic issues analysed and discussed in *Micropolitics*: the style of the headteacher and his relationship with staff; the nature of relationships among the staff; oppositions, conflicts and alliances; and male-female relationships within school organization. In some ways the nature of the interviews come close to life history methods. An account of the respondent's own career was usually a central part of the exercise and I often started the interviews with this, and the respondents own 'place' in the micropolitics of the institution was also important. It was both necessary to see the individual respondents as micro-political cases – being active, attentive or uninvolved, etc. – and in order to make sense of their view of things it was crucial to know their personal stance and role – head's confidant, part of the opposition, disgruntled about not being promoted, etc. I was also keen to ensure that as often as possible any general statements of view – 'The head is too susceptible to outside influence' – were related to specific instances – 'Can you think of a recent occasion when that was evident?'

It should be apparent that emotional issues were sometimes close to the surface in the interviews as respondents discussed strained interpersonal relations or 'spoiled' careers or tense and difficult meetings or strongly held values and beliefs. This was particularly the case in the work at Casterbridge. Here with the amalgamation of three schools some teachers had lost status and position, had lost control over their immediate environment or felt that their beliefs about education and professional practice were being debased. The stresses of amalgamation were evident in illnesses, absences and anger. Lives, careers and organization were very tightly interwined here (Draper, 1989). The English department was a particularly tense example of the interpersonal dimension. All three of the previous heads of English from the three amalgamated schools had applied for the new head of department post. The youngest, a women, had got the job. The other two, older men, remained in the new department as classroom teachers (although on protected salaries). A recipe for emotional conflict.

All of this raises issues about the conduct of such research. Especially the difficult questions of how deep and how far to pursue personal questioning. How much does the researcher need to know, as against how much should they be allowed to know? One response might be to say that in dealing with sophisticated adults the matter of how much to disclose can be left to the respondent to decide. But things are not that simple. The skills of interviewing built up over a number of years give the researcher an edge. The respondent may find themselves manipulated into saying more than they intended. The onus must lie with researchers to establish their own ethical code in such matters. Only once, I think, did I overstep the mark in the *Micropolitics* research, when, by repeated requests, I pushed one ex-head of department, who was very reluctant, into allowing me to interview him about his failure to become head of department in the amalgamated school.

ANALYSIS

I have mentioned several times already my commitment to the constant comparative method. Let me try to make the use of the method a little more concrete. Jacqueline Wiseman (1974, p. 317) puts this in graphic terms:

> The qualitative researcher is not unlike the detective in the classic murder mystery. Starting with a few clues, the detective questions persons connected with the case, develops hunches, questions further on the basis of these hunches, begins to see a picture of 'what happened' starting to emerge, looks for evidence pro and con, elaborating or modifying that picture – until finally the unknown is known. The murderer is caught; what was once a mystery is now understandable. The facts have been 'reorganized' in a way to connect – with as few contradictions as possible – the vast amount of empirical data.

As I see it, or prefer it, these processes are in part physical. The mechanics of analysis involve a literal manipulation of the data. This is part of getting intimately familiar with the data. When working from documents, observation notes and interview transcripts the first stage of the process is familiarization. The reading and re-reading of material in order to know what is what and where everything is. It is surprising how often, particularly with interviews, that reading the transcript draws attention to issues that passed by almost unnoticed in the interview itself. As I work through the material I use a highlighter to pick out 'slices' of data which seem important and interesting and make short marginal notes – often in effect labelling the data or beginning an analytical commentary. Two things are accomplished in this. The notes or 'memos' are part of theoretical development and take on a life of their own. Strauss (1987, p.18):

> theoretical ideas are kept track of, and continuously linked and built up by means of theoretical memos. From time to time they are taken out of the file and examined and sorted, which results in new ideas, thus new memos. As research proceeds to later phases, memo writing becomes more intense, more focused, and memos are even more frequently sparked by previous memos or sum up and add to previous ones.

Writing about data is a vital discipline. It encourages the

interrogation of data and facilitates creative thinking. (The comments and broken phrases in the second field-work diary extract above is an example of the early stages of this.) The other aspect of the reading and selecting process is coding or categorizing.

coding (1) both follows upon and leads to generative questions; (2) fractures the data, thus freeing the researcher from description and forcing interpretation to higher levels of abstraction; (3) is the pivotal operation for moving toward the discovery of a core category or categories; and so (4) moves towards ultimate integration of the entire analysis; as well as (5) yields the desired conceptual density (i.e. relationships among the codes and the development of each). (Strauss, 1987, pp.55–6).

When I have a significant amount of data which I have worked through highlighting and developing commentary I photocopy all the pages of data and then cut these pages up into data-bits. I then put these bits, according to initial categories into separate files or envelopes. If some bits of data need to go into more than one category then I take another photocopy. I also number each bit of data and where relevant use these numbers to cross-reference between the bits. I also make sure that each bit has an indication of its origin. It is very frustrating and time-consuming to have to work through transcripts to identify a quote one forgot to label.

The categories and their data then provide the basis for some writing and drawing. I try to map out pieces of analysis as diagrams which link together categories or concepts. As new diagrams or arrangements are tried I often go back to the collection of data to review the material. Some times there seems to be more 'in' it the second time or third time around.

Various kinds of visual devices conceived while doing analyses can be incorporated into the follow-up theoretical memos, among these devices are diagrams, matrixes, tables and graphs. . .Whether one uses them or not undoubtedly reflects personal though styles and predilections for various types of imagery. (Strauss, 1987, p.143)

I am particularly fond of the two-by-two table as a device for organizing and thinking about data.

As these processes of sorting and thinking about the data go on it is often the case that material which was originally not selected out assumes some significance and new categories are created or initial categories are subdivided or amalgamated. If this is being done, as it should, when data collection is still going on, the categories and the propositional relationships between categories can be tested out via specific data collection tasks. If change seems such a crucial factor in revealing or disrupting existing patterns of social relationships I should try to interview more people from schools which are in the throes of dramatic change. Or I need to talk to more people from low status subjects. Or I must try to get female respondents to talk more about being a woman in the organization. Or I should try to interview some union 'reps' about their role in schools. Various 'significances' are being identified, examined and if possible fitted into a larger whole.

As more data is added to the envelopes some categories fail to develop much analytic bulk and they may be abandoned, or they begin to assume a special significance as a negative case or aberration and can prove to be very useful as a basis for moderating generalizations. The search for the deviant case is a key aspect of the process of constant comparison, and any model, concept or typology must, unless clearly specified, be able to accommodate all the data in the relevant categories.

The very first list of code categories, noted in my field-work diary, is fairly primitive and mundane. It includes:

headteacher's roles,
previous school,
comprehensive education,
pupil abilities,
pupil behaviour,
pastoral care,
amalgamation,
morale,
career prospects,
career construction,
luck and chance,
timetabling,
the appointment of women.

Some of these later disappeared from view, as far as *Micropolitics* was concerned, but something of the process of refining, separating and relating such categories can be recovered from the final version of the book. Change, age, gender, leadership, opposition, control, career, resources and relationships are the major organizing and analytical categories employed – and several of these are crucially interrelated. (The origin of some is evident in the early list.) If we take career as an example, this emerged very early as a major aspect of organizational commitment, and as a basis for the 'interpretation' of organizational life for many respondents in the study (Where am I now? Where might I be? How are others progressing?). Gender quickly emerged as a concomitant category. Career also subsumed categories like; career strategies, awareness, commitment, sponsorship, promotion decisions, identity and patterns of advantage, and interrelated directly with interests, leadership succession, amalgamation, redeployment, stigma, teaching ideologies and innovation. Career in fact provided the primary conceptual link between individuals and organizations. A career is a social trajectory across one or more institutions. Thus, 'the analysis here rests on the interplay between personal aspirations and identities, and the micropolitical processes and constraints of the organization' (*Micropolitics*, Ball, p.167). The labelling and categorization of data, the comparison between data, the decision to collect more data of particular kinds, and the categorization of that, are the processes which link collection intimately with analysis. In these processes, 'the researcher will be making a number of interesting, if at first quite provisional, linkages among the "discovered" (created) concepts. The coding is beginning to yield *conceptually dense theory* which will of course become much more dense as additional linkages are suggested and formulated' (Strauss, 1987 p.17).

Once established categories and concepts developed in writing and drawing provide the language of analysis, they are the terms which stand for processes and relationships between things. But engagement with literature is also a part of the process of analysis and of the 'naming of parts'. There is always a huge resource of concepts 'out there' to be plundered. The basic integrating concept of my attempt to build a theory of school organization – micropolitics – was garnered from a paper by Eric Hoyle (1982), 'Micropolitics of Educational Organizations'. Reading the paper for the first time was a strange experience, it was like a gasp of recognition. 'That's it, that's what it's all about, micropolitics'. All the material I was writing on conflict, interests, careers, groups, alliances, strategies seemed to fall neatly into place behind the one organizing and integrating idea. I did not agree fully with Hoyle's use of the concept and I felt it could be developed further but it made sense, it was obvious. This obviousness, the recognition, is a part of the cognitive and emotional engagement with an analytical project and part of the creative process with integrates a new piece of research into a broader tradition of concepts, theories and substantive findings.

There were several other points in the analytical development of *Micropolitics* where the literature played a part. The data on teachers' perceptions of their headteachers and the contradictory expectations which were expressed left me perplexed for some time. Different bits of data did not seem to fit together. Here the breakthrough was provided by re-reading Anne and Harold Berlak's dilemma's analysis (1981). Their work on students' expectations of teachers spoke directly to teacher's expectations of heads. Hall's (1972), symbolic interactionist analysis of politics, also contributed to the development of the idea of the use and control of talk by heads. Elsewhere, Du Boulay's (1984) study of the role of gossip in a Greek mountain village, suggested by Sara Delamont, and other anthropological references on gossip provided by Martyn Hammersley, firmed up the analysis of other aspects of organizational talk.

As categories and concepts come to be grouped together then the first sense of a structure for writing up begins to emerge. A set of categories and concepts logically coalesce into a chapter (although pity on the reader for academic convention often leads to divisions into chapters which do not necessarily match the 'natural' structure of the analysis). I use this sense of structure as the basis for new groupings. A set of envelopes containing data go together with a set of analytical notes and interpretive asides into a folder. That is the basis for a chapter. Also what happens in this process is that sub-codes of major categories become clearer – career, gender, conflict, opposition, interests, alliances – as they are broken down into sub-headings and sections. This is the most intellectually challenging and frustrating stage in most ethnographic work, trying to make bits and pieces of analysis fit into an analytical whole.

Undoubtedly, *the* most difficult skill to learn is 'how to make everything come together' – how to integrate one's separate, if cumulative, analyses. If the final product is an integrated theory, then *integrating* is the accurate term for this complex process. This is why the inexperienced researcher will never feel secure in how to complete an entire integration until he or she has struggled with the process, beginning early and ending only with the final write-up. (Strauss, 1987, p. 170)

As well as providing a means for manipulating and reworking data in a very direct sense, this low-tech approach to data analysis makes writing up much easier, I believe, and more creative. (Of course it has to be weighed against the hi-tech possibilities of data analysis programs for use with micro-processors.) At the point when I want to attempt a full, first draft of a chapter, I start on the floor. The categories to be deployed in a particular chapter can be manoeuvred around like a pack of cards until a logical, sensible, narrative flow is arrived at. This first, then that, then that. The exercise can be repeated within the categories for each of the sub-sections. This can go one stage further and the data bits to be used can also be ordered. The data-bits are important in two ways as the writing begins. First, they serve for illustration of categories and issues, very rarely can a qualitative researcher display all relevant data, there is not enough space. Second, the deployment of the data drives the analysis as exactly what it is about each extract that is meaningful is explained. Again at this point I often find more 'in' the data than anticipated. New nuances, complexity or contradictions emerge, especially as each new piece of data is added to what is already displayed and said. Thus, writing up is not the mechanical process that it is sometimes presented as. It is not something done at the end of everything else, it is integral. It is part of the creative process of analysis. As Peter Woods (1986, p. 169) explains:

I am not arguing that we should not have a rigorous methodology, with due attention to matters of validity, access, ethics, data collection, etc., nor that we should not have tested and recognized techniques and routines. Rather that, as part of that methodology, we should give equal attention to the cultivation of mental states conducive to the production of theory as to the collection of data. One requires liberation, creativity and imagination: the other discipline, control and method. In some ways they tend to work against each other, and where we put more emphasis on one, the other will suffer.

THEORY

The final aspect of doing *Micropolitics* that I want to discuss briefly, is the status of the product as theory. The book has the tentative sounding subtitle 'Towards a theory of school organization'. One aim of the exercise as noted at the beginning was to provide an alternative to the functionalist, systems theories of organization which were prevalent in existing attempts to 'describe' schools as organizations. But I wanted that alternative to be theoretically sophisticated enough to stand on its own as a basis for the analysis of organizational life. Martyn Hammersley (1987) suggests that there are four elements to theoretical development in ethnographic work.

1 the addition of new concepts and relations;
2 the clarification of concepts and relations;
3 the development and testing of measures;
4 hypothesis testing.

Hammersley sees these as stages in a progressive hierarchy of worth with (4) as the ultimate goal. He uses the term theory in a 'strict' sense; 'The minimum requirement for a theory, as I shall use the term, is that is makes explanatory claims in the form: given the occurrence of $(A_1 . . . . A_n)$ then $(B_1 . . . B_n)$ will probably occur' (p.285). In contrast Woods (1985) has argued for a conception of theoretical development based on the generation of theoretical ideas and concepts. But what really separates the two is their definitions of theory and their views of the purpose of theory. Hammersley stresses explanation and predication. Woods highlights understanding and insight. For me, Hammersley's counsel seeks quite unnecessarily to bind ethnography, and social action, to the requirements of scientific methods modelled upon research of the natural world. Woods wants to retain a commitment to theorizing which is predicated on and compatible with particular theoretical conceptions of the social world (e.g. symbolic interactionism). The question is whether social life can only be or can be best know in terms of 'if. . .then', predictable relations? Is it really useful to reduce all social life to this form? It seems perverse and constraining to want to direct all social science into one model for understanding human action. Furthermore, the imposition of a testing mode fundamentally alters the inductive-deductive interplay which is the stuff of ethnographic method. The method, both the collection and analysis of data is modelled upon the diachronic/synchronic nature of social reality.

Thus, through ethnography 'the discovery of grounded theory' is a self-conscious replication of the processes of knowing and making sense which are common to all human actors. Theorizing must, I believe maintain this social authenticity, while Hammersley aims to divorce the form and nature of theory entirely from the methods and processes of qualitative social research.

> One of our deepest convictions is that social phenomena are complex phenomena. Much social research seems to be based on quite the opposite assumption; either that, or researchers working in various research traditions describe or analyse the phenomena they study in relatively uncomplex terms, having given up on the possibility of ordering the 'buzzing, blooming confusion' of experience except by ignoring 'for a time' its complexity. (Strauss, 1987, p.6.)

Thus, the claims I would make for micropolitics as a theory have little to do with cause and effect and there are few statements in the text which could be rendered into the form of predictions. Ethnography aims to capture, part at least, of a social totality. As Strauss indicates, complexity and interrelatedness rather than simplicity are the end points. The law of parsimony – that that theory is best which explains in the simplest way – does not apply. Concepts are the goal rather than law-like generalizations. The point of the exercise is transferability – the transferability of the forms of social action and social reasoning embedded in micropolitics from one school setting to another, and one organizational setting to another. Thus, micropolitics is a system for making sense of the complexity of organizational life. It is about reasons generally rather than causes specifically. 'Research which is geared primarily to hermeneutic problems may be of generalized importance in so far as it seems to elucidate the nature of agents' knowledgeability and thereby their reasons for action, across a wide range of action – contexts' (Giddens, 1984, p. 328).

The most satisfying forms of feedback on *Micropolitics* come in two varieties. First, there are the occasions of identification, that is when people see their own experience of organizations reflected in the analysis. This is a sort of *ad hoc* respondent validation. Second, some people have talked about reaching for the book as a manual, as a source book for micropolitical skills and strategies. Again Giddens makes the point 'Studying practical consciousness means investigating what agents already know, but by determination it is normally illuminating to them if this is expressed discursively, in the meta language of social science' (Giddens, 1984, p.328). In these terms, as theory, *Micropolitics* is an exercise in conceptual mapping. The aim is to establish a set of analytical tools – power, goal diversity, ideological disputation, conflicts, political activity and control – which can be employed in specific settings towards the understanding of social practices. The concepts are intricately related.

REFERENCES

Ball, S.J. (1981) *Beachside Comprehensive: A Case Study of Secondary Schooling*, Cambridge, Cambridge University Press.

Ball, S.J. (1982a) 'Competition and conflict in the teaching of English: a socio-historical analysis', *Journal of Curriculum Studies* 13, 4.

Ball, S.J. (1982b) 'Participant observation as a research method', in *Deakin University, Case Study Method: Readings 32–44. The Conduct of Fieldwork*, Geelong, Deakin University Press.

Ball, S.J. (1982c) 'The application and verification of participant observation case study', in *Deakin University, Case Study methods 26–33. Perspectives on Case Study 4: Ethnography*, Geelong, Deakin University Press.

Ball, S.J. (1983a) 'Case study method: some notes and problems', in Hammersley, M. (ed) *The Ethnography of Schooling*, Driffield, Nafferton Press.

Ball, S.J. (1983b) 'A subject of privilege: English and the school curriculum 1906–35, in Hammersley, M. and Hargreaves, A. (eds) *Curriculum Practice: Sociological Perspectives*, Lewes, Falmer.

Ball, S.J. (1984a) 'Becoming a comprehensive?: facing up to falling rolls', in S.J. Ball (ed.) *Comprehensive Schooling: A Reader*, Lewes, Falmer.

Ball, S.J. (1984b) 'The making of a school subject: English for the English 1906–82', in Goodson, I.F. (ed.) *Social Histories of the Secondary Curriculum: Subjects for Study*, Lewes, Falmer.

Ball, S.J. (1984c) 'Conflict, panic and inertia: mother tongue teaching in England 1970–83', in Herrlitz, W. *et al.* (eds) *Mother Tongue Education In Europe, Studies in Mother Tongue Education 1*, International Mother Tongue Education Network, National Institute for Curriculum Development, Enschede, Netherlands. pp.160–93.

Ball, S.J. (1984d) 'Beachside reconsidered: reflections on a methodological apprenticeship' in Burgess, R. (ed.) *The Research Process in Educational Settings: Ten Case Studies*, Lewes, Falmer.

Ball, S.J. (1985a) 'Participant observation with pupils', in Burgess, R.G. (ed.) *Strategies of Educational Research*, Lewes, Falmer.

Ball, S.J. (1985b) 'School politics, teachers' careers and educational change: a case of becoming a comprehensive school', in Barton, L. and Walker, S. (eds) *Education and Social Change*, London, Croom Helm.

Ball, S.J. (1986) Ball, S.J. 'Relations, structures and conditions in curriculum changes: a political history of English teaching', in Goodson, I.F. (ed.) *International Perspectives in Curriculum History*, London, Croom Helm.

Ball, S.J. (1987a) *The Micropolitics of the School: Towards a Theory of School Organization*, London, Methuen/Routledge.

Ball, S.J. (1987b) 'English teaching, the state and forms of literacy', in Kroon, S. and Sturm, J. (eds) *Research on Mother Tongue Education in an International Perspective*, Enschede, VALO-M.

Ball, S.J. (1988) 'Costing democracy: schooling, equality and democracy in Sweden', in Lauder, H. and Brown, P. (eds) *Education in Search of a Future*, Lewes, Falmer.

Ball, S.J. (1990) *Politics and Policymaking in Education*, London, Routledge.

Ball, S.J. and Larsson, S. (eds) (1989) *The Struggle for Democratic Education: Equality and Participation in Sweden*, Lewes, Falmer.

Ball, S.J., Kenny, A. and Gardner, D. (1989) 'Literacy and democracy: policies and politics for the teaching of English' in Goodson, I. (ed.) *Bringing English to Order*, Lewes, Falmer.

Ball, S.J. and Bowe, R. (1989) 'When the garment gapes: ethnography and policy as practices', paper presented to the Ethnography and Policy Conference, St Hilda's College, Oxford.

Berlak, A. and Berlak, H. (1981) *The Dilemmas of Schooling*, London, Methuen.

Beynon, J. (1985) 'Career histories in a comprehensive school' in Ball, S.J. and Goodson, I.F. (eds) *Teachers' Lives and Careers*, Lewes, Falmer Press.

Burgess, R.G. (1983) *Experiencing Comprehensive Education*, London, Methuen.

Burgess, R.G. (1984) 'Headship: freedom or constraint?' in Ball, S.J. (ed.) *Comprehensive Schooling: a Reader*, Lewes, Falmer.

Draper, J. (1989) 'Teacher adaptation to school merger', paper presented to the Ethnography, Education and Policy Conference, St Hilda's College, Oxford.

Du Boulay, J. (1974) *Portrait of a Greek Mountain Village*, Oxford, Clarendon Press.

Duverger, M. (1972) *The Study of Politics*, London, Nelson.

Freund, J. (1972) *The Sociology of Max Weber*, Harmondsworth, Penguin.

Giddens, A. (1984) *The Constitution of Society*, Oxford, Polity Press.

Glaser, B. and Strauss, A.L. (1967) *The Discovery of Grounded Theory*, Chicago, Aldine.

Hall, P.M. (1972) 'A symbolic interactionist analysis of politics', *Sociological Inquiry* 42, 3–4, 35–75.

Hall, P.M. (1979) 'The presidency and impression management' in Denzin, N.L. (ed.) *Studies in Symbolic Interactionism, Vol. 2*, Greenwich, Conn., JAI Press..

Hammersley, M. (1987) 'Ethnography and the cummulative development of theory', *British Education Research Journal* 13, 3, 283–96.

Hindess, B. (1982) 'Power, interests and the outcomes of struggles', *Sociology* 16, 4, 498–511.

Hoyle, E. (1982) 'Micropolitics of educational organizations', *Educational Management and Administration* 10, 87–98.

Pfeffer, J. (1978) 'The micropolitics of organizations', in Meyer, M.W. *et al.* (eds) *Environments and Organizations,* San Francisco, Jossey-Bass.

Radnor, H., Ball, S.J. and Burrell, D. (1989) 'The Certificate of Pre-Vocational Education: an analysis of curriculum conflict in policy and practice', in Hargreaves, A. and Reynolds, D. (eds) *Policy and Practice in Contemporary State Education,* Lewes, Falmer.

Riseborough, G. (1981) 'Teacher careers and comprehensive schooling: an empirical study', *Sociology* 15, 3, 352–81.

Strauss, A.L. (1987) *Qualitative Analysis for Social Scientists,* New York, Cambridge University Press.

Strauss, A.L. *et al.* (1961) *Psychiatric Ideologies and Institutions,* Chicago, Aldine.

Wiseman, J. (1974) 'The research web', *Urban Life and Culture* 3, 3, 317–28.

Wolcott, H.F. (1973) *The Man in the Principals Office: an ethnography,* New York, Holt, Rinehart & Winston.

Woods, P. (1985) 'Ethnography and theory construction in educational research', in Burgess, R.G. (ed.) *Field Methods in the Study of Education,* Lewes, Falmer.

Woods, P. (1986) *Inside Schools,* London, Routledge & Kegan Paul.

10

DOING EDUCATIONAL RESEARCH
IN TRELIW

David Reynolds

The very small group of people who started research in the field of school effectiveness in the early to mid-1970s were in many ways a highly unusual group compared to those who usually conducted conventional educational research in Britain. Michael Power and colleagues (1967, 1972), whose publication of an article which impertinently asked whether there were *Delinquent Schools* in Tower Hamlets resulted in them being ejected from those same schools, were members of a Medical Research Council Social Medicine Unit. Dennis Gath (1977) was a child guidance consultant in a hospital setting. Michael Rutter (1979) was a child psychiatrist. As for myself, I had been appointed as a member of the Medical Research Council scientific staff to see if it was possible to undertake work into school differences and school effects in South Wales which had been impossible for Michael Power to complete in London.

The professional location of being the only trained sociologist in an Epidemiology Unit with a staff of clinicians, a statistician and a field-worker trained in the detection of coalminer's pneumoconiosis from reading lung X-rays was a somewhat jolting experience intellectually. My own preference had been for the use of qualitative methods that had been a central part of the philosophical and educational ethos of the sociology department at the University of Essex where I had been an undergraduate, yet these methods were regarded as 'soft' or, to use more technical language, invalid and unreliable by those colleagues working within the conventional positivist paradigm that medical and medico-social research has been based upon. After a time, it became easier to see why these researchers viewed what they regarded as impressionistic data based upon utilization of professional sociological skills and sensitivities with grave disquiet, since the unit itself had been set up because of its Director's concern about the activities of chest consultants in the NHS who had used *their* professional judgements to argue that there was no such thing as coal miners' pneumoconiosis! Most important of all, the Director of the unit (the late Archie Cochrane) believed in the revolutionary or socialist potential of 'hard', numerical data in furthering social change, believing that Marxism was derived from empirical evidence which was to be obtained by the amassing of material about the realities of the inefficiency of the capitalist system. This commitment to socialist empiricism and Marxist positivism influenced me greatly and led to what has been a life-long distrust of those in the naturalistic or CARE traditions who seem to believe that the use of qualitative data or the interpretive approach is a necessary mark of a true radical. Positivism and its search for an objective truth, I believed, was capable of revealing social realities only hidden in the subjective, qualitative world of member accounts, definitions of the situation and multiple selves.

When it came to the choice of research paradigms within which to locate our proposed studies, it was therefore somewhat inevitable that I utilized a mixed methodology of *both* quantitative and qualitative orientation, representing the influence of both research traditions. Our aim was to use the quantitative data to generate and test hypotheses on the lines of the classic hypothetico-deductive model, and to use the qualitative data to explain the findings and processes at work in schools that lay behind the statistical relationships.

Taking this particular multi-paradigmatic road was particularly difficult for a researcher in the 1970s and early to mid-1980s, since sociology of education in particular and sociology in general was divided very much into two oppositional camps, which utilized naturalistic *or* positivistic methods. The strong tradition of the late 1960s where *both* methods were used, as in the quantitative and qualitative case studies of Hargreaves (1967) and Lacey (1970), had been replaced by an intellectual either/or situation where the two oppositional groups used only one method each, a method which in both cases was supported and buttressed by a supporting ideology about the nature of social science knowledge and indeed by a more general orientation also about the nature of society. Defending this mixed methodological strategy and also defending the view that adoption of the positivistic research strategy (among others) was the only place for a person with a radical or reformist social orientation to be, became an activity that naturally involved us intellectually in the late 1970s and early 1980s (Reynolds, 1981).

With our methodological orientation settled and our research interests – the possibility that schools as institutions had effects upon the development of their pupils – clarified with the help of some of the researchers mentioned earlier in this chapter, the next stage was the negotiation of research access to a sample of schools. It is easy to understand how this crucial area of the research process has received so much attention in the methodological literature, because the process in our case was extraordinarily complicated (see Walford, 1987 and Beynon, 1983 for other accounts). We first approached the local authority of 'Treliw', since it was this valley community that had been the location for all the unit's previous work into pneumoconiosis. We reasoned, as it turned out quite accurately, that any community where around 12,000 miners and their families had received payments from the Coal Board directly due to the unit's programme of chest screening would be eager and willing for further research! The meeting with the Treliw Education Committee which had been arranged as the first step towards access lasted accordingly thirty seconds and after the chair had said who we were, one councillor simply commented that anything that the MRC Epidemiology Unit might want to do was alright by the people of Treliw, which was followed by a loud murmur of support.

We chose as our target research sample and population a group of nine secondary modern schools, each of which (unlike the selective grammar schools) served a defined local catchment area which made possible an assessment of the 'intakes' of pupils that the schools were getting by looking at the characteristics of their local communities. In this homogeneous working-class community, our hypothesis was that we had 'controlled' scientifically for any variation in the calibre of the pupils entering the schools, with the result that any variations in the 'outcomes' in terms of the characteristics of the pupils was due to the institutions themselves. Delinquency data, which we had already collected through the local police records office, showed substantial school variation and in our meeting with the officers of the LEA we presented this data, asked for further centrally collected data on other school outcomes such as attendance rates and levels of academic achievement, and re-quested access to the schools to test our ideas about the importance of their institutional functioning.

The LEA officers agreed to allow access to their schools, but only went so far as to permit schools to take part. It was to be up to each school headteacher, using his/her own methods of determining the policy of the school, to decide whether to join the project. It turned out later that the officers agreement to participate was because the LEA itself was concerned about variation in the quality of its school provision, and in fact already had one of its senior officials engaged in a monitoring exercise looking at schools' examination passes. So sensitive was the issue within the LEA, though, that only one copy of a preliminary report was ever produced. The outside cover had an instruction written in red that the contents were 'for professional use only and no judgements should be inferred'.

Before approaching schools the local authority officers thought that it was vital to elicit the support and agreement of the local representatives of the teachers' unions, so that if there were any problems with their members once the research began in schools, these could be ironed out before potentially escalating and threatening the study's continuation. One teacher union agreed instantly: the National Association of Schoolmasters (as it was then titled) was pleased that there was to be research on school delinquency. The National Union of Teachers, though, were more difficult to convince and it took the intervention of a local Labour Member of Parliament to convince the local executive that we were interested in finding good practice rather than poor practice. The clinching argument with them was apparently that I was a 'good party man'!

Out of the nine schools, eight agreed to take part after the purposes of the research and the data collection instruments and procedures had been explained to them. In three of the schools the headteachers took the decision on their own, arguing that since it was 'their' school the buck stopped with them. In the remaining five, there was a degree of staff participation in the process, ranging from a vote at a full staff meeting in one to an informal discussion between the headteacher and her staff at another. One of the schools, however, refused to take part, the result of the staffs' feeling about an entirely spontaneous riot that occurred on the day that we had first visited the school to talk through what our research involved. Although many of the school staff insisted that the pupils had dropped concrete blocks and bricks through the roof of the main school buildings from a walkway above the building because of their knowledge that we were on the premises, our own perception was that the riot was the latest in a long line of trouble, a view that was supported by the existence of a school building that looked like a set being used for a Second World War film.

Keeping eight of the nine schools in the research programme was, we thought, a major achievement given that we had been open with all the schools that our aim was to find out 'what worked' and 'what didn't work' with adolescents in their school years. However, the research programme as it was undertaken in the schools during the whole of the 1970s generated many flashpoints, each of which could have cost us the participation of some of our sample of research schools. All eight schools were subject to a process of data collection involving:

1 Observation of school and classroom processes by a specially trained observer and myself.
2 Collection of data from the pupils on their levels of delinquency, attendance and academic achievement (as a check on the validity of the official records we had been using).
3 Collection of limited data from the pupils on attitudes to school, perceptions of teachers, etc.
4 Collection of data from the parents of senior pupils at the schools to see if the schools were taking from similar social backgrounds

In one school, some of the pupils went up to the headteacher and told her 'we told the researchers what we thought of you, Miss X'. In another school, the headteacher came into the room where the 'self report' delinquency data was being collected from pupils and began to look at the quite considerable lists of offences pupils were writing as having been committed. My reaction, which was to ask the head to leave the room, did not improve headteacher/researcher relations. In another school, we made the mistake of talking to pupils in the school 'smokers' corner' at breaktime, thereby validating the pupils' behaviour in the eyes of the teachers who were attempting to catch them. In all schools, we caused some offence by our dress, since we had attempted to deliberately show we were not professional teachers by wearing informal dress like t-shirts and jeans. In some schools teachers thought that this was a deliberate flouting of the conventions relating to adults/teachers dress in schools.

Perhaps the common factor across all eight schools that did most to create difficulties in our relationships with teachers in the schools was our attempt to gain the trust of pupils, a problem common in delinquency research in particular (Cohen, 1955) but in educational research also (Ball, 1985). We were not participants in the schools we were attempting to describe, so could not build on the natural relationships that might exist between a teacher and his/her pupils. We were clearly by accent, demeanour and life style 'outsiders' in what was a robustly working-class school community (since only perhaps 5 or 6 per cent of pupils would have had middle-class parents, although middle-class families made up about 20 per cent of the community as a whole). We were also, unlike virtually all other sociologists of education, attempting to collect data that might well get the children into serious trouble with their parents, their teachers and the local police if it were ever to be seen by them, since in our pilot studies of our questionnaires there were pupils self-reporting their crime on a scale that was probably up to twenty or thirty times higher than the actual official crime rate for the community of Treliw. We clearly needed the children to have absolute trust in us for them to fill in their questionnaires truthfully.

All these potential problems had made the gaining of the pupils' confidence a vital issue for us. Dressing as non-authority figures was part of the solution we chose, together with the cultivation of an easy relaxed style, drinking with pupils under age in public houses and even in one school our watching idly as the pupils destroyed a car that was somewhat past its sell-by date. We also attempted to spend part of each breaktime and lunchtime in the company of pupils in the playground, rather than just sitting in the staff room or at the teachers' lunch table . The price we paid for this necessary – we thought essential – over-identification with the pupils was of course a more parlous and threatened relationship with the staff and ultimately the generation of a body of knowledge which is quite strong on elaborating 'what works' from the pupils' perspective but which lacks a clear understanding of how individual schools and their teachers create, or fail to create, an effective and successful educational setting. This bias in our knowledge base was to cost us dearly when we later came to attempt to change 'ineffective' schools by changing their organization and their staff, since the latter were to display in our later improvement studies layers of what can only be called pathology and abnormality that took us completely by surprise.

The secondary modern schools had ceased to exist by the beginning of the 1980s, resulting in a feedback stage in which project reports, book manuscripts and papers did not need to be negotiated in their content by presentation to the research sponsors. The local Director of Education and a National Union of Teachers representative read all our published reports since we had agreed to their having the right to comment, and neither required any cuts, amendments or alterations. The fact that the schools were in the process of closing had also been a particularly fortunate situation for us when the research work began to become known by local and national media, particularly after one of our first publications (Reynolds *et al.*, 1976) prompted the headline 'Schools blamed for dull pupils' at the top of the main local news page of the Welsh national morning paper. Two national papers phoned at that time to find out which were the 'good' schools mentioned in our article and to find out where they were physically located, and on being politely told that we wished to retain the schools' anonymity then proceeded to telephone the local media to try to obtain information, making it clear that they really wanted to find out where the poorly performing schools were, in order to perform an educational crucifixion on them. To this day, the anonymity originally promised to the community, the schools, the teachers and to the pupils has been maintained. Publicly, the real location of 'Treliw' is still unclear.

Our work by the early 1980s had switched to a comparison of systems of education, rather than of schools *within* a system as with our first study of secondary modern schools. In spite of the publicity and the difficulties that this had produced for professional interaction with schools, again the approval of the local authority, the teachers' unions and five schools was given and the programme of work which formed the basis for *The Comprehensive Experiment* (Reynolds *et al.*, 1987) was undertaken in the early to mid-1980s. Our methodology was again mixed, although this time our research design was much stronger since it involved the study of a cohort of pupils passing through the comprehensive and selective systems, with a full range of intake data and a full range of 'hard' outcome data, backed by my and a new colleague's observations of the school system regimes.

Embarrassingly for a believer in the value of the comprehensive system (see my chapter in Hargreaves and Reynolds, 1989), the comprehensive system performed much worse than the selective system on all our measures of effectiveness, although it was in the pupils' social outcomes that the real superiority of the selective system showed. Given that our data showed that the groups of pupils entering the systems were very similar and that the catchment areas of the two communities were socially virtually identical, differences between the systems of over 10 per cent in their average pupil attendance rates and a doubled delinquency rate in the comprehensive system by comparison with the selective system made for depressing reading. When we fitted the process data which we had obtained from the five schools to the systems, though, what became immediately apparent was that the comprehensive system was in no way organizationally comprehensive as ordinarily defined. Curriculum change in the new schools had been minimal, modification of the ability grouping system had been marginal and the schools were organizationally very much like the grammar schools of the selective system. The rules were the same, the ethos identical. They were really 'grammar schools for all' and, since they were replacing secondary modern schools which would have been less alienating for lower ability pupils, the explanation for the new comprehensives' failure with the less able and their apparent success with the more able was clear.

Our argument that the comprehensives failed not because they *were* comprehensive but because they *were not* was obviously far too subtle for the local and national media. We had deliberately placed the book on publication in the *Independent*, giving the paper an 'exclusive' in return for a promise that our arguments and data were to be reported as we had written them and not commented upon. The aim of this exercise was clearly to attempt to set the ideological framework within which the study was going to be reported and to prevent distortion of our findings by the enemies of comprehensive schools. On the day the book was published, the strategy partially worked – the local morning paper was unhelpful, with a headline about the 'shock failure of comprehensive schools' but the 'Today' radio programme, the Jimmy Young radio show, Independent Radio News and the local radio and television programmes were all ideologically sound slots for the faithful portrayal of the 'grammar schools for all' thesis.

The next day this strategy was in ruins. The *Daily Mail* and the *Daily Express* gave banner coverage and editorials to the study, explaining quite erroneously that the schools had failed because they were comprehensive, not because they were not. Our attempted answer to this coverage and our restatement of our evidence and our conclusions in the *Guardian* two weeks later may have reached the liberal heartland but did nothing to reach the educational streets populated by those fed on the diet of distortion and appalling ignorance by other newspapers.

The effects of the waves of publicity that accompanied the first and particularly the second of our research projects described above were compounded in their effects upon research relationship, built up over a decade and a half, by my involvement in a third type of educational effectiveness study, this time comparing not schools or systems of education but comparing nations in their levels of achievement. This interest had started in the early 1980s when a 'mole' in the Education Department of the Welsh Office, the administrative location of central government in Wales, had leaked to myself and a colleague some unpublished statistics on the achievement of school leavers in Wales which showed that the proportion of pupils getting no qualifications whatsoever in schools in Wales had risen to 25.8 per cent in the most recent year the data had been collected. These Welsh 'failure' rates had customarily been higher than those of England but his increase in failure rate had to be set against a decrease in the English system's failure rate for the same time period, a decrease which had been occurring consistently for a decade.

The educational system, and its practitioners in Wales, had always generated two alibis to explain these high failure rates away, and up until the early 1980s had seemingly had the power to make the explanations stick. First, it was frequently argued that the high failure rate merely showed that the public examinations of Wales were still of a high standard and that paradoxically the high failure rate showed how educated a population the Welsh children were! Second, it was sometimes argued that Wales possessed higher levels of social deprivation which were the cause of the high levels of failure among lower ability children. Two further leaked Assessment and Performance Unit (APU) reports I had been given disposed of these alibis for the failure rate for the first time. One – on mathematical achievement at 15 – showed Welsh children doing appallingly badly when the *same* tests of equal difficulty were given to them and to children elsewhere in the regions and countries of Great Britain (APU, 1982). The second report – on scientific attainment at eleven – showed that Welsh children had at age eleven the *highest* attainment of children from all regions (APU, 1983). The high levels of social deprivation could not be a factor in explaining the poor performance by Welsh 15 year olds if the 11 year old pupils had such high scores. The explanation for failure, based on the APU data, had to lie within the processes of the secondary schools.

We took the three sets of data, linked them with the data on secondary school processes which we had gained both through the field-work for the comprehensive school study and numerous other more informal visits to schools in Wales, and proceeded to publish an article integrating the data and the processes with the history of education in Wales in the *Times Educational Supplement* just before Christmas 1981 (Reynolds and Murgatroyd, 1981).

Hostile letters appeared for six weeks in the supplement, the local morning newspaper began running stories each time a new APU report appeared and I became more and more involved in the 'Welsh Education Debate' as it became called (Reynolds, 1990), a debate about the possible under-achievement of the schools of Wales and the causes for it that ran throughout the 1980s in Wales in newspaper columns, radio and television programmes and in conferences and meetings. Counting up the personal involvement in these activities when writing this chapter was instructive, since I kept a record of all press, radio and television publicity concerning the debate: in eight years there have been 65 local radio appearances, 40 press stories that I was involved in and countless talks, conferences and public meetings.

Much of my involvement in the Welsh education 'debate', and in the publicity connected with the other research projects mentioned above, had been born out of my conviction that educational research and its findings should be more widely understood by the wider population. Particularly, I had believed – and still do – in the importance of feeding back the knowledge gained from research to teachers, in the hope that they would be persuaded to modify educational practices that may be unsound and that they might be persuaded to try new, potentially more effective forms of schooling. My own unwillingness to be a teacher was born out of the absurdly messianic, rather egotistical yet probably basically accurate realisation that a sound knowledge base which influenced teacher practice would affect many more children than I could ever have hoped to reach in classrooms by being a teacher.

Yet so great had been my exposure in Wales and so great had been the exposure for views and evidence which were clearly critical of the existing Welsh educational system that many of the people on which I had relied for research access refused to further allow that access if it was to be used for what they saw as the selling short of the schools. At one of the schools that had participated in the comprehensive school study, my visit for a re-study in 1987 generated an official protest about my presence on school premises from a National Association of Schoolmasters representative. I was told informally in 1988 that the authority of Treliw would never let me in their schools again and that the teachers of the area felt betrayed.

Because of a degree of guilt about the perceived 'hatchet job' that it was believed I had made upon the quality of Welsh schools and also to see if our conclusions on effective school processes were valid, from the mid-1980s our focus changed to the study of school improvement. The application of school effectiveness by means of school improvement programmes was of course the logical next step for school effectiveness research to take and has been attempted by others such as Rutter and colleagues in Britain (Ouston and Maughan, 1990) and by several American school systems (McCormack-Larkin, 1985). The belief was that the application of factors shown to be associated with being effective within schools that were ineffective would show if there was (using the positivistic paradigm) the causal relationship between school processes and student outcomes that many of us had hypothesized and tried to describe. Even if we were unable to generate much change, I reasoned we would generate substantial increments of knowledge, since the way to understand something is to try to change it.

Our chance of trying to directly improve schools came in the mid-1980s when a local school approached us to act as 'consultants' for their proposed major organizational review. On arrival at the school for informal discussion about what could be done to help it change, it was clear that the school showed a whole variety of pathologies that we had never seen before. There were fantasies around that change was someone else's job. There were the 'cling-ons' of past practice and the belief that existing practice was immutable. There was the 'safety in numbers' ploy, whereby individuals constrained their own freedom to change by an over emphasis on the constraints of their group membership. There was a widespread fear of failure and a corresponding reluctance to risk. The schools' staff employed scapegoating and a blaming of parents and children for its own collective deficiencies. There was closed leadership and a corresponding lack of knowledge within the school about the existing management practices, let alone the alternative practices that might have been adopted. The school relied on external authorities, and had always been used to innovative suggestions arriving from influential outsiders rather than from inside. The members of staff employed a tactic known as the

'yes-buts' which involved always being ready to change and introduce new policies (the 'yes') but finding important reasons why that
should not be done (the 'buts'). The staff feared the accountability
that was in their minds associated with such processes of school
evaluation and school change – many of them had gone into
teaching wanting an autonomy that did not exist in the evaluated
professions or in industry. The school was also isolated from its
markets, since it had limited feedback from the LEA or from the local
community about the acceptability of its products. There was a fear
of being 'taken over' by outsiders (like the MSC) if they were
allowed to get too close to the school. Finally the school had a large
minority of staff who exhibited the classic symptoms of the burnout
syndrome.

Involvement in the school had started when the headteacher of
the school approached University College Cardiff for help, about
two years after his appointment. He felt there was a lack of staff
commitment to change, that the school was academically and
socially underperforming and that a school change process which
involved all staff was essential in order to ensure a high take up of
innovations (the previous headteacher had been autocratic and
'top/down' in his attempts to change the school). Stephen Murgatroyd and I were to be the schools' sociological consultants.

The consultancy process began with a meeting of all staff at
which a diagnosis was made of the educational problems which
beset Wales at the time. The school effectiveness literature's
remedies at the level of the individual school were then outlined,
following which small group sessions of all staff were held with a
follow-up, feedback session to discuss the possible school change
strategies to be followed. At this meeting, it was agreed that the two
of us were to be invited in as observers, advisors and helpers of the
schools' change attempt – to be the facilitators for the developing
ways in which the school wanted to move.

All members of staff (except a handful of the older staff) were
then involved in the process of membership of working groups
which we set up. At the same time we got directly involved with the
senior management team and advised them as 'management
advisers' about how to organize their own work, liaise with the
remainder of the staff, etc. Further details of all this work are
available elsewhere (Murgatroyd and Reynolds, 1984; Reynolds and
Murgatroyd, 1985; Reynolds, 1987). The result of our consultancy
arrangement with the school was a large volume of recommend-

ations from the staff working parties concerning curriculum modification, assessment changes, pastoral care system improvement, more open management structures and change in school ethos. A process of interaction between the working groups and the senior management team was followed by the implementation of a wide range of changes such as the introduction of the five-lesson day, changes in form tutor systems, better communication of management decisions, a changed academic organisation that strengthened the role of the department and many others. Evaluation of these changes was undertaken, results were fed back to the school through meetings of the whole staff and attempts were made to ensure that individuals and sub-groups within the school who were attempting to introduce the changes received support and further help. The entire process ran for approximately two and a half years, with a progressive distancing of our involvement in the last six months.

The benefits for the teachers in the school were in our view substantial. Many began to acquire a more positive self image, with a more potent view of themselves and their potential power to affect educational outcomes. Many learnt to work with others in groups for the first time, beginning to lose their 'individual practitioner' notions at the same time. Teachers in the school learnt to share, to show their insecurities and doubts for inspection. They learnt to take power from authority figures, since they as a group of staff actually owned the change attempt – what was called an 'outbreak of line leadership' when the staff began to take on the senior management team over such issues as the publication of minutes of the team's meetings. Teachers also started to become more active outside the school; with an increasing number beginning to work through the teacher unions the change LEA policy (as in the redeployment of teachers for example).

It must be admitted, though, that there were also costs to the process of school change by means of sociological consultancy. Because of a fundamental error whereby we let members of staff actually choose the particular working group that they joined, the working groups themselves actually magnified the initial differences between members of staff in their recommendations. The English department (probably the most radical group in the school) tended to join the curriculum working party and they generated proposals for a much greater use of CSE Mode Three in the schools, proposals which the Mathematics department (probably the least radical group) found unacceptable. This latter department had not unsurprisingly gravitated to the pupil monitoring and assessment group, where they generated policy changes that the English department regarded as ideologically very unsound!

Other problems also revealed themselves over the course of our two and a half year involvement. There were the tears, hurt and pain for individuals when closer contact with others revealed for the first time what others really thought of them. There was the personal annoyance when cherished beliefs were threatened or when others refused to countenance deeply held views about the direction that educational change should take. The senior management team itself felt threatened by the forces it perceived it had unleashed, since a revolution of rising expectations led eventually to discussion of the goals of education, however much we had tried to avoid this happening in the early stages of the consultancy. As this goal based discussion began to start, the ideological dissensus that was created (with the English department arguing for an emphasis upon social goals and the mathematics department concerned to keep only academic goals) proved to very fragmenting of the staff group. Even though we attempted to draw staff discussion back to consideration of means, not educational goals, and towards practical means of accomplishment, the ideological differentiation was not something that the senior management team had expected and was not something that had been properly worked through by the time our consultancy was coming to its end.

In the school, then, the advantages of changed teacher practice, changed school organization, very different sets of interpersonal relations and a very different staff culture must be set against some of the problems that our liaison with the school produced. As the change attempt ran on, the old certainties of the institution fell apart, and were then partly re-created around a different collection of organizational arrangements. Inevitably in this process, there were – intellectually and personally – casualties.

Not all our attempts at school development and school improvement have been as unsuccessful and fraught with problems as the consultancy described above. We have gone on to run courses to train school change-agents whose goal is the organizational development of their schools. Evaluations of the effectiveness of these programmes show that two-thirds of the teachers on the courses have generated changes in their schools and that 85 per cent of these changes have survived in a six-year follow up (Reynolds *et al.*, 1989). Overall, though, our attempts to change schools have been characterized by growing realization of the complexity of the school as an institution and of the ways in which our school effectiveness research merely described the first dimension of an institution whose second dimension is cultural and whose third dimension is concerned with interpersonal relationships and interactions.

CONCLUSIONS

Looking back upon over fifteen years of doing educational research in Treliw, what strikes me now is the extraordinary riskiness of it all, both intellectually and personally. For the group of us starting to research school effectiveness, we had no agreed methodology, no knowledge of what to measure and no more than a rudimentary knowledge of schools as social institutions derived from the sociology of education of the 1960s. At any stage, the research might have been terminated by the local authority or the sample of schools might have been attenuated by sample loss, or the whole enterprise have ceased because of media attention and controversy. The school effectiveness paradigm was an extraordinary construction made possible by a few people who played the scientific hero, voyaging in strange disciplinary territories all the while knowing the historical tendency for heroes to meet tragic ends. It was only the size of our egos that made us think that we could escape the usual fates.

The achievements of school effectiveness research undertaken in Treliw and elsewhere are clearly not inconsiderable (see Rutter *et al.*, 1979; Mortimore *et al.*, 1988; Creemers *et al.*, 1989; Reynolds, Creemers and Peters, 1989). A knowledge base of reasonable validity both within and across cultures has been created which amounts to a valuable resource for professionals to use to improve their schools. Yet the direct *application* of that knowledge into programmes of institutional development has proved to be an elusive goal for us in Treliw, as we have moved on to try and apply our knowledge of 'what works' within schools. Our stance of over-identification with, and exploration of, the pupils' culture that was characteristic of our early work hindered our knowledge of the teachers world, and the excursions into the fantasy island of the media put further barriers in place.

We have therefore researched directly over a thousand teachers and have interacted with and worked with thousands more on INSET days and at local and national meetings, yet still without realizing quite *why* they have proven so reluctant to take up the insights of effectiveness work, although it is true to say that their take-up has increased over the years judged by our own experience in South Wales. As the study of school effectiveness moves from the elaboration of what makes a 'good' school to the vexed issues of what makes schools 'good' and to the problems of how to make schools good, the egos which were necessarily possessed by those who played the scientific heros voyaging in uncharted waters are now perhaps the biggest block upon further intellectual development, since the range of temperaments and characters that have produced a degree of success in one scientific field may be very unsuited for generating success in another. Teachers need now to be understood, not just preached at by those who have possessed messianic tendencies. Those of us who research in the field of school effectiveness need now perhaps to grow, adapt and change every bit as much as the teachers at whom we have lectured for so long.

REFERENCES

Assessment of Performance Unit (1982) *Mathematical Development, Secondary Report 2*, London, HMSO.

Assessment of Performance Unit (1983)*Science in Schools, Primary Report 1*, London, HMSO.

Ball, S. (1985) 'Participant observation with pupils', in Burgess, R.G. (ed.) *Strategies of Educational Research: Qualitative Methods*, Lewes, Falmer Press.

Beynon, J. (1983) 'Ways-in and staying-in: fieldwork as problem solving' in Hammersley, M. (ed.) *The Ethnography of Schooling*, Driffield, Nafferton.

Cohen, A.K. (1955) *Delinquent Boys*, New York, Basic Books.

Creemers, B., Peters, T. and Reynolds, D. (eds) (1989) *School Effectiveness and School Improvement: Proceedings of the Second International Congress, Rotterdam, 1989*, Lisse, Swets & Zeitlinger.

Gath, D. (1977) *Child Guidance and Delinquency in a London Borough*, Oxford, Oxford University Press.

Hammersley, M. (ed.) (1983) *The Ethnography of Schooling*, Driffield, Nafferton.

Hargreaves, A. and Reynolds, D. (eds) (1989) *Education Policy: Controversies and Critiques*, Lewes, Falmer Press.

Hargreaves, D.H. (1967) *Social Relations in a Secondary School*, London, Routledge & Kegan Paul.

Lacey, C. (1970) *Hightown Grammar,* Manchester, Manchester University Press.

Murgatroyd, S.J. and Reynolds, D. (1984) 'Leadership and the teacher', in Harling, P. (ed.) *New Directions in Educational Leadership,* Lewes, Falmer Press.

Ouston, J. and Maughan, B. (1990) 'Innovation and change in secondary schools', *School Organisation and School Improvement.*

McCormack-Larkin (1985) 'Ingredients of a successful school effectiveness project', *Educational Leadership,* March, 31–7.

Mortimore, P., Sammons, P., Ecob, R. and Stoll, L. (1988) *School Matters: The Junior Years,* Salisbury, Open Books.

Power, M.J. *et al.* (1967) 'Delinquent schools', *New Society* 10, 542–3.

Power, M.J., Benn, R.T., and Morris, J.N. (1972) 'Neighbourhood, school and juveniles before the courts', *British Journal of Criminology* 12, 111–32.

Reynolds, D. *et al.* (1976) 'Schools do make a difference', *New Society,* 29 July, 223–5.

Reynolds, D. (1981) 'The naturalistic method of educational and social research – A Marxist Critique', *Interchange* 11, 4, 77–89.

Reynolds, D. (1987) 'The consultant sociologist: a method for linking sociology of education and teachers', in Woods, P. and Pollard, A. (eds) *Sociology and Teaching,* London, Croom Helm.

Reynolds, D. (1990) 'The Great Welsh Education Debate, 1980–1990', *History of Education* (in press).

Reynolds, D. and Murgatroyd, S.J. (1981) 'Schooled for failure?, *Times Educational Supplement,* 4 December.

Reynolds, D. and Murgatroyd, S.J. (1985) 'The creative consultant', *School Organisation* 4, 3, 321–35.

Reynolds, D., Creemers, B. and Peters, T. (eds) (1989) *School Effectiveness and Improvement: Proceedings of the First International Congress, London, 1988,* Groningen, University of Groningen, RION.

Reynolds, D., Davie, R., and Phillips, D. (1989) 'The Cardiff programme – an effective school improvement programme based on school effectiveness research', in Creemers, B.P.M. and Scheerens, J. (eds) *Developments in School Effectiveness Research,* (Special issue of the *International Journal of Educational Research)* 13, 7, 800–814.

Reynolds, D., Sullivan, M. and Murgatroyd, S.J. (1987) *The Comprehensive Experiment,* Lewes, Falmer Press.

Rutter, M., Maughan, B., Mortimore, P. and Ouston, J. (1979) *Fifteen Thousand Hours: Secondary Schools and their Effects on Children* Cambridge, MA, Harvard University Press.

Walford, G. (1987) 'Research role conflicts and compromises in public schools', in Walford, G. (ed.) *Doing Sociology of Education,* Lewes, Falmer Press.

11

THE FRONT PAGE OR
YESTERDAY'S NEWS

The reception of educational research

Peter Mortimore

INTRODUCTION

British educational researchers are a relatively new breed. Although there is a rich tradition of writers, like Arnold of Rugby, addressing educational ideas, it is only in the last thirty or so years that educational research – as distinct from psychological, sociological or even psychiatric studies – has been funded from public sources and that the results of studies have begun to influence what goes on in schools. (A lucid account of developments through this time can be read in Shipman, 1985). Even so, it is sometimes difficult to identify clearly what makes up an 'educational research study' and to distinguish this from similar studies carried out in the general area of the social sciences. This is because educational researchers usually have taken their degrees in other subjects and have frequently worked in different traditions. It is a strength, in my view, of education that it can draw on the methods and concepts of other disciplines and that it can adopt – as appropriate – their perspectives, paradigms and theories.

This flexibility of approach, and youthful vigour, are helpful. But perhaps less helpful is the lack of collective experience of publishing work and disseminating findings. Furthermore, because education is such an important aspect of our society – especially in current times – publishing results and disseminating findings can take place in a highly charged political atmosphere. Alternatively, findings can be ignored – hence the title.

In this chapter, I will examine the publication of the results of research. I will draw on my experience as a co-author of two major studies of school effectiveness – *Fifteen Thousand Hours*, a study of secondary schools by Rutter, Maughan, Mortimore and Ouston, published in 1979, and *School Matters,* a study of primary schools by Mortimore, Sammons, Stoll, Lewis and Ecob, published in 1988 – rather than from the general repertoire of recent educational studies.

I have chosen to focus on these studies because, as someone involved in them, I was aware of the issues raised by their publication and kept records of the newspaper coverage. Authors of other studies might have different or more interesting stories to tell. For example the first researcher into school effectiveness in the United Kingdom was Michael Power. He analysed delinquency data and endeavoured to relate these to school and area influences. The work was highly controversial and a premature letter to *The Times,* appearing to lay blame for differential delinquency rates on teachers, virtually ended the study (Power *et al.* 1967).

Likewise the media reports that followed the publication of *Teaching Styles and Pupil Progress* (Bennett, 1976), were extensive – including a prime-time television programme – and contributed to a controversy over styles of teaching. The re-analysis of the data collected for this study using more sophisticated analytical techniques and the subsequent re-interpretation of the findings (Aitkin and Bennett, 1980), in contrast, never appeared to elicit the same media response. More recently, the publication of *The School Effect,* a research study exploring the relative strengths of the influence of individual secondary schools and of the race of secondary pupils (Smith and Tomlinson, 1989), received an enormous amount of attention in the press. The scope for exploring the role of the media in relation to these studies, therefore, is considerable but will not be dealt with here.

I should also make clear that while Rutter *et al.* (1979a) and Mortimore *et al.* (1988a) received a great deal of attention, a number of other pieces of work with which I have been involved, have not. In some cases this may have been because the work was smaller-scale or inherently less interesting. In other cases, however, it is more likely that they were less politically appealing to the newspaper journalists. Thus the work evaluating support centres for disruptive pupils (Mortimore *et al.,* 1983) received only academic book reviews and no coverage in the daily press. Curiously, I have also received a lot of publicity for a study which, though planned, was never undertaken. This was to have been a study of high achieving minority pupils which, because of a fear by some communities that the results might be used as an excuse for a lack of positive action, was not executed (see discussion in Swann, 1985).

This chapter will end by listing a set of recommendations for researchers. These will include precautions to be taken before the study is planned as well as during its active life and at the crucial time of publication.

THE FIFTEEN THOUSAND HOURS RESEARCH STUDY

The idea for a study which investigated how much individual secondary schools were able to influence the achievement and development of their pupils, can be traced to earlier work carried out by Michael Rutter and various associates. In particular, it can be recognized in the seminal Isle of Wight epidemiological study (Rutter *et al.*, 1970), and the subsequent Inner London Borough comparison (Rutter *et al.*, 1975). Having explored the influence of the neighbourhood on the lives of children and their parents, it seemed natural to explore, in more detail, the impact of the school – an idea enthusiastically sponsored by a group of the local head teachers. The investment in research on a cohort of 10 year olds could be exploited by a carefully planned follow-up study of those same young people as they progressed through secondary education. The Department of Education and Science grant was agreed and the research team appointed by January 1975. By this stage Rutter and colleagues had already collected a range of follow-up measures on the (by then) 14 year olds who made up the original 10 year old sample and who had progressed to twenty secondary schools. The measures collected included tests of reading and non-verbal intelligence, teacher ratings of behaviour, and up-dated background information.

Data Collection

Between January 1975 and June 1978, the research team, of which I was a member, collected a great deal more information on 12 of the schools selected to form a representative sample. With the assurance of complete confidentiality and using a variety of research techniques including classroom observations, interviews with head teachers and teachers, and a collection of pupils' views via questionnaires administered by the researchers, we established a large pool of pupil and school measures. This pool was enhanced with supplementary material from the census (using the Office of

Population and Census Surveys/Centre for Environmental Studies classifications); records of official delinquency (we were given access to data by the Metropolitan Police Juvenile Bureau) and the public examination results of the cohort's fifth year.

The co-operation extended by the head teachers and their colleagues to the research team was quite remarkable. No school dropped out; no class teacher refused access to their classroom. Considering the difficulties experienced by secondary schools – mainly through teacher turnover – during the 1970s this was very impressive as was the interest of the twelve schools in the preliminary results presented by the research team, in each school, at the end of the study. The findings of the study, as with most large-scale empirical work, were complex (for a full account see Rutter *et al.*, 1979a) but our four major conclusions were that:

1 secondary schools varied in respect of their pupils' behaviour, attendance, exam success and delinquency. . . even after taking into account differences in intake. . .
2 variations in outcome were systematically and strongly associated with the characteristics of schools and social institutions . . .
3 the research showed *which* school variables were associated with good behaviour and attainments. . .
4 the pattern of findings suggested that not only were pupils influenced by the way they were dealt with as individuals, but also there was a group influence resulting from the ethos of the school as a social institution. (p. 205)

Impact of Publication

The results of the study were made available to all those involved in the study in the summer of 1978 and, in 1979, a book aimed at wider readership, was published by Open Books. Accompanying its launch at a press conference on Thursday, 22 March were a series of accounts and commentaries – notably by Rick Rogers in the *New Statesman* (Rogers, 1979) and Caroline St John Brooks in *New Society* (St John Brooks, 1979) and a more varied batch of newspaper articles. The newspapers comments were led by the *Observer* which broke the publisher's embargo as early as January in an article headlined 'When potted plants are better than discipline' (Stevens, 1979). This was followed by an article on 18 March by Rhodes Boyson in the *News of the World* (complete with a photograph of the

Schools' (Boyson, 1979). Whereas Rhodes Boyson had focused on the negative findings, Alan Whitehouse, writing in the *Yorkshire Post* on 21 March, highlighted more positive aspects in an article headlined 'Lessons for a Perfect School' (Whitehouse, 1979). The *Nottingham Evening Post* (22 March) chose the headline 'Education Myths are Exploded' (Bailey 1979). In the *Daily Express* of 22 March, Bruce Kemble provided a seven point practical check-list entitled 'Your Good School Guide' (Kemble, 1979).

The *Evening News* of the same day carried a series of articles by their staff reporter, Tony Doran, with a headline 'Do as I do – not as I say' (Doran, 1979). Christopher Rowlands of the *Daily Mail* chose to widen the scope of the discussion with a headline of 'Schools that harm the gifted' and an opening paragraph that stated 'Gifted children do not achieve their potential in badly organized comprehensive schools' (Rowlands, 1979).

Another local paper – the *Southend Evening Echo* picked up the story on 27 March with a curious and somewhat inaccurate headline 'Less caning does not spoil the child' (Oswick, 1979). The review in the *Teacher* – the weekly paper of the National Union of Teachers – was supportive of the research in a rather lukewarm way, as illustrated by the headline 'Secondary findings stress the obvious' (NUT, 1979). Finally, *The Economist*, for the week ending 31 March, devoted three columns to a positive review entitled, simply, 'Schools count' (*The Economist*, 1979). the *Times Educational Supplement* was unable to report on – or discuss – the study since, like all *Times* publications, due to industrial action it was not being produced at that time.

Most of the press commentary on the study dealt only with the central findings: that individual schools varied in their effects though, as has been noted, the interpretations of these findings and their implications for schools, varied widely.

The extent of the coverage was surprising – at least to the research team. In retrospect, it may not have been as helpful as it may have appeared. To have so much space in the daily newspapers devoted to research findings means that the work will be taken seriously. It also means that critics will focus on the study and, to some extent, search for any possible weaknesses which can then be exposed!

Critiques by Researchers

The second wave of commentary on the study consisted of a series of critical articles by fellow researchers. Acton (1980), Tizard (1980), Goldstein (1980) and Heath and Clifford (1980) published major critical articles on the study. The research team felt bound to respond and, accordingly, a reply to Acton was printed in the same edition of *Educational Research* (Rutter *et al.*, 1980a). Likewise, rejoinders to the comments by Tizard and by Goldstein were included in the same edition of the *Journal of Child Psychology and Psychiatry* (Rutter *et al.*, 1980b). The reply to Heath and Clifford's critique in the *Oxford Review* appeared in a later edition (vol. 6, no. 3, Maughan *et al.*, 1980) and was immediately followed by a further rejoinder (Heath and Clifford, 1981).

Two collections of discussion papers were produced as a result of symposia devoted to debate on the study: one at the Thomas Coram Research Unit – Tizard *et al.*, 1980; and one at Exeter University – Dancy, 1979. Both provided space for our responses (Rutter *et al.*, 1979b; and Mortimore, 1979).

The *British Journal of Sociology of Education* devoted twelve pages to a Review Symposium on the study. Comments were invited from three sociologists: David Reynolds, whose evaluation was mixed; Andy Hargreaves, who was rather critical; and Tessa Blackstone who, on the whole, was positive (Reynolds, *et al.*, 1980).

Academics, however, were not the only reviewers of the work. Practitioners – especially from inner London – also expressed views: Peter Newsam, then the Education Officer of the ILEA, provided a positive half-page review in the *Observer* (Newsam, 1979); Trevor Jagger, then the Staff Inspector for secondary education in the ILEA, published a long and highly supportive review in *Education* (Jagger, 1979); Marten Shipman, the ex-Director of Research and Statistics in the ILEA, wrote a very positive review in *Research in Education* (Shipman, 1980).

As if all this was not enough, during 1980, *Education*, the *Times Educational Supplement* (now back in print) and the *Education Guardian* each decided to give space to a second look at the study. *Education* published a page article by Ted Wragg in which he summarized the arguments expressed at the Exeter Symposium (Wragg, 1980). In an article entitled 'Second thoughts on the Rutter ethos' in the *Times Educational Supplement*, Bob Doe also drew on the Exeter publication to summarize criticisms and replies (Doe,

1980). In the *Education Guardian*, Maureen O'Connor, in a delightfully headlined article – 'Fifteen thousand hours that shook the academics – drew on Goldstein's, Heath and Clifford's, Thomas Coram's and Acton's critiques and the responses to these (O'Connor, 1980).

In this chapter I am ignoring the equally numerous reviews and articles that appeared in American papers and journals. The fact that a British book received so much attention in the United States is unusual and, on the whole, comment by academics was more uniformly positive than in the United Kingdom. The most critical review carried in the organ of the American Educational Research Association – *The Educational Researcher* (Armato, 1980), was itself severely criticized by two other academics for its negative tone in a subsequent edition (Owens, 1981 and Gideanse, 1981).

Conclusions re the publication of *Fifteen Thousand Hours*

My aim in documenting all this material is certainly not to re-open these debates, but to illustrate what researchers can provoke when they publish their work! My personal view is that while some of the technical criticisms were justified – which research study could not be improved with hindsight – the enthusiasm with which such criticism was given was possibly a reaction to the positive press comments. It was probably fuelled by a variety of motivations, from the political to the personal. Looking back, more than ten years after publication, I consider that the book – and the study and reports – have stood up well to the tests of time. It was an ambitious study – probably attempting to solve statistical problems before appropriate methods and computer software had been developed – but certainly a worthwhile endeavour. *Fifteen Thousand Hours* has been cited a great deal in both the British and the North American educational literature and has been widely adopted by practitioners – at home and abroad – anxious to participate in school improvement work.

What then was the effect of the press coverage? In retrospect I think there were two main effects: one negative and one positive. The negative effect was that the complex findings of the study were trivialized and some journalists and other commentators seized the opportunity to claim support for their particular hobby horses – regardless of whether, in fact, the data lent any support to their cause. The positive effect was that a number of headteachers, teachers and inspectors/advisers were alerted to the study. The sales figures for the period indicate that many readers purchased copies. In a country where there was not a strong tradition of practitioners studying the results of educational research, this was very encouraging to us.

THE SCHOOL MATTERS RESEARCH STUDY

The study reported in School Matters – the Inner London Education Authority Junior School Project – stemmed directly from the research debates resulting from the publication of Fifteen Thousand Hours. The attraction of planning a study that could take advantage of the results of the methodological debate and emerging new methods of statistical analysis such as probabilistic cluster analysis and multi-level modelling was considerable and was discussed at the 1980 British Educational Research Association. The opportunity arose within the ILEA when – as recently appointed Director of Research and Statistics – I was able to plan the future research programme for the Authority. With support from the ILEA inspectors and senior officers, and from the then Education Officer and Chair of the Schools Sub-Committee, a longitudinal study – of two years in the first instance – was funded and undertaken.

The formal aims of the study were to:

1 produce a detailed description of pupils and teachers and of the organization and curriculum of schools;
2 document the progress and development of 2000 pupils;
3 establish whether some schools were more effective than others in providing learning and development, once account had been taken of variations in the characteristics of pupils;
4 investigate differences in the progress of different groups of pupils.

The study, in the event, ran for four years and was thus able to follow the cohort through the whole of their junior schooling. A related study – the Secondary Transfer Study – then exploited the data and studied the same cohort as they transferred from primary to secondary schools. (This was too good an opportunity to miss for carrying out a prospective study. Pupils, teachers and parents were interviewed *before* and *after* transfer, and comparisons drawn – see Alston, 1988, for full details).

Like the earlier study, confidentiality was assured to participants and a variety of research techniques were drawn upon: classroom *observations* – using the methodology created for Leicester University's Oracle Study was undertaken; interviews and questionnaires were used for teachers and pupils and – with the help of a special grant from the Leverhulme Foundation – home interviews with parents were carried out with interviewers speaking the language of the family.

Despite the difficulties facing schools in the early 1980s, the demands of the field-work were tolerated by the heads and teachers in the 50 schools of the sample. In the whole of the four-year time-span the research team was involved with field-work, only one headteacher found the demands so great that the school was withdrawn from the study. The reasons for this goodwill to the research are probably many but three, especially, seem important.

First, the heads and teachers accepted that the aims of the study were worthwhile (we had invested a great deal of time briefing heads with information about the proposed study and had visited each school prior to its start). Second, the project team was very fortunate in its staffing. We had been allocated four Field Officer posts for seconded teachers by the Authority and, without exception, over the four years we had attracted excellent experienced primary teachers to work in these roles. In fact, only one Field Officer stayed with the project for its duration; others moved on and needed to be replaced. This change of personnel during a project could have been disruptive but, in the event proved beneficial by ensuring that our links to current classroom practice remained active.

The third possible reason for the schools' co-operation was the policy of the research team of keeping heads and teachers informed about the progress of the study and about any new demands that we were likely to make. Thus we provided a regular bulletin which summarized all the research activity that had taken place that term and laid out our plans for the next term's collection of data.

Nevertheless despite the co-operation given to the research team, the period 1980–84 was an eventful one for the sample schools. In fact, we maintained a register of interruptions to each of the schools over this time. The result for many schools was a daunting list ranging from temporary closure due to emergency building work to – in some cases – an almost complete change to staff. It was during this time that the Brixton street disturbances took place though, as was noted at the time, the amount of damage inflicted on schools was minimal. Much more serious interruptions to the school life were caused by staff and especially, headteacher changes. The following extract from *School Matters* reports an extreme case that illustrates the lack of stability that can occur in some schools:

> the Deputy Head went on maternity leave and an acting Deputy was appointed during the first year of the study. In the second year, in this school, the Head Teacher left and was replaced, in an acting capacity by the original Deputy, who later became Head Teacher. An acting Deputy Head was appointed during this period but was replaced in the third year by a permanent Deputy. Therefore, two Heads and three Deputies or acting Deputies were in place over two and a half years! (Mortimore *et al.*, 1988a).

The progress of the study was also reported to the research community in a Symposium at the 1983 Conference of the British Educational Research Association (BERA) and in an introductory publication (Mortimore *et al.*, 1984). Further progress reports were presented at subsequent BERA conferences and at the first meeting of the International Congress of School Effectiveness held in London in 1988. A final progress report was presented at a series of local meetings for the head teachers and the staff of the sample schools.

The Main Findings

As with the earlier case study, the findings of the research were complex. Our interpretations of those findings are reported in various places: in the summary report (Mortimore *et al.*, 1986a) and in the four project reports – including the technical appendices – published by the ILEA (Mortimore *et al.*, 1986b) as well as in the book *School Matters* (Mortimore *et al.*, 1988a) produced for more general readership. In addition, some of the statistical issues are discussed in more detail in a journal article in *Research Papers in Education* (Mortimore *et al.*, 1988b). In terms of the four principal aims listed earlier:

1 we endeavoured to produce a detailed account of the life of urban primary school focusing, in turn, on the head teachers and deputies, teachers and pupils and we attempted to describe the organization of schools and of the curriculum not only as it was planned, but also how it was experienced by pupils;

2 we documented the progress of the targeted cohort through the four years of junior schools (and into secondary schools);

3 we showed that schools varied considerably in their effectiveness with some appearing to enhance pupils cognitive and non-cognitive progress and development far more than others even when initial intake differences to the schools had been taken into account;

4 finally, unlike some other research studies (e.g. Nuttall *et al.*, 1989), we found that schools that were more effective benefited all groups of pupils, though not necessarily to the same degree.

Reactions to the Study

The research findings were written up in a formal report to the 17 April 1986 meeting of the Schools Sub-Committee of the ILEA. Prior to this, a press conference was called by the Leader of the Authority on 14 April and journalists were briefed on the overall findings. Due to the recent industrial action, and the general newsworthiness of the Authority the press reaction to the research was partly overshadowed by the political context in which the study was presented.

On the day following the press conference, John Izbicki, of the *Daily Telegraph,* published an article in which he claimed our findings were 'contrary to the claims of so-called progressive educationalists' (Izbicki 1986). Walter Ellis, in the *Financial Times*, provided a short summary which included several quotations from the Leader of the Authority (Ellis, 1986). Sarah Boseley of the *Guardian* picked our several of the key findings of the study, but the headline carried was 'Traditional teaching values vindicated by ILEA study into pupils' achievement' (Boseley, 1986).

The *Evening Standard* carried two separate pieces by its Education Reporter David Shaw. One listed the twelve key factors identified by the research.

The other carried a story that 'education chiefs are planning a purge to improve primary school students in the wake of a 4-year research study' (Shaw, 1986). A similar story – reacting to a comment made at the Press Conference – was carried in the *Daily Express* with a punchy opening statement: 'The one-time trendy lefty leader of Britain's biggest schools' authority yesterday called for a return to basic 'three R's' teaching for primary pupils' (Wood, 1986). The same sentiment was echoed in its leader column. Similarly, the *Daily Mail* assured readers that the Authority 'is moving to ensure that youngsters in its primary schools once more get a grounding in basic learning' (Rowlands, 1986). The *Sun* was content with two paragraphs under the heading 'Poor Schools get a caning'. *The Times*, too, focused mostly on the comments of the Leader of the Authority but added a brief comment on two of the twelve key factors included in the study's report.

More serious comment was provided by the *Times Educational Supplement*. This devoted a page to a summary of the report, with only one column on Press Conference matters. The main leading article related the findings of the study to American research and to those of *Fifteen Thousand Hours* (TES, 1986). *Education*, devoted its 'document of the week' page to the study and provided a helpful quick summary *(Education*, 1986). *New Society* carried a two-column article relating the findings to discussion of *Fifteen Thousand Hours* and commenting on the statistical methodology used *(New Society*, 1986).

The danger of misleading headlines was well illustrated by a follow-up article by John Marks in the *Daily Mail* of 22 March entitled 'I expose the alibi of our failure schools'. In a wide-ranging whole-page article he cited two of the findings and added – with no relevance to the citations – 'many schools – both primary and comprehensive are also failing their pupils through politically motivated teaching' (Marks, 1986).

The March edition of *Good Housekeeping* contained a more factual article by Angela Neustatter. This discussed, in some detail, the findings of the study and sought to relate these to a particular London school (Neustatter, 1986). The July edition of *Junior Education* also carried a one-page summary of the study (Junior Education, 1986).

However, controversy returned with an article by John Clare published in the *Listener* of 31 July, 1986. In this article, Clare argued that 'progressive ideas' hindered the teaching of working- class pupils. He also used it to mount a personal attack on an educational statistician. Support for these somewhat different points was ostensibly culled from the findings of the Junior School Project and from the recently published Brent Enquiry (Clare, 1986). The succeeding edition of the *Listener* carried criticisms of Clare's arguments in the form of letters from a current and an ex-headteacher.

Finally, the third report from the Education, Science and Arts Select Committee referred on a number of occasions, to findings from the Junior School Project and related these to other published work concerned with primary education (House of Commons, 1986).

The report of the project was thus cited by journalists in support of a number of different arguments. There was very little serious analysis of its findings or even of its implications for schools. Whilst it is unrealistic, perhaps, to expect journalists writing for lay audiences to question the validity or reliability of findings, it is regrettable that only superficial accounts of a detailed study should be disseminated. However, it is only fair to point out that the summaries in *Education, Junior Education* and the *Times Educational Supplement* were accurate and provided basic information about the study. In this particular case, the Press Conference was probably unhelpful to the study, focusing attention more on political than on educational concerns.

Translation to book form

The work of the Project had thus been reported to its funding body (the ILEA), and details had been made available to the research community and to the media. There remained the task of converting a lengthy, and necessarily technical, report into a book suitable for a wider readership of practitioners. In particular, we were hoping to write something which would have been of interest to teachers, headteachers, advisers and inspectors as well as to education officers. As so often happens in such cases, however, all the research team had by this time moved on to other jobs and the task of re-writing and editing had to be undertaken in evening and weekend slots. Saturday morning breakfast meetings were used by the team to reach agreement on points of interpretation. Because of the pressure of other commitments, the manuscript was not ready until the autumn of 1987 and the book finally appeared on 24 March 1988.

Reaction to the publication of the book

Because of the earlier exposure of the Study's findings in 1986, the book was launched on Thursday, 24 March without a press conference and with relatively little expectation of media interest. Nevertheless, a number of comments about the book did appear in the media.

Curiously, the first comment preceded publication day and was not directly about the book but referred to a forthcoming article by the research team (Gow, 1988). This article (Mortimore *et al.*, 1988b) was mainly technical and dealt with different methods of analysis adopted in the Study. (See also the subsequent criticisms of this, Preece, 1988, and our riposte, Mortimore *et al.*, 1988c.) However, because of the sensational and misleading headline in the *Guardian* piece 'ILEA survey down grades social factors in pupil attainment', a letter of response, which attempted to sort our differences between attainment and progress, was immediately despatched to the *Guardian* (Mortimore and Sammons 1988).

The next comment – also prior to publication day – appeared in the *Evening Standard* on 14 March. Bruce Kemble (who had reported on *Fifteen Thousand Hours* for the *Daily Express*) provided a two-page fairly detailed summary complete with suitable quotations. Together with this article, Kemble listed a checklist for a 'Good junior school'. This had a scale of 1–15 and according to Kemble, a score of 9–12 indicated 'a good school' (Kemble, 1988).

The *Sunday Times* carried a thoughtful comment with quotations from eminent educationalists on the Sunday before publication day. This was written by Caroline St John Brooks, who had earlier provided a very clear summary of *Fifteen Thousand Hours* for *New Society* (St John Brooks, 1988a).

The *Daily Mail* also included six paragraphs on the study before publication day. These paragraphs were embedded in the text of an article about the pressure from right wing educationalists being mounted on the Secretary of State. The reporting of findings was reasonably accurate though the context may have been puzzling for some readers (Bates, 1988). The *Evening Standard* of the same day also ran a short leader on 'Social Classes' in which the Study was cited as supporting the notion of independent assessment through-out pupils' schooling (a point specifically discussed and rejected in the final chapter of School Matters (*Evening Standard*, 1988).

Perhaps the most thoughtful commentary on the book was published in the *Independent* on the day of publication – 24 March. In this article, the Education Editor, Peter Wilby, located the central findings of the study within the context of educational debate on the influence of homes and schools. He also used the book's comments on progress to advise the Prime Minister on how testing for progress would be far more sensible than testing for attainment (Wilby, 1988).

The *Times Educational Supplement* provided extensive coverage of the book on the day following publication. As well as an article commenting on the study and noting that plans to abolish the ILEA would prevent a longer term follow-up of the pupils at the end of their secondary schooling (Bayliss, 1988), and a personal column by Anne Sofer recalling that, while ILEA Chair of the Schools Sub-committee in 1979, she had agreed funding for the study (Sofer, 1988), three full pages were devoted to it. The first page contained articles which both described and criticized the research. These were written by the head of a Birmingham junior school (Winkley, 1988) and the Professor of Primary Education at Exeter University (Bennett, 1988). The second and third pages of the TES were devoted to an investigation, by one of the paper's reporters, of schools chosen to illustrate the project's findings. This included a description of two London primary schools chosen by the reporter because one appeared to possess the factors identified by *School Matters,* while the other did not (Hagedorn, 1988). There was also a further Document of the Week devoted to the study in *Education* the day after publication (*Education,* 1988).

A follow-up to publication appeared in the *Sunday Times* of 27 March in the form of an interview with me in which I tried to relate the findings to previous research and to the current situation facing teachers (St John Brooks, 1988b). A postscript to the *Sunday Times* coverage came in the form of a letter from Jakarta published on 10 April in which I was firmly taken to task for my comments in the interview that the research had found no support for rote learning and streaming. According to the letter, 'such views were not in line with employers, parents or even children' (Ishewood, 1988).

Further interviews were reported in two Ontario papers – the *Toronto Star* and the *Burlington Spectator* (Contenta, 1988; and Porter, 1988). In both cases these were stimulated by local conferences and sought to relate the research findings to the situations in Canadian schools.

A whole page article later appeared in the May edition of *The Teacher.* In this article, the Principal Officer with research brief provided a detailed commentary on the research and discussed it in relation to the reporting of the tabloid press. In comparison to the review of *Fifteen Thousand Hours* ten years before, the Union review was far more supportive of research (Barber, 1988). Similarly the largest American teacher union, the National Educational Association (NEA), published a positive review of the study in its

February edition of the Union paper (Needham, 1988). A full two-page article also appeared in the June edition of the *School Governor* (Taylor, 1988). From slightly further afield, the *New Zealand Herald*, in November, published a half page article on schools and the issue of parental choice. Embedded in this article was a detailed summary of School Matters together with a discussion of its implications for the New Zealand situation (Guy, 1988).

Critiques by fellow researchers

As may be expected, the more detailed and, in some cases, more critical comments came in the form of book reviews in academic journals. These included the review in the *Oxford Review* (Galton, 1988); the *British Educational Research Journal* (Davies, 1988); *Forum* (Simon, 1988); *Educational Research* (Boydell, 1988); and the *British Journal of Educational Psychology* (McNamara, 1988).

The most critical of these reviews was McNamara's. This was the only review that the research team felt deserved a ripost–mainly because the critic appeared to be unaware of the many related publications of the study and accused us of producing something that was data-free! Unfortunately, the *British Journal of Educational Psychology* policy was not to permit dialogue and therefore, would not publish our carefully drafted response, thus cutting off what might have developed into a fruitful debate (Mortimore *et al.*, 1989). Shortly after this, a long and critical review – not of School Matters per se – but of almost all research studies about school effectiveness appeared in *Research Studies in Education* (Preece, 1989).

Issues arising from press and journal comment

For research teams, interest in published work is always double edged. On the one hand, it is gratifying to have notice taken of one's work by the media. If findings make a contribution to the public discussion of educational issues this can be very satisfying. On the other hand , however carefully writers present their data, if it is given sensational or politically-biased interpretation, this is very distressing. Such coverage, in the media, also influences the way academics respond to the study and, as was seen with the *Fifteen Thousand Hours* study, encourages some reviewers to blame the research team for the biased reporting.

A problem for researchers concerns the audience to be targeted and the choice of the most appropriate publishing channel to be adopted. Fellow researchers will expect to hear of results through scientific journals; practitioners will look for useful summaries in the trade press; students, teachers updating their qualifications, and interested parents and other lay people will require a book. *Fifteen Thousand Hours* was reported through seminars for those involved, in the ILEA's House Journal, and in the book form.

School Matters, nearly ten years later, was reported through seminars, in the range of newly established ILEA House Papers – for teachers, parents and governors – through a series of journal articles (*Forum,* 1987/88) and a separate technical publication, as well as through the ILEA Reports and, finally, the book. In this way we attempted to write in the appropriate style, with the correct level of technical detail for the various audiences. Sometimes, as noted earlier, this policy fails as when a reviewer of a *general* publication criticises the lack of *technical* details.

A more fundamental problem is how best to present research data. Thankfully, the International Statistical Institute (ISI) has produced a code of ethics which has been widely discussed by statisticians and others with an interest in ethical aspects of research (Sammons, 1989). This code, and publications by the Radical Statistics Group (RSG, 1982), provide guidance to researchers on how best to present and process data and on the principles which need to be followed if statistics are to clarify rather than obscure relationships between variables.

It is obvious that criticism of published work is essential. It is only through criticism that work is improved, even though there is a danger that well-publicised disagreements may reduce public confidence in the value of research. Whether this risk can be reduced in any way is doubtful – given the situation in this country. In other countries, there is a sharper distinction between the popular press and academic journals than in the UK and academic disputes, therefore, may be carried out in a private rather than the public domain. However, in the UK, where publications such as the *Times Educational Supplement* and *Education* flourish, there is likely to be a blurring of this distinction, particularly as so many practitioners and academic researchers read these publications.

While the existence of this 'trade press' is a cause for celebration, it also increases the likelihood of researchers being involved in controversy when they publish their work. Such an experience can be very off-putting. Press conferences can be daunting and radio or television interviews frightening. What steps can be taken to maximize the chance of getting a fair hearing?

One obvious step is for the research team to build in regular meetings with a support group which can be used as a sounding board. Paradoxically, it is within such a supportive context that strong criticisms can best be made. If the research team gain the experience of having to respond to challenges in this way, then they gain the opportunity to build up the skills necessary to defend their work in the more public arenas occupied by the mass media.

In both the studies considered in this chapter such support groups were available. In the case of the *Fifteen Thousand Hours* study, it consisted of a group of primary and secondary head teachers together with the local education officer and inspector. For the *School Matters* study, it was the School Differences Research Group that had been established and supported under the auspices of the Association for Child Psychology and Psychiatry that provided the necessary support and criticisms.

What then are the lessons that can be learned from these case studies? The general lessons for good research, perhaps, are obvious: sound preparation; methodical work; statistical caution; careful interpretation and simple jargon-free writing! Some of the specific lessons of how best to deal with media attention to research findings are also obvious; others are less so.

The following list of recommendations has been compiled after my experience of 'publications' in order to assist researchers to deal with these issues. There are probably many other ways researchers could prepare for publication but this list identifies a number of actions that are possible and may be helpful.

As will be clear, the actions contained in the list cannot all be dealt with in the weeks before publication: some need to be considered even before the start of the study, and others are best dealt with during the course of its progress.

Recommendations

1 Before committing oneself to the study, invest time in thinking about the area and its key issues. Try to gauge how sensitive an area it is and how strongly people feel about the issues.

2 Think through possible results for your study: is it likely that clear answers will emerge? If clear answers were to emerge would they be likely to cause a furore? Would they be likely to offend a particular group in society?

3 If your planned study is likely to lead to controversy decide if you have the temperament to cope with it: seeing your name in the papers can be stressful, especially when it is the subject of a vitriolic or personalized attack.

4 During the planning of the study set out clear aims and provide a simple statement of how these are to be achieved. Have copies available to give to people who show an interest in the study.

5 During the course of your work consult with those who believe they have a right to be involved. You clearly cannot see everyone and will need to chose carefully those who are representative and sometimes, those who are powerful. Use an advisory group to sound out ideas and to give you warnings of potential problems. If at all possible, consult with other researchers at the key stages of your work and, especially, when crucial decisions over field-work or methods of analysis are about to be taken. For this reason, it is very helpful to provide progress reports at conferences or in preliminary papers. These can provide a vehicle for discussion with others working in similarly fields and also serve to advise the research community as to your future findings.

6 Always take criticisms of the study received through these mechanisms seriously. Use your advisory group to discuss whether you need to modify your programme, or whether you should keep your nerve and continue. Pay adequate attention to the validity and reliability of any measures collected and of any statistics being used. Refer to the ISI code.

7 Keep all those participating in the study informed of what you are going to do next. Never trick or deceive your respondents. Recognize their privacy and their rights.

8 At the time of publication write as clearly as possible and use data and statistics only to clarify your findings. Try out drafts on your advisory group and remember you will have to write for different audiences who will need different formats and styles. Ensure that you are prepared to stand by what you claim.

9 Brief journalists *before* publication. It has to be realised, however, that it is difficult to accommodate them with their different publication deadlines. If you go for the *Times*

Educational Supplement your press conference will have to be on a Monday or Tuesday; if you go for the Sunday papers – their circulations are large – then you have to choose a different day.

10 Prepare for possible controversy ahead of time (although you may still be surprised at what does turn out to be controversial). Make sure your arguments are marshalled and rehearsed – again use your advisory group to play the devil's advocate. In any arguments in the public forum always remain polite – whatever you are feeling. Nothing dispels an aggressive question as much as a polite answer. Always be sensitive and considerate to any parties who come out of the study badly. Whenever possible accentuate the positive and thank your respondents for their time and trouble.

These ten points might not prevent your work from being mis-interpreted in the press; they might not protect you from the experience of controversy, but they may aid you by ensuring that you are better prepared to deal with it.

REFERENCES

Acton, T. (1980) 'Educational criteria of success: some problems in the work of Rutter, Maughan, Mortimore and Ouston', *Educational Research* 22, 163–9.

Aitkin, M. and Bennett, T.N. (1980) 'A theoretical and practical investigation into the analysis of change in classroom based research', final report to the SSRC for Grant No. HR5710.

Alston, C. (1988) *Secondary Transfer Project Bulletin 17 Improving Secondary Transfer*, London, ILEA.

Armato, B.J. (1980) '*Fifteen Thousand Hours:* a review', Educational Researcher, September.

Bailey, R. (1979) 'Education myths are exploded', *Nottingham Evening Post*, 22 March.

Barber, M. (1988) 'What makes a good school', *Teacher,* 23 May.

Bates, S (1988) 'Right wingers set out to teach Baker a lesson', *Daily Mail,* 21 March.

Bayliss, S. (1988) 'Vital research threatened by plan to abolish ILEA', *Times Educational Supplement,* 25 March.

Bennett, N. (1976) *Teaching Styles and Pupil Progress*, London, Open Books.

Bennett, N. (1988) 'What about the teaching?' *Times Educational Supplement,* 25 February.

Boseley, S. (1986) 'Traditional teaching values vindicated by ILEA study into pupils' achievement', *Guardian*, 15 April.

Boydell, D. (1988) 'Review of *School Matters: The Junior Years*', Educational Research 30, 3, 235–6.

Boyson, R. (1979) 'Secret shame of Britain's schools', *News of the World*, 18 March.

Clare J. (1986) 'Schools of scandal', *Listener*, 31 July.

Contenta, S. (1988) 'Putting schools to the test: a simple 12-question quiz', *Toronto Star*, 16 April.

Dancy, J. (1979) '*Fifteen Thousand Hours*: a discussion', *Perspectives* 1, Exeter University.

Davies, J. (1988) 'Review of *School Matters: The Junior Years*', British Educational Research Journal 15, 1, 95–6.

Doe, B. (1980) 'Second thoughts on the Rutter ethos', *Times Educational Supplement*, 13 June.

Doran, A. (1979) 'Do as I do – not as I say', *Evening News*, 22 March.

Economist (1979) 'Schools count', *The Economist*, 31 March.

Education (1986) 'Document of the week: ILEA primary progress', *Education*, 18 April.

Education (1988) 'Document of the week: what a good school can do', *Education*, 25 March.

Ellis, W. (1986) 'Importance of primary education underlined', *Financial Times*, 15 April.

Evening Standard (1988) 'Social class', *Evening Standard*, 21 March.

Forum (1987/88) Articles in Vol. 29 and 30 on the Junior School Study.

Galton, M. (1988) 'Writing effectively about school effectiveness', *Oxford Review of Education* 14, 3, pp.377–9.

Gideanse, H.D. (1981) Letter to Editor, *Educational Researcher*, January.

Goldstein, H. (1980) '*Fifteen Thousand Hours*: a review of the statistical procedures' *Journal of Child Psychology and Psychiatry* 21, 4, 364–6.

Gow, D. (1988) 'ILEA survey downgrades social factors in pupil attainment', *Guardian*, 23 February.

Guy, C. (1988) 'Best school formula is a tough equation', *New Zealand Herald*, 29 November.

Hagedorn, J. (1988) 'Great expectations', *Times Educational Supplement*, 25 March.

Heath, A. and Clifford, P. (1980) 'The seventy thousand hours that Rutter left out', *Oxford Review of Education* 6, 1, 3–19.

Heath, A. and Clifford, P. (1981) 'The measurement and explanation of school differences', *Oxford Review of Education* 7, 1, 33–40.

House of Commons (1986) 'Third Report from the Education, Science and Arts Committee', *Achievement in Primary Schools*, London, HMSO.

Ishewood, J. (1988) 'Viewpoint', *Sunday Times*, 10 April.

Izbicki, J. (1986) 'Best schools give priority to 3R's', *Daily Telegraph*, 15 April.

Jaggar, T. (1979) 'The school factor,' *Education*, 25 May.

Junior Education (1986) 'Effective schools', *Junior Education* 10, 7, July.

Kemble, B. (1979) 'Your good school guide', *Daily Express*, 22 March.

Kemble, B. (1988) 'The school matters – official', *Evening Standard*, 14 March.

Marks, J. (1986) 'I explore the alibi of our failure schools,' *Daily Mail*, 22 April.

Maughan, B., Mortimore, P., Ouston, J. and Rutter, M. (1980) '*Fifteen Thousand Hours*: a reply to Heath and Clifford', *Oxford Review of Education* 6, 3, 289–303.

McNamara, D. (1988) 'Do the grounds for claiming that school matters, matter?', *British Journal of Educational Psychology* 58, 3, 356–60.

Mortimore, P. (1979) 'The Study of secondary schools: a researcher's reply', *Perspectives* 1, Exeter University.

Mortimore, P., Davies, J., Varlaam, A. and West, A. (1983) *Behaviour Problems in Schools: An Evaluation of Support Centres*, London, Croom Helm.

Mortimore, P., Sammons, P., Stoll, L., Lewis, D. and Ecob, R. (1984) 'The ILEA Junior School Project: an introduction' in D. Reynolds (ed.) *School Effectiveness*, Lewes, Falmer.

Mortimore, P., Sammons, P., Stoll, L., Lewis, D. and Ecob, R. (1986a) *The ILEA Junior School Project: The Summary Report*, Research and Statistics Branch, London, ILEA.

Mortimore, P., Sammons, P., Stoll, L., Lewis, D. and Ecob, R. (1986b) *The ILEA Junior School Project: Main Report Parts A, B, C and Technical Appendices*, Research and Statistics Branch, London, ILEA.

Mortimore, P., Sammons, P., Stoll, L., Lewis, D. and Ecob, R. (1988a) *School Matters: The Junior Years*, Wells, Open Books.

Mortimore, P., Sammons, P., Stoll, L., Lewis, D. and Ecob, R. (1988b) 'The effects of school membership on pupils' educational outcomes', *Research Papers in Education* 3, 1, 3–26.

Mortimore, P., Sammons, P., and Ecob, R. (1988c) 'Expressing the magnitude of school effects – a reply to Peter Preece', *Research Papers in Education* 3, 2, 99–101.

Mortimore, P., Sammons, P., Stoll, L., Lewis, D. and Ecob, R. (1989) 'A Response to McNamara's Essay Review, (unpublished).

Mortimore, P. and Sammons, P. (1988) 'Snapshots of a pupil's path to progress', *Guardian*, 24 February.

Needham, N. (1988) 'What makes good schools (surprise!)', *National Education Association* (NEA) Today, February 1989, 17.

Newsam, P. (1979) 'Teacher knows best after all', *Observer*, 25 March.

Neustatter, A. (1986) 'What makes a good school' *Good Housekeeping*, March.

New Society (1986) 'Could do better', *New Society*, 18 April.

NUT (1979) 'Secondary findings stress the obvious', *The Teacher* 30, March.

Nuttall, D.L., Goldstein, H., Prosser, R. and Rasbasm, J. (1989) 'Differential school effectiveness', *International Journal of Educational Research* 13, 7.

O'Connor, M. (1980) 'Fifteen thousand hours that shook the academics', *Education Guardian*, 22 July.

Oswick, C. (1979) 'Less caning does not spoil the child', *Southend Evening Echo*, 27 March.

Owens, R.G. (1981) 'Letter to the Editor', *Educational Researcher*, January.

Porter, B. (1988) 'Effective schools make a big difference', *Burlington Spectator*, 4 May.

Power, M., Alderson, M., Phillipson, C., Schoenberg, E. and Morris, J. (1967) 'Delinquent schools?', *New Society* 10, 542–3.

Preece, P. (1988) 'Misleading ways of expressing the magnitude of school effects', *Research Papers in Education* 3, 2, 97–8.

Preece, P. (1989) 'Pitfalls in research on school and teacher effectiveness', *Research Papers in Education* 4, 3, 48–69.

Radical Statistics Education Group (1982) *Reading Between the Numbers: A Critical Guide to Educational Research*, London, BSSRS.

Reynolds, D., Hargreaves, A. and Blackstone, T. (1980) '*Fifteen Thousand Hours*: a review symposium', *British Journal of Sociology of Education* 1, 2, 207–219.

Rogers, R. (1979) 'How good schools can change children', *New Statesman*, 23 March.

Rowlands, C. (1979) 'Schools that harm the gifted', *Daily Mail*, 22 March.

Rowlands, C. (1986) 'School chiefs back return to three Rs', *Daily Mail*, 15 April.

Rutter, M., Tizard, J. and Whitmore, K. (eds) (1970) *Education, Health and Behaviour*, London, Longman.

Rutter, M., Cox, A., Tupling, C., Berger, M. and Yule, W. (1975) 'Attainment and adjustment in two geographical areas', *British Journal of Psychiatry* 126, 493–509.

Rutter, M., Maughan, B., Mortimore, P. and Ouston, J. (1979a) *Fifteen Thousand Hours*, London, Open Books.

Rutter, M., Maughan, B., Mortimore, P. and Ouston, J. (1979b) '*Fifteen Thousand Hours*: school influences on pupil progress: research strategies and tactics', *Journal of Child Psychology and Psychiatry* 2, 4, 366–8.

Rutter, M., Maughan, B., Mortimore, P. and Ouston, J. (1980a) 'Educational criterion of success: a reply to Acton', *Educational Research* 22, 3, 170–4.

Rutter, M., Maughan, B., Mortimore, P. and Ouston, J. (1980b) 'The reseachers response', *Bedford Way Papers* 1, London, University of London Institute of Education.

Sammons, P. (1989) 'Ethical issues and statistical work', in Burgess, R., *Ethics of Educational Research*, Lewes, Falmer.

Shaw, D. (1986) 'Purge on schools, the ABC of good teaching', *Evening Standard*, 14 April.

Shipman, M. (1980) '*Fifteen Thousand Hours*: a review article', *Research in Education*', May.

Shipman, M. (1985) 'Developments in educational research', in Shipman,

M. (ed.) *Educational Research: Principles, Policies and Practices*, Lewes, Falmer.

Simon, B. (1988) Research Report, *Forum*, Summer.

Smith, D. and Tomlinson, S. (1989) *The School Effect: a Study of Multi-racial Comprehensives*, London, Policy Studies Institute.

Sofer, A. (1988) 'Matter of facts' *Times Educational Supplement*, 25 March.

Stevens, A. (1979) 'When potted plants are better than discipline', *Observer*, 7 January.

St John Brooks, C. (1979) '*Fifteen Thousand Hours' (review)*, *New Society* 20, 493–4.

St John Brooks, C. (1988a) 'Quality of school lessons the effect of class,' *Sunday Times*, 20 March.

St John Brooks, C. (1988b) 'Shedding light and optimism on the class of the future', *Sunday Times*, 27 March.

Swann Report (1985), *Education for All: The Report of the Committee of Inquiry into the Education of Children from Ethnic Minority Groups'*, London, HMSO.

Taylor, F. (1988) 'What makes good schools?', *School Governor*, June.

Times Educational Supplement (1986) Leader and articles by Sarah Bayliss, *Times Educational Supplement*, 18 April.

Tizard, B. (1980) '*Fifteen Thousand Hours*: a review', *Journal of Child Psychology and Psychiatry* 21, 4, 363–4.

Tizard, B., Burgess, T., Francis, H., Goldstein, H., Youngs, M., Hewison, J. and Plewis, I. (1980) '*Fifteen Thousand Hours*: a discussion', *Bedford Way Papers* 1, London, University of London Institute of Education.

Whitehouse, A. (1979) 'Lessons for a perfect school', *Yorkshire Post*, 21 March.

Wilby, P. (1988) 'The myth exploded: schools really do matter', *Independent*, 24 March.

Winkley, D. (1988) 'Handle with care', *Times Educational Supplement*, 25 March.

Wragg, T. (1980) 'Second thoughts on the Rutter Report', *Education*, 14 March.

Wood, N. (1986) 'Go back to 3Rs, says top Lefty', *Daily Express*, 15 April.

INDEX

234

Printed in the United Kingdom
by Lightning Source UK Ltd.
134386UK00001B/126/A